The Siren Years
A Canadian Diplomat Abroad
1937-1945

D0096104

Charles Ritchie

With a foreword by D.O. Spettigue

FITZHENRY & WHITESIDE
Canadian Biography Classics
Large Print Library

The Siren Years
© 1974 by Charles Ritchie

This edition published 1995, Fitzhenry & Whiteside,
by arrangement with Macmillan of Canada
Editorial material © 1995, Fitzhenry & Whiteside

Canadian Cataloguing in Publication Data

Ritchie, Charles, 1906-
   The siren years: a Canadian diplomat abroad,
1937-1945 [text (large print)]

(Fitzhenry & Whiteside large print library.
Canadian biography classics)
ISBN 1-55041-306-6

1. Ritchie, Charles, 1906-   . 2. Diplomats –
Canada – Biography. 3. Large type books.
I. Title. II. Series.

FC581.R5A3 1995   327.71'092   C95-930563-7
F1034.R5A3 1995

95 96 97 98 99 ML 6 5 4 3 2 1

Printed and bound in Canada

Fitzhenry & Whiteside
195 Allstate Parkway
Markham, Ontario
L3R 4T8

This edition of The Siren Years *is part of the Fitzhenry & Whiteside Large Print Library, Canadian Biography Classics Series. The publisher gratefully acknowledges the assistance of the National Library of Canada, Large Print Program, in the publication of this book. It has been set in 16/18 point Plantin type and is intended for those who need or prefer Large Print. For information on additional Large Print titles, please contact the National Library of Canada in Ottawa.*

Cover design: Darrell McCalla
Editing: Nicole Hesse
Production: Arnold Diener
Typesetting: Falcom Design & Communications Inc.

CONTENTS

Other titles in the series:

Grace MacInnis

Canadian Literary Classics:

Barometer Rising
Leaven of Malice
The Loved and The Lost
Two Solitudes
The Stone Diaries
Swamp Angel

FOREWORD

IT WAS in adolescence," Charles Ritchie tells us, "that the diary addiction fixed its yoke on me." But, he adds, "the habit had begun even earlier."

What prompts an otherwise normal-seeming schoolboy to keep a diary? Ritchie does not explain, although he does let us see that he has no ability in sports or other expected boyish interests and acknowledges his penchant for "secresy." The diaries, in other words, were intended (at least at first) for himself, not for publication. At one point he describes them as being "stacked up" in his room, yet he cannot bring himself to destroy them. Perhaps there was too much of Charles Ritchie in them and their destruction would have been a kind of symbolic suicide.

Ritchie was a Nova Scotian by birth, raised mainly in Halifax and Wolfville, with interludes on the west coast and in England and France. His family was not wealthy, but they were well connected, conservative, genteel — and had that touch of the eccentric, in the person of Uncle Harry, that seems to go with old families.

Born in 1906, Ritchie was twenty-eight when he began his career as an "acolyte third secretary" in Ottawa. His first posting was to Washington as "a sort of private secretary" to Sir Herbert Marler. There

The Siren Years begins. It is 1937, and the diary passes quickly to the next posting, the one that shaped his life, to the office of the Canadian High Commission in London. The war would keep Ritchie in England until 1945, and there was no place he would rather have been.

When, in the early 1970s, Ritchie began preparing his diaries for publication, it was the London years he chose as the first of what would prove to be five published volumes. *The Siren Years* (1974) was followed by *An Appetite for Life* (1977), dealing with the youthful period of 1924-27, by *Diplomatic Passport* (1981), covering postings of 1946-62, and by *Storm Signals* (1983), describing his last years in the service, 1962-71. Perhaps because these diaries were filled with the familiar names and events of Canadian diplomatic history, they were judged to be of greatest public interest, and so were published first. At any rate, the childhood volume, *My Grandfather's House*, was published in 1987 as the last in the series. Oddly, a ten-year gap remains, 1927-37; perhaps the diary-obsession flagged in that interval.

But why publish diaries? There was a time when "journals" were fashionable, and "memoirs" still are. A journal is not very different from a diary; both terms derive from the word "day," and both are daily records. The journal, however, is usually kept by a person of social or political importance—we have Lady Simcoe's Canadian journal, for example—as a record of an historical period or event, and meant to be circulated or published. Diaries are thought of as more intimate. Samuel Pepys' diary, written in an elaborate code, likely to prevent anyone in his household from ever interpreting it, is world-famous; it is both a revelation of Pepys' secret life and a record of public personas and events of seventeenth-century London by someone close to the centre of Restoration political, social and literary life. Ritchie's *Siren Years* stands in that tradition. A middle-level diplomat in wartime London on Vincent Massey's staff, Ritchie shares with us the experience of surviving the blitz, having his apartment destroyed, accepting the death of friends. He gives us the current news and speculations, and fills in the social life: dinners with the Dukes of Sutherland and Bedford, or with the Rothschilds; friendship with a Romanian princess: weekends with literary personalities —the Sitwells, Cyril Connolly and, most satisfying for him, the novelist Elizabeth Bowen. While Ritchie was strongly attracted to Elizabeth Bowen and she planned to write him into one of her books, nothing came of the relationship.

If Ritchie's diaries are characteristically candid, they are also cautious. He acknowledges his many sexual affairs, apparently necessary to him. Yet he was forty-four years old before, without any preparation in the text, he tells us that he has married and embarked on a happy domestic life. We never see his wife, Sylvia, in the diaries, however. There are scattered references— he is away on duty and misses her—but she never appears as a character in the way, for instance, the

American ballerina does. Perhaps that is because Sylvia is too important to treat lightly. And this of course is a difference between the Pepys diaries and Ritchie's. Pepys' were edited centuries after his time and produced whole; Ritchie's are edited by himself, so we cannot know what may have been omitted.

Ritchie does, however, add explanatory prefaces indicating the years covered, and his motives, and giving us increasingly his thoughts on the importance of the diaries to him, and on the nature of diaries. He insists that the diary is not "literary," but a form of autobiographical record that interests us because it tells us concisely, without embellishment, what was important to the writer on a given day. Still, Ritchie often embellishes; he likes to recreate the mood of an evening, the scent of wet lilacs, the atmosphere of London streets or someone's country mansion, or of an exotic personality. This is one of the attractions of his prose. Another is the reported conversations that catch the essence of a person, a situation, a love-affair, or social undercurrents. Another is sheer politics: the frustration with which those in the know watch the cynical posturing of politicians on the world stage. Ritchie helps us to see exactly how personalities, and secret personal agendas, can dictate world affairs.

Most of all, of course, because this is a diary, it shows us Ritchie himself. Diaries are confessions, all the more intimate for being directed not to a listener but to the writer. Here is a man close to the heart of world affairs, and yet, as we all are, he is concerned primarily with the self. What makes a diary worth reading is the quality of that self. What emerges from Ritchie's diaries is the double nature of the man: both the civilized, Halifax side and the irrepressible, Uncle Harry side. Ritchie recognizes not only the cool, diplomatic, even timid element of his character, but also that element that delighted in excitement and romantic affairs and exotic people, and knew the importance, the necessity, in every life, of the occasional fling.

Of the five Ritchie diaries, *The Siren Years* perhaps best combines the man and the world stage. Winner of the Governor-General's Award when first published in 1974, it remains today an eloquent record of rich experience.

D.O. SPETTIGUE
Queen's University

THE AUTHOR

CHARLES RITCHIE was born in Nova Scotia in 1906, the son of a prominent Halifax barrister. He received his education at Oxford and Harvard before embarking on a career as a diplomat, accepting a position with the Department of External Affairs in 1934. In the course of his career he acted as Deputy Under-Secretary for External Affairs, Ambassador to the Federal Republic of Germany and Head of the Military Mission in Berlin, Permanent Representative of Canada at the United Nations, Ambassador to the United States, Canadian Representative to NATO, High Commissioner for Canada in London, and Special Adviser to the Privy Council.

Winner of a Governor-General's Award in 1974, *The Siren Years* was the first volume of Ritchie's diaries to be published. It was followed by *An Appetite for Life* (1977), *Diplomatic Passport* (1981), *Storm Signals* (1983) and *My Grandfather's House* (1987).

AUTHOR'S
FOREWORD

It was with adolescence that the diary addiction fixed its yoke on me – a yoke which in the succeeding fifty years I have never been able entirely to shake off, although there have been merciful intervals of abstinence. The habit had begun even earlier – had sprouted furtively when I was a schoolboy. Its seed was perhaps already sown when I would write on the front of school books, Charles Stewart Almon Ritchie, King's Collegiate School, Windsor, Nova Scotia, Canada, North America, The World, The Universe, September 23rd, 1918, 3:17 p.m. – an early compulsion to fix myself in space and in time. Once given over to this mania there was no cure for it. With obstinate obsessiveness I continued to scribble away. Now the toppling piles of my old diaries are mountains of evidence against me, but I still postpone the moment to destroy them. Their writing and subsequent concealment were intentionally secretive – to have them discovered and read would have meant to be caught in the practice of 'solitary vice'.

1

The dairies included in this book begin in Washington in 1937 and end in Ottawa in 1945 but are in the main my record of the years I spent in London during the Second World War. They show the scenes and people described as viewed by an outsider-insider—one immersed from boyhood in English life but not an Englishman.

The writer was during these years an officer of the Canadian Foreign Service but these are not diplomatic diaries in any sense of that word. The deliberate exclusion of official business from the record leaves the odd impression that I was floating about London in idleness. One might well ask not only, 'What was his war effort?' but 'What did the Canadian Government pay him for?' The answer is that I was an obscure and industrious junior diplomatic official who was thrown by chance and temperament into the company of a varied cast of characters who lived those years together in London in the stepped-up atmosphere of war with its cracking crises, its snatched pleasures and its doldrums. The diaries are personal – too personal to see the light of day? I once would have thought so. Now thirty years later the personal seems to me to merge into 'we' of wartime London days. I resist any temptation to patronise or justify the writer. His faults, follies and errors of judgement show plainly enough. To paper them over would seem a smug betrayal of my younger self. The diaries are as I wrote them at the time save for occasional phrases which have been altered for the sake of clarity.

While I spare the reader a leisurely tour of my origins, childhood and early manhood, a brief backward glance may be helpful in making the narrative and the narrator more comprehensible.

I was born at our family home, The Bower (which crops up from time to time in these diaries) then on the outskirts of Halifax, Nova Scotia, in 1906. The Halifax of those days – at any rate the Halifax of my mother and her friends – looked back to its past as a garrison town and a base for the Royal Navy. I was brought up in an atmosphere – which must be incomprehensibly remote to modern Canadians – in which everything British was Best and 'Upper Canada' was a remote and unloved abstraction. Yet my family had been in Nova Scotia for four or five generations. Their devotion to Crown and Empire was a romantic fidelity, quite different from the satisfied acceptance of the English by themselves as English. They might look to England but it was hard for the individual Englishman to pass through the eye of their needle. They were Nova Scotians first, Canadians second. They were North Americans with a difference and they clung tenaciously to the difference. They belonged to Nova Scotia, the land where memories are long, legends, loyalties and grudges unforgotten, a land where a stranger should tread warily.

My mother was widowed when I was ten. My father, twenty-five years older than she, was a barrister and a brilliantly effective one to whom the law, which he had in his bones from generations of lawyers and judges, was a devotion. My mother was left with two boys to bring up, my brother Roland and myself. She tackled the job with love and a touch of genius. Never possessive, she held us by the magnetism of her personality.

Our home always seemed full of people coming and going, relations and near-relations, friends young and old and those whom my mother was sorry for or thought to be lonely. Then there was our own coming and going as a family to and fro from England in the slow boats from Halifax to Liverpool until England began to seem the other half of one's life.

Our education never stood still in one place – in and out of schools – on and off with tutors – now at a preparatory school in England, then back to Nova Scotia, then to an Anglican concentration camp of a boarding school in Ontario.

It was in 1921 while at the squalid age of fifteen I was incarcerated in this establishment that an envelope emblazoned with the Arms of Canada reached me as unexpectedly as the invitation to Cinderella to attend the court ball. The letter within was from Sir Robert Borden, then Prime Minister. He and my father had been law partners and lifelong friends. His kindly letter now informed me that he hoped in due course to see established a Canadian Foreign Service and that hearing (from my mother) of my interest in international affairs he suggested that one day I might be interested in such a career. Thus was planted the germ of an ambition.

As for my later education it seemed destined to extend to infinity, from King's University in Halifax to Oxford – to Harvard – to the École Libre des Sciences Politiques in Paris and back to Harvard. In no hurry to earn my own living, I was in danger of becoming a perpetual student. There were intermissions, a short-lived spell of journalism in London, an amateurish but exhilarating bout of teaching French irregular verbs in an 'experimental' school in Canada but no settled profession until the Victorian Gothic portals of the Department of External Affairs opened in August 1934 to receive me as an acolyte third secretary.

The Department of External Affairs at that time was small as was Canada's place on the map of international politics. Its future was being shaped by a handful of unusually gifted men who shared the belief that Canada had its own role to play in the world and a conception of what that role should be. They worked together without feeling for respective rank, without pomposity, with humour, despising pretence, intolerant of silliness and scathing in their contempt for self-advertisement. They were my mentors and later to become my friends.

My first posting abroad in 1936 was to the Canadian Legation (now Embassy) in Washington. At first this was a sunny and enjoyable interlude.

Not overemployed, the diplomatic bachelor had a full and easy hand to play in that sociable city. It was by fits and starts that the approaching war made its presence felt. Ominous newspaper headlines came and went and then business continued as usual, but by 1938 reality was coming inescapably closer. The Americans whom I knew in Washington and the American papers which I read were vehemently opposed to the appeasement of Germany. Their anti-Nazi feeling was more intense than what I was to meet on arrival in England. They felt that compromise with this evil was immoral and unforgivable. Perhaps they understood the implacable nature of the enemy better than the rest of us did. But there was this difference: emotionally committed as they were, it was not their war that was at stake.

In January 1939 I was transferred from Washington to the Office of the High Commissioner for Canada in London. The London to which I came turned out to be less concerned with the likelihood of war than the Washington I had quitted. We were permitted, indeed encouraged, to hope that the danger had passed. Whether anyone fully believed this is another matter. People behaved as if they did.

Nowhere was this state of mind more firmly ensconced than at Canada House and in this the High Commissioner Vincent Massey accurately reflected the views of his Government and in particular of his Prime Minister, William Lyon

Mackenzie King – himself a fervent supporter of the Munich settlement.

On my arrival at Canada House I found that in addition to my diplomatic work I was to act as a private secretary to Mr. Massey. Despite occasional explosions of irritation to be found in the diaries I was devoted to him. I was attracted by his personality, his sense of drama (he was a born actor), his susceptibility, the alternations of closeness and coolness in his dealings with people and the delight of his company. It was not an uncritical devotion, but no man is a hero to his private secretary, especially a private secretary who was not himself cast in the heroic mould.

It was impossible to think of Vincent Massey without his wife Alice. The contrast between them was as striking as their deep mutual attachment – his fastidiousness, her impulsiveness, his discretion, her outspokenness. There was a physical contrast too between his meticulous almost finicky gestures and her exuberant smiles and greetings. She was a handsome woman, prominent eyes of piercing blue, abundant reddish hair piled high. He had the austere visage of an Indian chief belied by his small, frail-appearing form. She was, or seemed to be, the stronger nature emotionally and physically. She wore herself down in the war by hard work for Canadian servicemen in England. I see her plodding along Cockspur Street laden with provisions for the Beaver Club which the Masseys founded for

Canadian soldiers, sailors and airmen, or at her desk writing hundreds of letters to the relatives of Canadians serving abroad.

The Masseys made their successive homes my second homes. When I was bombed out in the blitz they put me up as their guest in the snug safety of the Dorchester Hotel where they lived at the time. Their sons, Lionel and Hart, were my friends.

The second in command at Canada House was Mike Pearson, the most stimulating of companions in and out of the office. He was at the beginning of a career which was to see him become Prime Minister of Canada. In all the changing scenes of that career he remained the same Mike I knew in those days, incapable of self-importance, ready in wit and undaunted in the pursuit of his objectives and ideals.

The position of the High Commissioner and his staff in wartime London was not made any easier by the ambivalent attitude of our own Prime Minister Mackenzie King. *Canada at Britain's Side* was the title he chose for his own book on Canada's war effort. The title was certainly justified by the contribution made by Canada to the defence of Britain and to the conduct of the war. Yet Mr. King was obsessed through these years by the suspicion that Whitehall was plotting designs against Canada's independent nationhood and trying to draw us back into the old imperial framework. Unfortunately for us at Canada House the Prime Minister came to believe that his representative, Vincent Massey, had succumbed to these sinister British influences. Even Mr. Massey's successes in London were held against him. He had during his time there consolidated his personal and official position in the inner bastions of pre-war London. Cabinet ministers, editors of newspapers, directors of art galleries, the higher ranges of the peerage, not to mention Royalty itself, enjoyed his company and respected his views. This did him no good in the eyes of his own Prime Minister who reacted with intense irritation to the Masseys' familiarity with the Great.

To mutual resentment was added a difference of political views. Vincent Massey was a stout defender of Canada's interests, but believed in Canada as an actively participating member of the British Commonwealth. Mr. King emphatically did not. Whatever the rights and wrongs of their respective opinions, the resulting estrangement between them put the staff of Canada House in a difficult position. The disembodied presence of the Prime Minister brooded over us. It was not a benevolent influence. In the flesh he was thousands of miles away, but he needed no modern bugging devices to detect the slightest quaver of disloyalty to his person or his policies. Perhaps through his favoured spiritualist mediums he was in touch with sources of information beyond Time and Space. As will be seen these discords did not unduly affect the diarist. London scenes and people and the conduct and misconduct of his own life were too absorbing.

9

In these diaries people appear and disappear. For a time one character occupies the centre of the stage only to vanish as if down a bolt-hole. Intimacies develop quickly and sometimes dissolve as quickly. Wartime London was a forcing ground for love and friendship, for experiments and amusements snatched under pressure. One's friends came and went, some to war zones, others evacuated to the country. There was an incessant turnover of occupations from civilian to military and sometimes back to civilian. People drifted apart and together again as the war pattern dictated. This sometimes leaves the diary record disconnected. Situations are left up in the air; questions are not answered. All one can say is that this is what that life was like.

A diary is not an artistic creation. It has – or should have – a breath of immediacy but at the expense of form and style. Life is not transmuted into art. Anyone who wishes to see how that miracle can be achieved should read the work of genius set in the London of those years, *The Heat of the Day* by Elizabeth Bowen.

1937-1938

1 July 1937. Washington.

The Canadian Legation is housed in the former home of a millionaire, one of the palaces in such varied architectural styles which line Massachusetts Avenue. The Legation is both office and also the residence of the Minister, Sir Herbert Marler, and his wife. Sir Herbert is an impressively preserved specimen of old mercantile Anglo-Saxon Montreal. He looks like a painstakingly pompous portrait of himself painted to hang in a boardroom. He is not a quick-minded man – indeed one of my fellow secretaries at the Legation says that he is 'ivory from the neck up'. Nevertheless he has acquired a handsome fortune and his successful career has been crowned with the diplomatic posts of Tokyo and Washington and with a knighthood.

I am acting as a sort of a private secretary to him for the time being. He is extremely nice to me although each has habits which irritate the other. He has large square hands of immaculate cleanliness with the largest, broadest fingernails I have ever seen on a hand. When reflective or puzzled he has a habit of snapping the end of his index fingernail with his thumb making a distinctly audible clicking sound while gazing meditatively into space. This little repetitive clicking echoes through the large panelled office ornamented with elaborate carved foliage in the manner of Grinling Gibbons. I stand attentively before him awaiting his command and choke back the words, 'For Christ's sake stop doing that.'

If he is unconscious of my irritation I have been equally unconscious of a trick of my own which must madden him. One day last week Lady Marler drew me aside and said that the Minister had wanted to speak to me about something personal but had asked her to do so instead. Her manner made me wonder whether it was halitosis or a moral misdemeanour of mine which had offended him, but she said, 'His Excellency would much appreciate it if you would stop whistling in the hall outside his office.'

The Marlers are quite strong on the use of the word Excellency. Once when they were leaving the Legation with their small son I heard Sir Herbert say to the chauffeur, 'His little Excellency will sit in the front with you.'

There are two other junior secretaries at the Legation with me. We share offices on the top floor. When I arrived they told me that it was a tradition in the Legation that the most newly arrived officer must walk along an extremely narrow parapet running under the office windows. I obediently climbed out of the window and took a few precarious steps looking down at a drop which would have brained me if I had faltered. Then I climbed back in again to be told that I was the first person to be such a bloody fool as to believe this story.

16 July 1937.

Staying in the house in Georgetown which Dudley Brown has lent me. Woke in a state of stupid irritation with Dudley's Negro manservant who had neglected to call me. He is a handsome creature with a peculiarly rich voice and a glib talker. His name is Vernon.

19 July 1937.

There was no hot water. Vernon's face was thunderous. I ate breakfast nervously conscious of his mood and feeling unable to cope with it. 'There's a heap of small things in the house that just have to be attended to,' he said. 'Mr. Brown forgot to have the boiler filled. I spoke to him about it before he went away too.' He spoke with the grim, tight-lipped disillusionment of the stern father of an incurably feather-brained offspring. I felt that I could hardly admit this tone in speaking of a fellow 'white master'. 'Oh, he forgot,' I said, with a nervous attempt at nonchalance. 'Yes *indeed*,' said Vernon, allowing his magnificent, sultry, dark eyes to dwell on me for a moment in contemptuous disapproval.

Then he withdrew to the pantry. I turned again to *Anna Karenina*. In a minute or two I would have to shave, but what with? There was no hot water. Then unfortunately for my peace of mind it occurred to me that Vernon could quite easily heat up some water – not that it really mattered – I have often shaved in cold water. Why go and face him? Am I afraid of him? I thought, putting down *Anna* to look this disagreeable thought in the face. No, of course not, but I do not like meeting those sullen, disgusted eyes. This is getting too much, I thought, and went into the pantry. 'Vernon,' I called in quite a loud, confident voice. He was in the kitchen sitting beside the table with a black silk stocking twisted around his head – I suppose to keep the kink out of his hair. 'Vernon.' He did not get up, but rolled his eyes at me. 'I wonder if you could heat up a little water to shave in.' I spoke rapidly. 'Well, I will have to get some kind of a pot or pan, and it will take some little time to do.' This brought me to myself. I said sharply, 'Of course, only get it heated up.' I felt better after that. Later I was able to go down to him and in quite a calm voice ask him the road I should follow to get to the town in Virginia where I was lunching. Feeling my change of mood he became more amiable himself and gave me the directions I asked for. 'What is there to do when I get there?' 'Well, there are some places of considerable interest,' he said gravely, 'there is the home of Nathan Freeman, the great Negro Emancipator,

14

now turned into some kind of *mu*seum, and then also there is St. Elizabeth's Hospital for the *In*sane.' 'Indeed,' I said politely. I was so pleased with this information that on impulse I nearly asked him to make me a small picnic luncheon, but although I felt better about Vernon I did not feel equal to this.

3 November 1937.

Michal Vyvyan[1] said on the telephone that he would come around in twenty minutes to show me the draft of the telegram of greetings to Canadian War Veterans. With him came a new man just out from the Foreign Office, a smooth-faced Etonian with an air of sophistication. What happens to them at Eton? However innocent, stupid or honest they may be they always look as though they had passed the preceding night in bed with a high-class prostitute and had spent the earlier part of the morning smoothing away the ravages with the aid of creams, oils and curling tongs. This graceful young man handed me an elegantly worded little draft message typed out on a piece of paper. I said it was very pretty – 'Good morning' – and when they had left went down to tell the Minister about it. 'What,' said he, 'was the significance of this move on the part of the British Embassy?' 'A gesture of politeness – of co-operation,' I hazarded. But no, it was not as simple as all that. He had to be very careful in his dealings with the Embassy. 'They are a queer lot, Ritchie.' I was to call Vyvyan and ask him the significance of the whole thing. On second thoughts he would do it himself. Then Vyvyan must needs come down and explain it in person and the Minister explained that we would have to consult our Government. And this was all because they had shown us a message of welcome to Canadian Veterans. The Minister is obsessed with the dangers of any dealings with the British Embassy.

Miss C. the accountant is reading a book on *How to Make Friends and Influence People.* She says that she goes down to see the Minister and after five minutes, despite all the lessons she has learned from the book, she is longing to say, 'Oh, to hell with you, you damned old fool.' He wears down one's tolerance and amiability like a dentist's drill.

17 November 1937.

The secret telegrams sent by the Dominion Governments to the Government of the United Kingdom during the Rhineland occupation crisis in 1936 have been an eye-opener to me. I have just been reading them. Not much 'rallying around the Mother Country in time of danger', and if a similar crisis blew up tomorrow would it be the same song? If the United Kingdom Government could publish these telegrams it might give their Collective Security critics something to think about. The Dominions are not going to fight on account of the rape of Spain nor an indecent assault on Czechoslovakia. The United Kingdom must choose her ground very carefully. I am not sure that a German invasion of France would do the trick. Perhaps not until the first air raid on London.

I was sitting at the bar in the Club tonight beside a man on a visit from New York. 'So I took this woman out to dinner,' he said, leaning his two elbows on the bar and looking into his brandy and soda. 'Marvellous-looking woman and from what my brother had told me I thought it was, well, a foregone conclusion.' 'An open and shut proposition,' I suggested. 'Exactly as you say – an open and shut proposition. First of all she ordered three chops straight off like that. That was not all.' He twisted his ragged moustache in an agony of remembrance. 'I picked up the menus – one was table d'hôte. I really shoved the other at her more as a gesture. It was à la carte – everything three times as expensive in it, of course. She chose a dollar apéritif – there were several at forty cents – then right the way through, a three-dollar entrée, lobster mornay, always the most expensive thing in sight, and after dinner seven double whiskies in the course of the evening, and I never came near to first base.' He said, 'There must have been something wrong with the woman – physically I mean.'

17 February 1938.

At the Soviet Embassy hordes of fat, bespectacled women, young and old, 'Radical' newspaper columnists with jowls and paunches shouting their phrases the second time lest they should not be heard or appreciated the first time, a few senators and political big-shots whose faces give one a feeling of familiar boredom like picking up an old twice-read newspaper.

The Soviet Embassy was first the house of Pullman, the inventor of the Pullman car, and then the Imperial Russian Embassy. It is full of tasteless carving, red silk panelling, heavy chandeliers and marble. Now everything is slightly soiled and shoddy, the silk is frayed, the carved floral designs are encrusted with dust. Paunchy Russian Jews wander about through the marble halls in their shirt sleeves with cigars dripping ashes on their ties, or muttering together in the corners of the big saloon.

18 February 1938.

Reading Shakespeare's *Henry IV*, the scene between Hotspur and his wife. From that glimpse we know what Hotspur is in bed and at table, how he would make love, how he would nick impatiently through his morning paper, how he would drive a car, how he would bring up his children. Hotspur the falcon-eyed aviator, reckless skier is easy to imagine. The jesting, unsentimental tone when talking with his wife and his quick come-backs are startlingly 'modern'.

7 March 1938.

I went for a walk in the country with the

Australian Minister at the British Embassy. His blue, candid eyes, his silver hair, his ruddy cheek, his kindly, wholesome air all announce the fair-minded man of good digestion. He takes snapshots of old forts and churches, he observes the lie of the land, the names of the plants – he walks a steady pace, stout stick swinging at his side, pausing to appreciate a pretty stretch of country or to smile with good humour at a child playing in the village street. He is so nice – why then does one feel stealing over one a faint disgust at the man? Is it because for the best of all possible reasons his bread is always buttered on the right side? His house is in excellent taste, his dinners are not fussy but well cooked, suitable for a manly bachelor, his guests are sensibly chosen, the conversation is cheery and pleasant. On his shelves are Foreign Office reports, official war histories, biographies and the novels of Galsworthy. In his garden are crocuses planted by an ambassadress. In the mirror in his neat, manly dressing-room are stuck dozens of invitation cards from those who appreciate his jolly niceness. He is too shrewd and too dignified to let the cat out of the bag, but it is for these invitations he lives. They are wife and children to him. The man of the world with his silver-clasped evening cloak, his signed picture of the Duke of Gloucester on the drawing-room mantelpiece, his brandy in old glasses. The Australian without an Australian accent.

8 March 1938.

I went to the district jail to see a Canadian who had been kept thirty-five days awaiting trial for illegally entering the United States. I sat on a bench in the stone-flagged rotunda where visitors may talk to prisoners. The rotunda is in the centre of the prison and is lined with iron grating, beyond which one floor on top of another of the prison is visible, rising right up to the glass roof of the rotunda five floors above your head. The floors are connected by iron staircases. It is like being in the central hall of a zoo, an impression which was heightened by the figures sprawling on the staircases in attitudes of recumbent boredom. They were some of the prisoners and seemed mostly to be Negroes. Why they were sitting about on the stairs instead of being in cells I do not know. It is one of those illogical details which usually occurs in dreams. My prisoner came towards me across the floor. He was a pale boy with romantic, brown eyes and a shadow of a moustache. His features were delicately chiselled and rather trivial. He had on a very clean shirt open at the neck. He must have put it on a minute or two before coming to meet me. He seemed from his name to be of Greek origin and was in show business. 'My brother,' he said, 'had sworn out a warrant for my arrest.' 'What did he do that for?' I asked. 'I do not know what he would do a thing like that for,' the boy replied in a gentle, speculative tone as though pondering the vagaries of human nature. I felt my question had been impertinent. His reply was so gracefully said that it could hardly be called a snub, but I did not pursue the subject. I left him a tin of cigarettes. 'It has made me feel good to have you come here,' he said with cordiality as I got up to go.

9 June 1938.

How many nights have I sat alone in my room listening to the laughter in the streets, looking furtively at my watch to see if I could get up and go to bed. All those nights in my stuffy little room in Paris, in my room at Oxford with the clock of Tom Tower striking nostalgia on the night air, at school with the movements and muffled voices of the boys in the corridors, and at home at the table which faced the window looking out on the lawn with the single oak tree. And always this piece of staring, white paper in front of me with the few and feeble words strung across it. These wasted nights are most remarkable. Nothing could be more stubborn than my devotion, nothing more stupid than my persistence. After all, I have written nothing – I will write nothing. Twenty years have not been enough to convince me of my lack of talent.

23 June 1938.

After dinner at Dumbarton Oaks[2] our hostess Mrs. Robert Woods Bliss led us by circuitous paths to the little lake in the 'wilderness' beyond the formal gardens. The night was cool, the sky clear, and there was no shiver of breeze among the box hedges that line the path. When we reached the lake she went ahead of us alone with a flashlight to spot the path under her feet. We remained standing in a little group on a high bank that overlooked the water. We watched her treading lightly and gracefully in the spots of torchlight as she went around the edge of the lake to the other side. There she vanished beyond a tree and touched a switch so that an electric light cleverly placed high in the trees above shone down with a clear, bright, but not too bright, light on the surface of the water. She pressed another switch and a second light shone. The lake and the trees around it were illuminated so that every shadow was given its precise value. When our hostess was within earshot again we murmured our admiration of the ingenuity of the lighting and the beauty of the scene. Quietly she accepted our praise. There was a pause while we stood there gazing at the discreetly illuminated lake conscious of a scene which must be photographed on our memories. In the silence created by our dumb appreciation our hostess's voice sounded in a tinkling falsetto, 'It has I think a quality of stillness about it which is most appealing.' We nodded agreement. It was a sentiment which could not be enlarged upon. Meanwhile with surprising stealth the moon had slid up over the trees and was regarding us with an expression of indifference.

3 July 1938.

We walked beside the lake arm in arm and stopped every now and then to kiss. The lake and its surrounding circle of trees was still as the empty sky. We saw a white house on an incline among the trees with a big plate glass in the front like the window in a shop. The glass was a blinding gold from the setting sun. 'What a view they must have from there over the lake.' We wished the house was ours, but then we had said that about so many houses and we nearly always found some objections. This time it was the mosquitoes. 'There must be clouds of them rising off the lake in the summer.' Instead of the houses we would have we talked for a little about trips to Bermuda, to Provence or to rocky coasts with inlets of pale sand somewhere in Donegal or Nova Scotia. One place would be too far, another too expensive, another perhaps dull. It was not that we disagreed, but we both knew that none of these things would happen to us – that we would not have a house together nor visit the coasts of Donegal or Nova Scotia.

5 July 1938.

With no rules that I put faith in, no instinct to guide me except the instinct of self-preservation, a soft heart, a calculating head and a divided mind, is it any wonder that I cause confusion when what I want is so simple – a woman who will love me and who will sleep with me sometimes, who will amuse me and listen to me and not flood me with love.

9 July 1938.

Until I touch her she seems not to be made of flesh – her clothes are of one material, her skin is of another. It seems madness to kiss her cheek, which is made of some soft stuff not silk or velvet. As one might put a piece of velvet to one's face to feel its texture I put my lips close to her skin. I feel a casual pleasure in the softness of her cheek. A moment later a miracle has been achieved – her body is no longer a stubborn material thing of painted wood covered in velvet. It is now fluid and sparkling and electric with life. I can bathe in this moving stream and drown in this strong current.

12 July 1938. Dance at the Leiters'

The house built in the nineties is rightly famous for its appalling ugliness. The ballroom of inlaid marble was a monument of frigid vulgarity. Other interesting features included the enormous green malachite mantelpiece in the dining-room and the portrait of old man Leiter in the hall which justifies the worst that could be said of the Leiter family.[3] I suffered less than usual during this party as a result of consuming one glass of champagne after another in quick succession. I realised that this was necessary when somebody came up to me and said, 'You look like Banquo's ghost.' After that I felt I must go home immediately or get tight. I am glad I chose the latter course. I danced with Mrs. Legare who was the local beauty. Platitudes dropped from her lovely lips, each

24

platitude as smooth and flawless as a perfect pearl. 'Paris is so beautiful in spring when the chestnuts are out.' 'Women should wear what becomes them not what happens to be the fashion.' Her beauty too is that of a pearl – smooth and flawless. She wore a full-skirted dress of some stiff, shiny material which seemed to radiate a sort of moonlight brightness. Her gestures with her arms and hands, her way of dancing, were of a liquid grace.

15 July 1938.

I am longing to get to Nova Scotia. I want to breathe air from the Atlantic, to lie in bed at night and listen to the fog bell's warning and to live in a family again – tea and gossip in the middle of the morning – my mother sinking exhausted into a chair, lighting a cigarette, beginning an impassioned attack on the stupidity or the ingratitude of the wordly-wise or telling one of those spontaneous masterpieces of mimicry, humour and pathos, which give such depth of variety and colouring to a small incident.

23 July 1938.

Walked home last night through the dark jungle of the Negro quarter. The groups of Negroes – women sitting on the steps of their houses, young braves under a street lamp at the corner – are waiting for an artist who can render the grace of their movements, their natural nobility of posture or repose.

31 July – 1 August 1938. Newport (Staying at The Breakers, the Vanderbilts' house.)

When I stepped out of the station there was the car gleaming like patent leather and a small chauffeur in a greying livery, a pink and crumpled face and an accent which I presumed to be Hungarian.[4] 'Two things in the United States not good – dogs and children – both too fresh,' wheezed the chauffeur in a piping, choking voice as he swerved the car to avoid a dog and again to miss hitting a child. 'How much must I tip you?' I thought. 'There is the home of Mrs. Vanderbilt.' he said. Our Mecca was in sight. In another minute we passed through high iron gates, past great trees – even the grass was a rich man's grass. No house was grander than ours I thought, as we curled in through the iron gates under the massive trees. After glancing at the immense marble hall, I was in the lift and then along a red carpeted corridor and then in my room. It appeared to have been designed for an Edwardian lady of fashion. It was panelled in faded chintz. There was her upright piano, her chaise-longue with its frilled and faded pink cushions. On the walls hung the pretty pictures which one sees nowadays only in the darkest corner of a second-hand dealer's shop where they are piled on dusty shelves asking a shilling a lot for them and glad to get rid of them. I went out into the upper stone terrace and looked over the perfection of green lawns, the fountains and two little groves of trees which framed the seascape beyond. There was the sea – a magnificent blue carpet spread in front of the house, the breakers broke obediently at the foot of the cliff as if performing for the special benefit of the Vanderbilts and their guests. It was all very gratifying.

On my breakfast tray was a gardenia in a glass of water. Anxious to miss nothing I was sniffing at it when the footman appeared. I felt that I looked slightly silly sniffing at the gardenia and I hastened to engage him in conversation about the day's boat race.

On the doorstep that morning we all stood waiting for the car to arrive. My host in white flannels had a cotton cap with a small, transparent, green window in its peak, my hostess in a pink dress and her little girl who was like an old-fashioned doll with circular pink cheeks, china-blue eyes and golden ringlets. A Hungarian nurse went with the child as though they were two pieces of the same set of chinaware as she too had the pinkest of cheeks and the bluest of eyes. The nurse and child both shone with cleanliness. I am not particularly fond of sailing, and I know less than nothing about boats, but the day was agreeable. I was sustained by the sensation that people would envy me seeing the America's Cup Races on such a fine, fast boat and with such knowledgeable and truly sporting men. I was sustained too by the caviare and champagne and by the slightly heady feeling of association with people whose incomes outdistanced my own by astronomical proportions. The harbour was full of ships, and people kept on saying, 'This is the sight of a lifetime.' I believed them readily enough. There was in fact nothing remarkable to see. The two yachts were somewhere on the horizon, the English one well in the rear.

That night there was a dance. It took all my energies to wear an easy, pleasant expression. I was frightened of catching a glimpse in one of the mirrors of a pallid, ghost-like face and recognising with horror that it was my own. As I knew hardly anyone there it was necessary to hide the anxious and slightly embarrassed air of one 'who does not belong', particularly in this case because in the eyes of the guests those 'who did not belong' at this party could belong nowhere mentionable. All were talking the same unmistakable cosmopolitan language of the dollar, but it was not their money that filled me with exhaustion – it was their vitality.

In the garden I was led up to old Mrs. Vanderbilt who received me with the cordial simplicity of royalty. Her husband with his seedy beard does in fact look like an eccentric member of the German ruling family. One suspected him of epileptic attacks and a passion for collecting birds' eggs. I was paired off with a woman who had recently with unflagging zest embarked on her fourth marriage. She was one of those invulnerable American women set in motion by some secret spring of energy who go dashing through life at such high speed that it is impossible to think of them except in terms of motion – from hotel to hotel – from party to party –

from cocktail to cocktail – from bed to bed – and doubtless too from book to book, for American women have of course read *everything*. Her present husband is a pink-cheeked and amiable guardsman who, with a reckless courage which does more credit to a stout heart than to any appreciation of the laws of possibility, seeks to satisfy her.

The young girls at the dance had skins the colour of warm sand which the sun has burnished and the grace of movement and easy buoyancy of those who swim through life on golden tides.

9 August 1938. Halifax, Nova Scotia.

The clammy air comes in through the windows. There is fog in that air, and at intervals there is the melancholy mooing of the foghorn. A tram goes by in the quiet street. As it recedes its sad monotonous chant grows thin upon the air. When it stops at the corner it puffs like a stout woman with too many parcels. All sounds here are in a minor key, all colours dimmed by a slight disparaging mist.

10 August 1938.

The miasma of the small town – the terror that comes as you are shaving the next morning and remember the things you said the night before. Will it be repeated and distorted? Will your employer hear of it? Will it cause people to think you odd or affected or depraved? Will people say you are a communist or an advocate of free love?

Have you *hurt somebody's feelings?*

The last of the three old Miss Odells is dead – foolish, ugly, innocent ladies coming down the aisle after Holy Communion their silks creaking, their gold bangles tinkling. Now their big solemn town house is for sale and its contents will be offered at an auction next Wednesday, the proceeds to go to the cathedral diocesan fund. Already the china, the glass and the silver are laid out on tables in the dining-room in preparation for the sale. The little silver vinaigrettes and snuff-boxes on the occasional tables – each has attached to it a numbered cardboard label as big as itself. Even the old mourning ring enclosing a twist of chestnut hair belonging to some dim great-aunt is labelled for the sale. A group of ladies of the diocesan guild of the cathedral are supervising the arrangements. Some are enthusiastic and stand in ecstasy before the Crown Derby dinner service. 'Oh, what lovely old things,' they say. Others are disparaging, 'I must say I thought the silver would have been finer than this – it is mostly plate and the dining-room chairs are falling to pieces.' One lady in particular richer than the others insists that the Waterford glass decanters are modern imitations. Her attitude is felt to be too superior and is resented accordingly.

The Miss Odells during their lifetime had no desire to make new acquaintances. Most of the women who wander briefly through the bedrooms would not have been invited to tea in that house because they were 'new people' and one did not know them. Now they open private little drawers in the old desks and stare at the religious prints over Miss Ella's bed. An auctioneer pulls books out of the shelves in the library. The maids still kept on until the house is sold laugh and call out to each other in the upper rooms. I do not think the old ladies looking down from their Anglican heaven can escape being pained at the intrusion and the noise but perhaps as it is for 'the dear cathedral' they do not mind. Most of the things in the house are not beautiful, but in the drawing-room placed on the closed top of the piano is a dessert service of ivory white Wedgwood with urn-shaped sauce-boats painted in Pompeian red with classical motifs of helmets, laurels and harps. It gleams immaculate among the heavy furniture and carved oriental screens. And high on the walls of the tall library are hung plates of Old Blue patterned in willows and waterfalls. From the bedrooms where every table is petticoated in white muslin one can see the wet lawns, the dripping trees and (for the gardener cannot yet have been dismissed) yellow chrysanthemums tied neatly to small stakes. Then the fog rolls in from the harbour and all vanishes in a white mist.

It is hard to open the heavy front door – there are so many polished brass bolts and bars – enough perhaps they thought to keep out time and change. As one walks away down the street the grave, pillared portico and the elms beside the stables disappear in mist. When the fog dissolves the house may have gone and in its place will be an ugly shadow that haunts all private homes. There will be a boarding-house leering and shabby with an ingratiating grin and frowsty smell.

12 September 1938. Washington.

I had my first taste of Hitler's style today. I heard the broadcast of his eagerly awaited speech at Nuremberg dealing with Czechoslovakia. He is certainly remarkable entertainment value. I listened for nearly an hour to him speaking in German with brief interpretative interpolations. At the end of that time my nerves were jumping so that I could hardly sit still. This was not because of the subject with its implied danger of war – it was that voice, those whiplash snarls, those iron-hammer blows of speech. What a technique! The Germans get their money's worth all right – the long-drawn sentences with the piled up climax upon climax until the nerves are quivering – shudders of hate and fear and exaltation going through the audience. This cock-teasing oratory drives its victims frantic. If they do not have their grand orgasm of war soon they will burst.

But every good story must have a point and the point of Hitler's story is the outbreak of war. Instinctively every listener longs to get to that point. I heard an American woman say today, 'I could not sleep a wink last night after reading the papers and listening to the broadcasts. I was so worried about

32

this war scare.' How much anticipation do you suppose was mixed up with this genuine dread?

As I believe that England will not fight for the Czechs if it is possible not to do so I think it probable that there will be no war at present. The above reflections can be kept in cold storage until *der Tag* comes. What is striking is the lack of a moral cause for and also the absence of any objective to be gained by, a war. If war comes it will be an exasperated reaction to continuous blackmail.

14 September 1938.

This may be one of those historical dates and may be fated to figure in future schoolbooks as the beginning of the Second Great War. The various steps leading up to this climax have had the dramatic excitement of a grand historical drama. One is prepared for the blood-and-thunder finale and it has become almost unbearable to have it so often postponed. We have been going about for months pulling grave faces about the horrid possibility of war, talking about the destruction of civilisation, etc., etc., but deep down in our jungle depths have we not been longing for what we fear? Have we been willing this war? This is the same impulse which makes Emerson's saying true, 'A person seldom falls sick but the bystanders are animated with a faint hope that he will die.' It is human love of disaster to others, and living on this continent it has been possible to feel that one is watching a distant drama. This emotional desire for a climax has been heightened by the newspapers. The familiar vocabulary of exaggeration and dramatisation, the horrific illusion are all employed to build up a story – the story of the European crisis, the outbreak of war – the greatest *news story* in the world.

28 September 1938.

We are now on the very edge of war. Already my feelings have changed since I last wrote. Perhaps I am already beginning to suffer from war blindness. I feel more and more part of my generation and my country and less an individual.

The war offers us no ideal worth dying for – we make no sacrifice for a noble cause. We fight with no faith in the future. It is too late to pretend (though we shall pretend) that we are defending the sanctity of international obligations or the freedom of individuals. We are fighting because we cannot go on any longer paying blackmail to a gangster. Whoever wins, we who belong to what we call 'twentieth century civilisation' are beaten before we start. We have had our chance since 1918 to make a more reasonable and safer world. Now we have to go and take our punishment for having missed that chance. We have willed the ends but we have not willed the means to attain those ends. That must be our epitaph.

Here in America it is 'business as usual'. Tonight I have been listening to the radio for hours. It reflects the stream of normal American existence, the advertising, the baseball games, the swing music, but every few moments this stream is interrupted by a press bulletin from Europe. More mobilisations. Hitler may march before morning. These warnings from another world give Americans shivers down their spine, make them draw the curtains closer and huddle around their own fireside thanking God that they are safe from the storm outside.

29 September 1938.

Today it seems as though we are not going to have our war after all. I feel tired and slightly hysterical now that the strain is released. The crisis that we have been through shocked some of us temporarily at least out of a lot of our nonsense. Perhaps all this gab about the uplifting effects of war has something in it.

15 December 1938.

I am to be posted to London to the High Commissioner's Office, leaving next month. This means the end of this holiday in Washington, for no one could take too seriously my marginal responsibilities in the Legation. If I have learned anything here it is thanks to Hume Wrong, the Counsellor of the Legation. Each of my draft despatches has been returned to me with detailed emendations in his elegant script. He has applied acid to what he terms my 'impressionistic' manner of expressing myself. He will not allow the word 'feel' as in 'there is a feeling that the United States Administration's attitude is hardening'. 'Members of the Canadian Foreign Service,' he says, 'do not feel – they think.' The most gratifying moment of my time here has been seeing his report on my work which states that I have 'an instinct for political realities'.

I have loved Washington – the beautiful city itself. I have made friends here, friends made in this happy interlude who may last a lifetime. I shall miss Nora very much.[5]

I feel a strong tug of attraction to this country and these people, yet I know that it is time for me to go. The prospect of London means taking up the real pattern of my life and responsibilities again. It has its dreary side – the oyster-coloured skies, the waiting for buses in the rain, the staleness and *main morte* of the class system everywhere. All the same I cannot wait to get back.

1939

17 February 1939. London.

Being a Private Secretary is a busy unreal sort of life – unreal because it makes one's day such a programme of events. One does things in a certain order not because one feels like doing them at the time or even because this is the order of their importance, but because they appear in that order on the day's programme. This programme is dictated by the engagements of the Chief, who is in turn a victim of his engagements and spends most of his day in doing unnecessary things which he does not want to do. Yet neither of us is unhappy. We feel that the ritual of our lives is obligatory – we grumble but we submit with satisfaction to the necessity. A day of telephone conversations, luncheon parties, notes acknowledged, visitors received, memoranda drawn up. Exhaustion is merely staleness – we return with zest to the game. What an extraordinary amount of time is spent in saving our own face and coddling other people's vanities! One would really think that the people we deal with were a collection of hypersensitive megalomaniacs.

28 February 1939.

Levée at Buckingham Palace. I fancied myself in my diplomatic uniform hired for five guineas from Morris Angel, theatrical outfitters, Shaftesbury Avenue. With me was my French-Canadian colleague. We waited for upwards of an hour standing about in a succession of dull rooms in the Palace – the ceilings were ornamented with plaster nymphs of pallid respectability – the walls with portraits of the Royal Family through the ages by artists who were very consciously on their best behaviour. The crowd of well-brushed men in the Army, Navy and Civil Service did not make a striking colour scheme. It was only saved from drabness by the strong note of scarlet supplied by liveried footmen, beefeaters and officers of the Guards. These latter were magnificent – the old ones who were court officials seemed as inhuman as heraldic birds with their tall white plumes, their wasp-waisted uniforms with monstrous epaulettes. Their aristocratic beak noses were so appropriate that they might have been ordered for the occasion with the rest of their costumes. The young guardsmen glistened with superhuman elegance – their crimson faces matched their uniforms – their hair and moustaches had been worked over by scrupulous hands. They did what Englishmen wished to do – they looked their part.

The rest were middle-class and muddled by comparison. Groups of officers in khaki were as out of place as stage-hands who had strayed into the midst of a gala performance. Judges pushed back their wigs and looked irritable – their stooping backs and loose bellies in contrast with the military rectitude of the rest. One thin little man with horn-rimmed spectacles wore white duck and carried a topee under his arm. A doctor from Borneo? Civil Servants in knee-breeches had to be careful not to be mistaken for the Palace waiters. It was boring waiting like that and exchanging stares of assumed hauteur with other nonentities. My French-Canadian colleague paused before each mirror to examine his legs – he was worried about the prominence of his calves in their tight casing. 'And this is costing me five guineas,' I said to him. 'Cinq femmes,' he answered. At last we trooped into the picture gallery – Rembrandts, Vermeers – but we were too close to the Royal presence for aesthetic appreciation. Before I had time to take in how the man in front of me was executing his bow I was walking across the floor standing a second and bowing, I fear from the waist, instead of from the neck only, as I had been taught. As I raised my head I had a glimpse of a surprisingly unreal and kingly figure in a scarlet tunic with a pink face. There was a flash of Royal azure eyes, a half-smile and I was walking out like a patient emerging from ether.

George VI looked his part. I am told that his

ruddy air of health was due to make-up. This gives that touch of unreality which to my mind is a principal charm of royalty.

The distinction of the occasion lies in incongruities – the superb pictures in the gallery and the Victorian clocks and vases on the tables, the splendour of the Guards, the shabbiness of the judges, the Tudor beefeaters, the Regency Hussars and the Great War khaki, the mixture of style and colour which would be unthinkable if it had been planned, but which has grown up with the monarchy. Beside all this how made to order is the best of dictatorial display!

5 March 1939.

In the Park on a windy, spring day shadows come sliding along and vanish again, the breeze shifts, and the faces of people change with the light and shade. Everywhere is movement – nothing to seize. A painter was sitting with his canvas facing the bridge and the distant towers, ignoring the life around him. Ducks on ruffled cold-blue water, men rowing with certain strength as though we were in leisured summer. Three sailors sitting on a bench – two reading papers – one his legs apart and his elbows on his knees gazing at the ground, safe from the sound of command. A fair goddess of a woman – how unjust to be so sure that she was stupid. Little laughing cockneys with mis-shapen teeth – city-bred runts enjoying jokes. Two well-bred friends or flirts or lovers exchanging smiles of radiant supremacy as they watched the bouncing or slack-bellied nobodies riding in The Row. A young man with a neck of strength and a head of arrogance riding a fine horse. The shuttered pride in a few ruling faces – the quiet joy in moving within their well-cut clothes. The gazing, haunted, jeering, half-impressed, half-sardonic German Jews who move in and out of the English cavalcade. In the middle distance the black trunks and branches of trees backed by a mist of poetic blue. Damp fresh grass. From beyond the Serpentine came the pulse of a distant band and one's feet fell obediently into step.

15 March 1939.

Posters in the streets announce German troops enter Prague. My neighbour said at lunch, 'It may seem cynical but I really cannot get excited over this. I do dislike all this sentimentality about the Czechs – as long as the Germans are going towards the east...' This seems to be the general view among the 'people one meets at dinner'.

Went to the House of Commons. Chamberlain spoke of the disappearance of Czechoslovakia like a Birmingham solicitor winding up an estate. Eden was moved – even eloquent. I wish I could get rid of the haunting impression that he is still an undergraduate. Looking down from my place in the gallery in the House of Commons on the pomaded ringlets of a brace of young Conservative M.P.s who were lounging below I reflected on the excessive attraction which style exercises over my imagination. I would not like to be on the opposite side of the fence from beings so elegant, however clumsy and vulgar the ideas inside those sleek heads.

The moral weakness of the government's foreign policy lies in the fact that they talk the language of trust while arming to the teeth. If Chamberlain believed in Hitler's good faith we would not need our big guns. He does not believe in it, but wouldn't it be better to give up a pretence which takes in nobody? Where are politeness and consideration for German susceptibilities getting us? The Germans evidently consider this façade meaningless.

Yet I cannot forget the remark of a middle-aged woman I met one day at a cocktail party. 'If we had gone to the help of the Czechs my twenty-five-year-old son might be dead fighting in Central Europe by now, and what good would that do the Czechs?'

Chamberlain, if he used phrases, might have said, 'Czechoslovakia is not worth the bones of a British Tommy.' That is what he means, and most Englishmen agree with him. They do not think of the corollary, 'England is not worth the bones of an American or Canadian soldier.' They know that while the second proposition may seem as sensible as the first it is not true politically.

19 March 1939.

This latest crisis was at first exciting. One had the illusion of participating in 'an historical event'.

42

As I hurried from Trafalgar Square to the Foreign Office[1] my brain was buzzing with clichés 'The Chancelleries of Europe are humming' – 'The hour of destiny is at hand', etc. The wireless transmitters over at the Admiralty would soon be tingling with commands to the fleet. This was the 'pulse of the Empire'. It was in these buildings, the Admiralty, 10 Downing Street and the Foreign Office, that fateful decisions would be taken. I hastened to the Foreign Office, my mind moving among images consecrated by historians, journalists and radio broadcasters. This feeling of excitement and importance underlay my pessimistic language and my grave actor's face. It was only today that I got bored with my role and bored with the crisis. I wanted to close the book, leave the theatre, turn off the radio. But I am no longer in America, so I cannot do any of these things. Boredom, worry, bewilderment, fear – these unpleasant sensations will be with us for months.

6 April 1939.

This is to say what it was like to be sitting in my office this afternoon after lunch, looking out of the window and wishing that I could settle down to work. There were memoranda of telephone calls which must be made immediately and notes for a speech to be ready by tomorrow morning. I would not touch this welter of paper but stared gloomily, nervously, out at Trafalgar Square. The sky was a stale grey of three days' standing. St. Martin-in-the-Fields and the National Gallery were grey too, so was the water in the fountains – so were the pigeons. People passed in their dreary mackintoshes; the traffic filtered around the Square. There were sudden flights of pigeons – false alarms started by some panicky bird and obeyed in a perfunctory fashion by the others. As they flew they showed the paler grey of the underside of their wings. A wet wind blew the water in the fountains in fine showers over the passers-by. A man and a woman with their arms around each other stood near one of the fountains. He bent his head to her with some lover's joke which made them laugh a little. Her arm tightened around him. Scarlet buses supplied the invariable London colour combination and the note was carried out by the red letters of the posters telling Londoners that Civil Defence is the business of every citizen. The day was too sterile to breed even a good war scare. Who could be frightened when there seems so little to lose? A good bomb I thought is just what this Square wants.

16 April 1939.

My mother is here[2] and I refuse to wear an overcoat because I will not have my health fussed over. I refuse to turn out lights because of resentment at bourgeois economies. I also resent being waked up and being told I am late for breakfast. With this goes a revival of adolescent escapism. I wish for a new mistress or to risk my life in an aeroplane stunt. At the same time I insist on lecturing her on modern painting, reading aloud to her passages from Auden when she likes Shelley.

17 April 1939.

Quite another story. My mother and I went to a movie, came home, sat by the fire and talked – and this time it was like my youth again, but like the happy part of it. My mother seemed, as she does every now and then, to come back to herself. The ailing old woman disappears. She starts on one of her anecdotes full of mimicry, with a cruel eye for the comic effect – and sentimentality like a chapter of Dickens. She seems then for the moment as strong in vitality as ever she was.

20 April 1939.

Went to the Foreign Office to get telegrams.[3] Hadow, who is in charge of the Foreign Office relations with the Dominions, looked grey with fatigue and says that the Chief of the Southern Division, who is the man most responsible in this crisis, has been working until two or three in the mornings for days.

10 May 1939.

Lunched at the Ritz in the Edwardian Louis Quinze dining-room. The women in feathered and flowered straw hats seem pre-last-war. It was like the opening chapter of an old-fashioned society novel. The London season seems unrealistic in the face of anti-gas precautions and evacuation orders. Snobbery must indeed be a lusty plant that grows even on the edge of the precipice.

14 May 1939.

Family life makes me long for the brothel or the anchorite's cell.

16 May 1939.

I said to Mike Pearson today, 'Well, we are out of danger of war for the time being.' 'Do not be so sure,' he said, 'if the Germans attack the Corridor, Poland will fight, and so will France, and then we shall be in.' One of the few independent acts in recent French foreign policy has been the guarantee to Poland to fight if the Germans seize Danzig and their definite promise to send army divisions. These assurances were given only four days ago. They may not keep their word if the British refuse to promise their support. Plainly the British attitude towards the threat to Poland is the most important question of the moment. I cannot believe that this country will go to war for the Polish Corridor. Therefore, I think the French will probably desert their Polish allies.

29 May 1939.

To be always patient, to win all the skirmishes with one's own irritability and selfishness is to drain family life of its vitality. One has no right to pose for one's obituary fan-mail to those one loves.

9 July 1939.

A picnic lunch party in the gardens of Eccleston Square – pickled herrings, meat pies, lemonade and laughter. I shall remember this sunny week in the London season of 1939. It seems to belong to the past almost before it has had time to happen – sometime before the war – the next war I mean. The London season survived the last war and may survive the next. Will there always be cultivated rich girls who have read all this year's books and been to Algiers and will not admit to themselves that marriage is now as tiresomely inevitable for them as it was for their grandmothers? And clever young men in the Foreign Office? And little luncheons of eight in Bryanston Square with an actress, an M.P., a girl three years 'out' and getting on with her conversation, an American married woman and a vigorous Edwardian hostess?

Bernard Shaw passed me today bowling down Jermyn Street in a grey tussore silk suit like a man of twenty-four with false eyebrows and a cotton beard.

And Margot Asquith[4] sat next to me in the cinema treating the performance as a background for her showing-off. No one shushed her – I suppose they recognised her and knew that it was useless, as no one in the last half century from King Edward VII on has succeeded in shutting her up.

Edwardian London,

Between interruptions - the first one 1914-1918 - the next 1939—.

The pink and white telegrams in the worn Foreign Office leather boxes – 'Urgent and Secret', 'According to your Lordship's instructions I sought an interview with Signor Mussolini', 'The situation has deteriorated', 'His Holiness said', 'Monsieur Molotov with his habitual mixture of peasant naïveté and cunning'. For a mixture of naïveté and cunning give me any British Ambassador – and their prose – the casual style, the careful avoidance of purple patches and fine phrases, and every now and then the rather wry, tired, little joke.

I went down to Southampton to see my mother off – the usual discouraging lot of passengers – yellow discoloured American women of no particular age. On the way home the tube was full of soldiers and young men in suits carrying rifles and kitbags. Someone said, 'They have called up the militia.'

9 July 1939. Sunday.

Took a solitary walk by the river at World's End – swans making scanty meals in the mud flats craning their necks after filthy crusts and paddling about on their clumsy snow-shoes. In Chelsea Old Church elderly women with wispy hair were squatting on their haunches to read the inscriptions at the base of the monuments.

The dreariness of these slum streets on a Sunday

afternoon is something almost supernatural. The pubs are still closed, but here and there a small magazine and sweet shop is open, the overcrowded little interiors give some colour for the eye – bright, shiny, flesh colours of nudes on the backs of magazines – the yellows and reds of candies in glass jars.

At World's End a Salvation Army band was practising in a drizzle of rain – trumpet notes and the tumpity-tumpity tune – the women of the Army in their bonnets seemed a piece of Victorian London.

10 July 1939.

To the House of Commons where Chamberlain made his statement of support for Poland over Danzig. It was in so tepid a tone, delivered in such a mechanical manner and received in such silence that one felt chilled. The German Ambassador must have felt relieved – the Pole disappointed.

29 July 1939.

From my port hole window at the top of Stansted[5] I could admire the grand park in the manner of Le Nôtre with its noble avenues sweeping through the Sussex woods into the mist.

The Bessboroughs have made me feel at home at Stansted – Lord Bessborough has been kindness itself and is relaxed away from the fetters of Governor-Generalship.

Moyra was there. I am getting more and more

devoted to her. She has a charm compounded of candour and courage.

Lord Bessborough is a mixture of Whig magnifico and a modern businessman – the ruby ring on his hand – the occasional resonance of a phrase and amplitude of a gesture reveal his origins under the surface of a director of city companies. Someone said they had seen Lord Portarlington at Goodwood wearing a straw hat with a ribbon around it – 'Such a paltry hat!' said Lord Bessborough. He puffed at his cigar and repeated with satisfaction 'a very paltry hat'. When I asked him what he thought of Sam Hoare[6] he said he shared a study with Hoare at Harrow. 'He was always the same – twitter, twitter, twitter.'

Lady Bessborough glides through the flower-filled rooms of Stansted in an ever-changing succession of costumes. Her effects are calculated with French flair – the right jewels with each dress, the right flowers for each room, the right sauce for the fish.

9 August 1939.

Dined with Tony Balásy, Counsellor of the Hungarian Legation. He feels, coming from Washington where he was posted, the oppression of the preparation for war. He talked about the Hungarian minority in Romania. 'Dear old Charles,' laying his long hand on my arm, 'I should not perhaps pretend to be impartial but there are two million Hungarians in Romania – that dates to the Peace Treaty. Well, you know these countries in Central Europe, how many hatreds there are among them. What do I mean? Since the day that England gave her guarantee to Romania the Romanians have begun ill-treating the Hungarian minority. They say now, 'What does it matter about those damn Hungarians? We have the British guarantee.'

'Then you must not judge Hungary by what you read in the newspapers. What do I mean? Hungary has no freedom of choice. We export sixty per cent of our products to Germany. Before these exports were divided among Czechoslovakia, Germany and Austria. Now they are all Germany. What I mean is, take a look at the map. As for the Hungarian Nazis they have forty seats out of a parliament of two hundred and sixty. If Hungary was Nazi, why don't the Hungarians vote Nazi?'

I did not tell him that the statistics of votes cast for the Nazis and Fascists did not strike me as conclusive. Poor Tony! He will soon be in a concentration camp if the Nazis get in. There is not much place for gentle liberals in Central Europe, and unless he is harder-boiled and more unscrupulous than he seems he will never stand the pace.

14 August 1939.

Lunched with Robert Byron[7] who is going on a visit to the Kaiser. He hopes to be at Doorn when the next war breaks out (this September). He went last year to the Nuremberg Conference 'disguised as

51

a Mitford' with Lord Redesdale.[8] The latter, he says, treated the Nazi Party Conference as though it were a house party to which five hundred thousand rather odd and unexpected guests had turned up.

Looked at Poussins in the National Gallery. My heart swelled at their beauty and was subdued by their finality. This is art in the grand manner – no restlessness.

15 August 1939.

We are to sell out the Poles apparently although I still find it hard to credit, but the advice going out to them from the Foreign Office over Danzig is just what we told the Czechs this time last year over the Sudeten crisis. Hitler says that if absolute calm prevails and his prestige is not attacked the problem can wait, but at the slightest incident he will attack Poland. Hadow at the Foreign Office says we led the Poles down the garden path and now we must lead them back again. He was always against the Polish guarantee. He said then, 'We shall promise them too much and go back on our word. Better make a realistic settlement now.' He may be proved right. It is sickening. But how can one blame the Government with the sneaking desire inside one that they behave dishonourably as long as they avoid war. 'Let them do the dirty work and then we will curse them later for it.' Such must be the subconscious feelings of many critics of the Government.

21 August 1939.

An ominous, thunderous, heavy day – close grey weather – a weight on one's chest – not panic but a dull certainty that it is coming. This is a most peculiar crisis. It has not broken yet – it is like one of these heavy, leaden clouds which have been hanging over London all day and which must break in loud thunder and lightning. People are mystified and bewildered by the news. It is menacing but imprecise. No one has defined the immediate danger. Hitler has not said a word in public about Danzig or about Poland. There is nothing ostensible to make this immediately necessary – simply 'his patience is exhausted'. 'We cannot go on like this' – that is what everyone is saying. With fatalism we drift into the alternative; we almost embrace the alternative. This tragedy which, when I was in America, seemed too stupid to be true now seems inevitable. I could no more go back to America than I could leave this planet. There will be a war.

22 August 1939.

Coming down Hollywood Road on my way to the bus I saw the placards 'Russo-German Pact'. During the morning several journalists came to my office – they were as stunned by the news as I was. It is probably no exaggeration to say that a war to defend Poland with Russia benevolent to Germany would be suicide for this country. The present Government will in the end do anything to stay out of such a war. They should never have given the guarantee to Poland without a prior arrangement with Russia. However we get out of it, it will be so discreditable that the Government will not be able to go on unless they could participate in some kind of European Conference which would save their faces – 'undoing the wrongs of Versailles'. The results would be a further and far-reaching surrender to Germany who would promise for the time being to leave us alone. This seems the most likely upshot unless Beck, the Polish Prime Minister, either cannot or will not give in to the Germans.

Mr. Massey went to a High Commissioners' Meeting. The British Government pointed out that if Germany had access to Russian raw materials it would be impossible to blockade her. They said, however, that they were going to issue a press communiqué stating that they would stand by their obligations to Poland. Bruce, the Australian High Commissioner, protested against this and said it would lead Poland to resist and she would then be destroyed. Halifax was impressed and took him to put his arguments to the Prime Minister. He should find a ready listener. Of course there is the possibility that Parliament will revolt against the Government and then we shall have a war. If we can still get Russian support we should not discourage the Poles, but unless we can get Russia or the United States to come into this I suppose we must tell the Poles to give in. It all depends how far the Russians are committed. If they are really deep in with the Germans we might as well climb down. If they are likely to switch to us if it comes to a war, then we should fight. My God, how often have I heard the Foreign Office say that a Russo-German pact was an impossibility. They do not seem to have believed what any journalist in London or New York could have told them was likely to happen. Poor Mr. Massey – he has a cold and no role to play and no idea what he would do if he had such a role. He is as undecided as I am as to what is the proper line for the Canadian Government to take. He put the pros and cons to me without any idea of interpreting them and said pathetically, 'Of course Bruce' – the Australian High Commissioner – 'has a fine mind.' He left relieved at my view that in the end the Poles would have to give in.

23 August 1939.

Week-end in the country – When Sally Gordon-Ives met me at the bus stop at Chippenham she had a stranger with her, a man with the oval face of a Gainsborough portrait, an impression partly derived from his white, wavy hair. As he drove the car he kept waving his long fine hands. 'Where are we to turn now, Sally?' 'This is where I always get confused.' 'Oh, this is *worse* than death.' We arrived at the house before dinner in time for passion fruit and gin cocktails. The small white drawing-room was sweet with the smells of lilies and carnations. Sally's son, Victor, came downstairs in a dinner jacket with a carnation in his button-hole – long legs, lounging Eton manners and abundant dark locks. He seemed dripping with softness like a young Orsino. He is a caricaturist, a lover of music and a photographer of talent. 'Let's play Beethoven's Eighth on the gramophone just once, Mummy, before dinner. I do so love the part that goes...' and he hummed it in a pure, rounded, full voice. No doubt when war breaks out he will be among the first killed leading the lower classes into action.[9]

At dinner we had a discussion of literature. It crackled up quite suddenly and spread like a forest fire, started by John Davies (who is also staying here) saying that Dostoevsky was superior to Tolstoy. After drinking some sparkling hock I demolished him entirely.

John had just come back from exercises as a trooper – 'For three days I only slept three hours a night carrying a weight of fifty pounds all the time. Nothing saved my bottom but wearing silk pyjama trousers under my cavalry breeches. One morning I was so weak with exhaustion that I wept into my gas-mask. Have you heard about the cavalry officer who was so stupid that the other cavalry officers noticed it?' The white-haired man's name was David. He kept on saying, '*Worse* than death' and 'Too tiresome for words to tell' all the week-end. John says he really is a typical New College highbrow. There was a girl there whom they called

'Society' because she was a débutante. 'Society will not play tennis with a man in braces.' After dinner we played bridge and danced to gramophone records in the drawing-room. Young Victor and Society danced with grave seriousness – he a sensitive dark youth, she the perfect answer to his question. She had been to forty-five débutante dances and never leaves until they are over. She dances with a somnambulistic certainty of timing. I went out and stood in the garden, searchlights guarded our revels. I could hear the music of the *Kleine Offizier* coming through the window and could see the lighted, flower-filled room with the figures dancing and David's lounging figure. I went back to my pub through the empty streets of the village. They were still dancing and I could hear the drawing-room floor vibrating as they practised new tap-dancing steps. When I got into bed the sheets were damp as they always are in village pubs, and I soaked up my French three-volume saga by the light of a candle.

26 August 1939.

Yesterday Hadow of the Foreign Office suggested that the High Commissioners should ask Mr. Chamberlain to represent to Poland the full danger of the Russian position. It was a way of asking them to climb down. As I walked back across the Horse Guards I thought, 'Should I suppress this suggestion?' but I passed it on to Mr. Massey. If I believed that nothing must be done to discourage the Poles I would not have passed it on. I knew that I had to make up my mind in a hurry. I suppose my feeling was that as a Canadian I should be right in doing anything, however small, in the direction of postponing war. Mr. Massey took up the suggestion with Bruce, the Australian High Commissioner. Bruce took it up with the Prime Minister. Mr. Massey himself had the idea at second hand and understood it very imperfectly. Bruce must have understood it even less. They just got the essential part of it – to warn off the Poles. Mrs. Massey said, 'I saw the film of Mr. Bruce going to Downing Street – the irony of it that he should have the credit of making this suggestion to Mr. Chamberlain which really originates with Vincent.' As a matter of fact it is a double irony – the idea originated with Hadow, was brought from him by me to Mr. Massey, and Bruce made the effect. That is a historical fact for you – like a stone dropped in a pool.

Still not a word of enquiry or guidance from the Canadian Government. They refuse to take any responsibility in this crisis which endangers the future of Canada. Mackenzie King is condemned in my eyes as unworthy to hold office as Prime Minister.

Mrs. Massey and I sat up until eleven p.m. drinking whisky and water in the High Commissioner's big Mussoliniesque office awaiting his return from his meeting with Halifax.[10] London seems very calm – everyone appears resigned to war if it comes. They have lost any positive will to peace. The last year of peace has been too insufferable. If Russia was on our side I think people would not be sorry that war had come at last.

29 August 1939.

This is like one of those dreams in which images appear in incongruous juxtaposition. One sees one's maiden aunt riding through the park naked on a polar bear.

At the end of the quiet stuccoed streets hang the great silver elephants of the balloon barrage floating airily high in the evening sky. These captive monsters may be seen between their ascents pinned to the ground in the parks or public places – lying exhausted, breathing faintly with the passing puffs of wind. While the general London scene is the same, there are oddities of detail – brown paper pasted over fan-lights and walled-in windows on the ground floors of the buildings, the sand-bags around hospitals and museums, the coffin-like enclosures around the statues in the central court of the Foreign Office. And there are odd tableaux too – glimpses of people in shirt-sleeves digging air-raid shelters in their back gardens, or offices debouching typewriters and desks for removal to country premises. Then there is the outcropping of uniforms, raw-looking young soldiers in very new uniforms unload themselves from Army trucks and stand about awkwardly in front of public buildings. Women in uniform looking dowdy as old photographs of the last war, full-bosomed, big-bottomed matrons who carry their uniforms with a swagger, and young girls copying their brothers – a spectacle to make their lovers quail.

1 September 1939.

A day which may have lasted a week or a year. It began when that severely black-clad spinster in my office handed me the *Evening Standard* with the text of Hitler's proclamation to the German army. Until then I suppose I had not really taken in that there would be a war. There followed an interminable period of sitting about. It was like waiting for a train that would not turn up. People made their appearances in my office, stayed and disappeared. Voices from what seemed to be every part of my life spoke to me on the telephone. It was like the anteroom to Hades in which one expects to run into an ill-assorted variety of company.

This drawn-out waiting in the close, grey day was interspersed by my visits to the Foreign Office where Hadow was sitting, stunned, among his telegrams. 'These bloody pigs,' he said of his Foreign Office colleagues, 'want to set up a Jewish-cum-Leftist régime in Germany.' Like a man possessed he repeated his old anti-communist ravings but weakly like a gramophone running down.

At seven in the evening Mr. Massey came back from the House of Commons. By then there was a black-out. Three or four of us gathered in his huge office, its walls marked where the oil paintings had been removed to safety, its windows curtained. Mr. Massey stood under the vast chandelier. He was excited – unnatural or too natural 'We shall be at war some time tonight.'

I dined in the candlelit gloom of Boodle's Club dining-room. All but two waiters had been called up. It was the first time in history that members were permitted to dine in the dining-room in day clothes. After dinner I emerged into the coal-black St. James's Street of Pepys or Dr. Johnson. Through the driving rain I walked along the Mall. I half expected to see a crowd outside the Palace, but its grey mass did not show a light. I hailed passing cars, unable in the black-out to see whether they were taxis or private cars. As I squelched through the mud by the park railings I thought that this compact city civilisation, inter-related like a switch-board, is overturned. One's friends join up or go to the country, sail to America, or evacuate school children. If you see a friend you cling to him. For when he is gone he is swept away, and God knows when you will see him again. Telegrams are not delivered, telephones not answered, taxis do not run. I suppose once the war gets under way we shall get back to more normal conditions.

3 September 1939.

The war feeling is swelling. I believe it would sweep aside any compromise with Germany if the

Government at the twelfth hour could secure one. I think we may have cheering, weeping crowds in the streets yet. This thing is a drug which alternately depresses and elates its victims and which gives them release from the slow death of their daily lives. No one who has not felt this war-feeling inside him can know how it shakes the foundations and lets loose hate, generosity, lust, fear, courage, love – all the bag of human tricks. Some thought they had been analysed away, but it was just that the right button had not been pressed.

At the doors of the houses in my neighbourhood stand cars laden with luggage. Little groups of Kensingtonians are evacuating their aunts, their canaries and their small dogs.

8 September 1939.

Is that humming an aircraft? That faint fluting sound – is it a siren? Our ears have been sharpened. Who would have thought of using 'our' of Londoners before?

Was there a time when we did not all carry gas-masks? Only a few days ago.

The liner *Athenia* has been sunk by the Germans. The absurd wicked folly of these utterly unwarlike people being drowned. This war has a quality which no other had. We do not approach it with our former innocence. We are in cold blood repeating a folly which belongs to the youth of mankind. We are driven to it by the force of sheer human stupidity, laziness and error which we have been unable in the last twenty years to overcome.

We awake at three in the morning to sirens. I go for my overcoat, my gas-mask, my shoes and stumble through the french window into the garden where the other inhabitants of this boarding-house are already in the shelter. They are making jokes and meeting with sleepy or nervous responses from their neighbours. The cook says, 'We shall be used to this in ten years.' Then she goes off to the kitchen and comes back with a tray of tea. I get bored with the shelter and come up for air in the quiet garden. The old man we call 'Uncle' is looking at the stars. He has appointed himself an outside watcher. He often thinks he can hear sounds of enemy planes coming over. So far he has been mistaken. His wife 'Auntie' talks all the time in the shelter. She gave us quite a clear little description of different kinds of poisonous gases. I think she has a relish for horrors. 'Chris' appears in the shelter with her hair tied up in a pink gauze scarf. She looks better like that than she does in the daytime with her blondined curls – a little better but not enough to matter. I came in and had a bath before the all-clear signal went. People will get less careful each time – especially if we have so many false alarms.

15 September 1939.

Living in London is like being an inmate of a reformatory school. Everywhere you turn you run into some regulation designed for your own protection. The Government is like the School Matron with her keys jangling at her waist. She orders you about, good-humouredly enough, but all the same, in no uncertain terms. You need look no further to know what British fascism would be like. Nothing but acute physical danger can make such a regime bearable. So far we have had the restriction without the danger, and there is healthy discontent as a result. After the first air raid we may feel differently. Meanwhile London is a waste of dull desolation. Never has there been such a colourless war – not a drum, not a flag, not a cheer – just sandbags and khaki and air-raid shelters and gas-masks and the cultivated, careful voice of the B.B.C. putting the best complexion on the news. London is waiting for the first raid like an anxious hostess who has made all the preparations to receive formidable guests – but the guests do not seem to be going to turn up. Every time the door-bell rings she thinks, 'At last there they are,' but it turns out to be the grocer's boy delivering a parcel. So the days pass. We look at our watches, turn on the wireless, pick up a novel and wait. There are reports in from Denmark that five hundred German bombers are collected in the Sylt and that we may expect a raid in a few days. Meanwhile the Poles have begged the British Ambassador to press the Government to raid German military objectives as the one action which we could take which would really be helpful to the Poles. I do not see how we can avoid doing so any longer unless—Is this a token war fought to save our faces to be followed in a few weeks by a peace conference? The suspicion exists in England and is strong on the continent.

What a relief to be spending an evening alone in my room without thinking, 'the so-and-sos are giving a dinner-party – I should rather like to have gone'. There are no dinner-parties.

I have been reading '*New Writing*' which is full of bloody death and the symbolism of decay and destruction. The editors have collected the omens of our impending disaster from China and Spain. This monster which was grazing in exotic fields is now approaching England's garden cities.

16 September 1939.

I went to a typical American comedy film with Ginger Rogers in it. There is a country thirty-eight hours away by Clipper where it is still important that women should be smart and attractive, where the most irreverent wisecracks are permitted, where people are still trying to get rich, where individual happiness is still an aim. The selfish, free world of America seems electric with vitality and with hope compared to this scene of grey submission. All this comes from going to an American film. The truth is that I would not leave this country now if I was presented with a ticket to America and a cheque for one hundred thousand pounds.

17 September 1939.

Week-end with the Masseys. Mike Pearson was there. He went to a night-club last night and says there was a crowd of R.A.F. chaps all having a good time pretending to be tight, pretending to fight over the girls, etc. This was fine and as it should be. But he was disgusted by a group of middle-aged men, survivors of the last war, back in uniform again, singing the old songs of the last war, trying to fancy themselves heroes to the night-club hostesses, trying to get back the glamour of their own youth. Certainly one war generation should be allowed to die off before another war is started.

18 September 1939.

Dined with Robert Byron.

He was very amusing in his richly baroque style with his love of exotic places and extravagant episodes. He is an English eccentric – there is nothing quite like them – with their fear of losing face, their wit, their courage, their thin skins and their thick hides, the rudeness they dole out to others and their own palpitating sensitiveness to the snub.

19 September 1939.

I saw Hadow at the Foreign Office today. He says that the Germans and the Russians will merge into one barbarian horde. They will sweep into the Balkans on a tide of pan-Slavism. Turkey will never fight Russia – her western frontiers are too vulnerable to Russian attack. Therefore, the Turks will not come to the help of Romania when it is attacked by Germany and Russia. We may be able to hold the old line of the Roman Empire along the Rhine against the barbarians. Michal Vyvyan on the other hand says that the Russians and Germans will never be able to agree, and that the Russians must know that they have everything to gain from an eventual German defeat. I dined with Michal last night. He wants to join the Army as a private but at the moment he is employed by the Ministry of Economic Warfare. He says there is no use clinging to comfort. It is all so bloody anyway that one might as well enlist. He says he will not mind seeing people in uniforms killed half as much as it makes one lose one's sense of their individuality whereas if a bomb landed in this restaurant it would be awful watching all the people in their different clothes and with their various manners of suffering making different kinds of faces over it.

There is no war spirit as there was at the beginning. We are just jogging along in a state of some mystification about this peculiar contest. There seem to be such a lot of cultivated intelligent, youngish men about who have nothing to do in this war. They cannot *all* get into the Ministry of Information.

27 September 1939.

Jock Colville[11] told me of a communication from the Shah of Persia to a Victorian Foreign Secretary which he had seen in the Foreign Office Archives. The Shah wrote as follows:

'Last night I dreamed a dream. I was walking in my garden and I saw a great tree growing whose branches overshadowed the lily pond and the rose garden. Lo, as I approached nearer I saw that it was no tree but Queen Victoria of England. Then I gave orders that it be cut down and cast into a pit.'

19 October 1939.

I shall be sorry to leave this quarter for my chic new flat.[12] I have got attached to the dowdy, genteel streets off the Fulham Road. It is part of the ritual of life here to have a stack of pennies for the telephone and a stack of shillings for the gas fire. The boarding-house breakfasts are all right too. I do not mind the young men existing on three pounds a week, keeping their umbrellas rolled and their shoes shone and living for the week-ends of golf in the country. And the daughters of small-town doctors and country clergymen who have taken jobs at Harrods. They may be dull but at least they want things – to have enough money for smart cars and smart restaurants, to chat easily with earls or live in sin in Mayfair flatlets. They get a kick out of thinking of things like that. Far be it from me to look down on them on that account. Earls and Mayfair flats floated before my youthful eyes.

14 November 1939.

When she appeared at the door of my flat I was taken aback to see how smart, how almost beautiful, she looked. In two minutes she had the valet and myself moving sofas and chairs and changing the look of the flat. Tonight the Irish maid said to me, 'It is better this way – before it looked too much like a bachelor's flat – a real bachelor's flat I mean, sir.'

29 December 1939.

She and I went into the sitting-room and drew back the curtains and saw Arlington Street covered with snow and the beautiful sun in the sky. I ate toast and spoonfuls of honey and blissfully drank the unpleasant, cold coffee. Then we went out. She wore a fur cap that covered her ears and that checked blue coat I am not sure of and fur-lined boots that made her stumble. She clung to my arm. I was seized with irritation at this woman stumbling along beside me, clinging to me. Then when I looked into her bright, gay face, with her dark, witty eyes and her pink cheeks I felt proud, amused, happy and loving. We went into St. James's Park. The canal was frozen over – the sea-gulls were sitting perfectly immovable on the ice like birds made of white china. We walked all the way to the end of the canal and back. We passed a lot of Canadian soldiers who stared at her. 'People are looking at me,' she said, 'it must be my fur cap.'

1940

13 February 1940.

The man in the room next to Miriam at Claridge's sleeps with his mother in the same bed. The maids do not like it.

Dined with Victor Cazalet. His overbearing flouncings nonplus me. The party was for Lord and Lady Baldwin.[1] He seems less gaga than I had expected and said in tones of evident sincerity, 'The loneliness of living in the country is past belief.' There were a lot of Members of Parliament there. The more I talk to M.P.s the more the House of Commons sounds like a private school in which everyone has his rating. 'So-and-so is a swat', another 'a good sort', another 'a teacher's pet'.

13 March 1940.

Mr. Massey wanted me to include in my despatch something to contradict the illusion that England is a class-ridden society. Why illusion? He says that the majority of Civil Servants did not go to the public schools. This may be true of the obscurer clerks, and is obviously not true of the men at the top. Lunched with John Tweedsmuir.[2] He does not agree that England will be much changed after the war. 'People who hunt six days a week will only hunt four days and when things pick up again they will hunt six days a week again.'

Everyone is stunned by the Finnish surrender. The Foreign Office only a week ago had no idea of Finland suing for peace with German connivance. The Foreign Office has had more disagreeable surprises in the last twelve months than ever before in its history. The dictatorship countries move suddenly, boldly and secretly. We carry on our fumblings in an irritating half-light of partial censorship.

17 March 1940.

She has gone. There is nothing to show that she has been here except the toothbrush glass of faded violets and some talcum powder on top of the dressing-table – that and my own feeling that other people do not exist, have no solidity or meaning, that they are figures cut out of illustrated papers, photographs of people. I am alone in the flat. I wonder whether I could sit through a dinner at the club. No – I do not think so. The sight of those pink-faced, silver-haired, old boys and those well-kept young men drinking their claret and eating their jugged hare would be too much. The whole settled order of daylight comfort and daytime wisdom has become insufferable. I am beyond any consolation to be derived from the cosiest and most sympathetic friend. My heart hurts – I should like to have it removed and taken away on a silver salver.

3 April 1940.

The housekeeper in these flats is like the enchanted woman in the fairy tale. Every time she opens her mouth toads drop out. As she does not seem to dislike me particularly I think this must be simply 'her way'. Today she came in to arrange my chestnut branches in a vase. 'Very pretty they are, but it was naughty of you to pick them. Why it is a whole branch taken off.' 'Well Mrs. Haines,' I said, 'I need them to brighten up my life.' '*You* need brightening up', she cried with a raucous laugh. Whether she meant that I was a particularly dull dog or whether this was a sarcastic reference to my life of immorality I cannot quite make out. To any complaint she always has an answer ready. A lifetime of dealing with complaining lodgers has taught her the technique of always keeping on the offensive. For instance, one day I said that my room was rather stuffy. 'It is because you keep the electric fire on. It is not 'ealthy.' The price of the fire is included in the rent so that every time I burn it they lose money. I gained this arrangement after long-drawn-out fencing with Mrs. Haines. The other flat dwellers pay for electricity by the hour.

4 April 1940.

Dined with Jock Colville who is in the Prime Minister's Office. He sees everything that is going on in home and international affairs, but tells one nothing, and the questions that one is too much of a gentleman to ask hang heavily over the conversation.

8 April 1940.

Went to the House of Commons to the last day of the great debate on the conduct of the war. There they sat on the front bench – the three of them – Chamberlain, Simon[3] and Hoare, the old-fashioned, solid, upper middle-class Englishmen, methodical, respectable, immovable men who cannot be hurried or bullied, shrewd in short-term bargaining or political manipulation, but with no understanding of this age – of its despair, its violence and its gropings, blinkered in solid comfort, shut off from poverty and risk. Their confidence comes from their certainties. They are the old England. When Chamberlain goes, that goes and it will not return.

Lloyd George attacked the Prime Minister – that old poseur, that mischievous mixture of statesman and minor prophet and tricky Welsh politician. But what an orator! His speech made me think of King Lear's ranting – shot through with gleams of vision. He and Churchill are the only orators in the House. As for Chamberlain, he has authority when he speaks and a sense of the weight of words and an admirable precision. He has at least a standard of speaking.

13 May 1940.

The war has begun all over again in these last few days with the invasion of Holland and Belgium. Events have the same air of unreality that we experienced in the first week in September after the declaration of war. One has the dazed feeling of being dragged in the wake of a runaway destiny. On we go bumping along at a terrific rate with the dust of passing events in our eyes. We are trying to clutch at some meaning in the landscape that rushes past us but it is no good. We are too close to what is happening. This closeness to history puts everything out of focus.

War itself is not unnatural, only the modern weapons of war are unnatural. The weapons dominate us. The pilot is the tool of his plane, the gunner of his gun. That is what makes modern war a new predicament. We are caught in the same trap as the Germans, and we are closer to them than to any neutrals and having got into this mess we long to drag in everyone else. The Germans know the same joys and sorrows that we do. They are the mad dogs who have bitten us and infected us with their madness.

15 May 1940.

They tell us that the greatest battle in history is

beginning. London is sultry with the rumour of it. The possibility of defeat appears in whispers and averted glances.

18 May 1940.

I cannot believe that the French are as demoralised as I hear they are. If they have gone to pieces, we have not been beaten yet, and we will have to go on fighting. We know the history of conquered races, the eternal resentment and the eventual revolt. Better to let this generation go through hell and beat the buggers.

22 May 1940.

Last night I wrote a speech for Mr. Massey to deliver to Canada on the general theme of 'the darkest hour before the dawn', 'British spirit is unbreakable', 'the nightmare of horror and destruction that hangs heavy in the air in these lovely days of English spring'. Mr. Massey delivered it. It was a great success, I believe. Writing these speeches gives me an outlet for my feelings. Hume Wrong says I shall develop into a jelly-bellied flag flapper. Before the war I used to say that I could not understand how any man of conscience could write propaganda, and in my mind I was always critical of my father for the recruiting speeches he made in the first war and *he*, unlike me, was trying to go to the war himself.

Bad reports on French morale, which is said to be undermined by subterranean communism and fifth column activities. Poor old Franckenstein, the Austrian Ambassador, came to see me today. He wants now to get out to Canada. He is usually so suave and mannered but today he looked shattered. He is partly Jewish and he knows that if the Germans come he will be shot at once. N. says, 'Well, he has had a pretty good time all his life. Now he is old – why shouldn't he be knocked on the head? Look at all the chaps who are being killed in France.'

A Canadian R.A.F. pilot came back on leave. He seemed a dull young man, but he and the rest of them are our only hope. All I could do was try to talk to him normally, as he must find it awkward to be treated with the reverence he deserves.

19 May 1940.

When Haines, the valet who works in all these service flats, came to see me this morning he was in a state of high excitement. 'The news this morning is awful. We have got the men and the spirit, but we have not got the planes. *Somebody* is responsible for this.'

Michal Vyvyan said today at lunch, 'How absurd to blame a liberal social democracy for not being organised to deal with war. It is like blaming a fine flower garden for not moving at sixty miles per hour.

Meanwhile two French journalists who attended a lunch in Lord Athlone's[4] honour the other day returned in a state bordering on nervous hysteria. They found all the Blimps at the luncheon discussing sports for the British troops behind the lines. 'Men must have some rugger and cricket. Keep them fit,' etc.

Refugees are beginning to arrive from the Continent – tough-looking Norwegian seamen with shocks of coarse blond hair, dressed in blue serge suits, lunching at Garland's Hotel – Dutch peasant girls in native costume like coloured photographs in the *Geographical Magazine* – walking down Cockspur Street carrying their worldly possessions tied up in bundles. A group of Dutch soldiers in the street in German-looking uniforms gives one a turn. (Shall we see German soldiers in London streets?)

My brother Roley[5] has cabled asking me to do my best to get him a commission in the British Army to get him over here quicker than he could with the Canadians. Why should he be hurled into that hell in France? Why can't he wait until his turn comes to come over with the Canadians? It is not *his* England. It would be more appropriate if I went, as I have always been so bloody English.

I cannot get out of my mind my cousin Jack Grant's face when I saw him the other day. He came over from Canada to join the R.A.F. and has been with them in France since October and now in the Battle of Britain. Earlier he was beginning to have a good-natured, gross look. Now he is pale with fatigue and thin. His eyes look blazing blue and he has two clearly-defined and quite new lines at the corners of his mouth.

This office is being invaded by women of the aristocracy wanting to send their children overseas. Lady S. who came in today is typical of the old-fashioned kind. She was most anxious not to do anything which might divert English currency from this country. But they are all looking to Canada now. We are to provide them with men and ammunition, take their children, intern their fifth column, etc.

29 May 1940.

I could hear the guns plainly tonight as I sat writing in the club library – I suppose at the mouth of the Thames. Natalie Hogg says that last week-end she sat in the garden at her place in Kent and could hear the gunfire from France all afternoon long.

The Canadians here are becoming disillusioned about the English. Mike Pearson says, 'Never have I been so glad to be a Canadian as in these last days – at least we are not responsible for this mess.' Patterson of the C.P.R. says, 'If I ever have to go through another war let it not be with the English – their slowness drives me mad.' Even the loyal Mr. Massey (more in sorrow than in anger) admits the flaws. But so do the English themselves. Lord Davies[6] said today, 'Things must go better now – after all we have made every bloody mistake that can be made so that we shall be reduced to doing something right in the end.' What makes one fear for the result of this war is not merely Nazi military success but the fact that they have faith in their rulers and we have not – or should not have. Yet we may win in the end because inertia rolling at last into action will be heavy with reserves of strength and wealth, whereas the German will keyed to this tremendous tempo must crack unless it has respite. Perhaps it is nearer cracking than we dream of. To me it is a sheer impossibility that Nazi power, if it triumphed in this war, could live for more than fifteen years. Because it cannot rest. It has no principle of growth in it and so must always be moving on until it meets an immovable object against which it is dashed to pieces. May the British Empire be that immovable object.

2 June 1940.

Went with Mike Pearson to Dover. There we really had the feeling of being in an extension of the actual war zone. Destroyers were coming in and out of the harbour, going to Dunkirk to embark the remains of the British Expeditionary Force and the French Army of the North.[7] As we walked along the pier we saw one of the destroyers returning, its stern had been blown clean off by a bomb. It was limping home with flags still flying. We went alongside two more destroyers, one English and one French. They began landing French soldiers who were herded into a troop train by a thin young officer in riding breeches. Looking down on the decks of the British destroyer we could see a bearded sailor lying asleep beside his gun. On the French destroyer the sailors were clustered in a chattering group – one was showing the others a postcard of a nude woman and they were gossiping and laughing. Soon a tug drew up alongside and began to debouch German prisoners. They were pallid and grimy and looked as if they had been kept underground for a year, the result I suppose of being packed together under the hatches while they were being bombed by their own people from the air. They came shambling out on to the deck in the sunshine and began running up the companion-way as if they had the devil behind them. There they formed into a file waiting to be taken away in buses. I remember the German prisoners-of-war at Calais, when I was a boy after the last war, carrying slop-pails around the British camps. They had shaven heads. These men had long hair which fell over their eyes as they stumbled along the gangplank. Some were aviators, and these had an air of arrogance. The privates ran and huddled like sheep. Prisoners without their guns and helmets have the look of having suffered an amputation, as if they were deprived of a vital limb or had been castrated. Then came the German wounded. They were swung from the decks of the ship by a crane. None of them moved or cried out but lay in waxen immobility as if they were already dead. While the procession of prisoners and wounded moved by, the Tommies who were guarding the pier remained silent. Anyone who spoke spoke in lowered tones. Out in the harbour a mist hung over the smooth sea and dozens of craft lay there at anchor after coming and going to Dunkirk time after time. About the cliffs the eternal gulls circled. Two little girls were shrilly calling to each other from their bicycles as they rode in and out of the small gardens in front of a row of houses at the foot of the great bluff of cliff behind the docks. These docks, and in fact the whole of Dover, are now within range of German shell-fire from Boulogne. But the life of the town is going on just the same. We could see the groups of old ladies coming out of church after eleven o'clock service and standing for a minute to chat in the sun. In the field of butter-cups outside the town some little boys were rolling about wrestling – they each wore their little card-board gas-mask case.

From Dover they can see Boulogne at night burning across the Channel and hear the bombs as they fall. Why the Germans do not bomb the small inner harbour at Dover, so crowded with shipping, one cannot guess. The naval officer who took us around, a lean individual with a sardonic, leathery face, indicated the cliffs of Dover with a wave of the hand, 'They may come over here,' he said, 'but if they do, not one will get out alive.'

6 June 1940.

Having half an hour to spare this afternoon I strolled down to the Foreign Office. No one would have thought that a German invasion is just around the corner. There were three or four pleasantly satirical and studiedly casual young secretaries draped about the room drinking their tea and eating strawberry shortcake. It might have been a scene from a skit on His Majesty's Diplomatic Service. In fact I am sure they are all conscientious, hard-working civil servants more aware than most people of what is at stake. After all their cup of tea and their ironic little jokes are pleasures shared by this whole nation and are no doubt part of *What We Are Fighting For*.

Our standards are being overturned. What is brought home to me is my existence as a member of a community in a way that I never dreamed of before. I rather fancied myself as a cosmopolitan who laughed at blimpish patriotism. Now I subscribe to all the old cries – 'My country right or wrong,' I could have my room plastered with these cracker mottoes which have now become for me eternal truths. Meanwhile we are all waiting, almost longing for these bombs. Hart Massey said to me today, 'I wish they would start bombing us.' And Michal said with relish, 'Soon the bombs will be landing on our heads.' This must be the mentality of the civilians behind the lines. The soldiers do not swell the chorus, nor have I heard any women express a pious hope for a bombing raid. The soldiers and the women must be right.

15 June 1940.

Lunched with Mrs. Andreae. She wanted to ask me about taking her grandchildren to America to escape the war. She is a shrewd, worldly, old woman but she is waiting to make her decision until she has consulted a fortune-teller. I should not laugh at her as for the last few days I have had a sort of obsession that the continuation of Hitler's successes was bound up with this unnaturally fine weather that goes on and on. 'Hitler weather' they call it. It is not only the effect of the weather in speeding up the movement of his mechanised forces but a purely silly and superstitious association in my mind.

17 June 1940.

The French have declared that organised resistance is at an end and the French Government have asked the British Government if with their approval they may sue for an armistice. The British Government have replied, 'Yes, provided the French fleet is handed over to us intact.' Apparently the French do not intend to resist in North Africa. It is difficult to see how they can hand over their fleet to us if they are going to make peace with Germany. A full-dress German attack on England is expected this week or the next. We have about five divisions trained and equipped. The Germans have one hundred divisions. They have a pronounced superiority in the air and in equipment. It is estimated that by bombing they could reduce the produce of our factories to twenty-five per cent of the present output. It would take the Americans at least six months to begin supplying this country on a scale equal to the needs.

Whatever the odds this country is not prepared to surrender and would not stand for it, although there are elements at the top and bottom of the social scale who secretly lean towards it. If after three months of total war this country cannot take it (any more than the Finns or the French could take it, and they are both brave races) then I suppose we shall make peace as France is doing now after thousands of men, women and children have been killed. Mike Pearson says, 'If this country makes peace I hope Canada will become a republic and that would be the end of this business of our duty to the Empire.'

I got my promotion today as Second Secretary – an odd time to get it.

22 June 1940.

Several exhausting days during which the office has been flooded with people trying to arrange for their children to get out to Canada. I have been impressed by three things:

1.The unnatural coolness of English parents – no broken voices or tear-filled eyes.

2. The incredible confusion caused when civil servants are taken by surprise and by a sudden onrush of events. I see how 'government' breaks down. The picture of such a breakdown is a queue of people with urgent problems and a distracted civil servant, his desk covered with forms and regulations, cornered by 'reality'.

3. I am impressed by the sacrosanct importance of the British Nanny. People here would rather let their children run the risk of being bombed than send them out on a sea voyage without their Nanny.

Refugees are arriving from our Legation staff in Paris. They have left most of their possessions behind them. Madame Vanier, the wife of our Minister to Paris, stood at the front door watching the boxes of documents from the Paris Legation arrive. Suddenly she gave a cry of emotion, threw herself upon one package – 'My hat-box – my hat-box. I never thought I would see it again.'

Saw Roger Makins of the Foreign Office at the club today. He says the French Government are completely demoralised and will accept anything the Germans dish out to them. He says it is a question of the collapse of the whole fabric of the Third Republic.

If these politicians of ours ever read any serious modern literature they might not be so surprised at what is happening in France. For years now there has been bad news from France. Their best writers have given a shaking picture of the dry rot which has overtaken the French bourgeoisie. The fascist and communist undercurrent in French literature has been quite audible. Books like Céline's *Voyage to the End of the Night* are social documents as important as white papers or ambassadors' despatches.

Mr. R. B. Bennett[8] has just made a speech at some school prize-giving saying that there can never be a fifth column in England because it is such a land of liberty, etc. Let him go and take a look at the slums in this country.

I dined with Tony Balásy of the Hungarian Legation. He talked about the overthrow of the small states in Europe by Hitler, and said that to understand the mentality of the people of those states one would have to have lived there through the post-war years. He said, 'You have the Big Power point of view. If the British Empire were destroyed you would have all lost something real, but it is not the same for us – we have known all along that our independence, the independence of a country like Hungary, depended on a precarious balance of Big Power rivalries. Such independence was always something of a fiction, although we might come ahead of Germany or England in the alphabetical lists for committees of the League of Nations. Our politicians had to repeat that we would die rather than give up a lot of this precious independence – still at heart we knew we had it on sufferance.'

I can see that despite his hatred of Nazis Tony is half fascinated by the idea of a united European bloc by whatever means achieved. Some Europeans may be tempted to think that if the small sovereign state entities can be broken down and Europe united it is worth the price of temporary Hitler domination, because Hitler will not last forever, and after he is gone it will be as impossible to reconstruct the Europe of small states as it was to reconstruct feudal Europe after the fall of Napoleon.

26 June 1940.

Walked today along the Broad Walk through Kensington Gardens. It was thronged with soldiers, the remains of the shattered continental armies, Dutch, French and Norwegian. Then the Canadians who have become almost part of the London streetscape and the newly arrived New Zealanders including many Maoris and then, the altogether more solid, as if carved out of some other material, Guardsmen. Moving in this procession of soldiers of the nations I had the sense of swimming in the full tide of history.

My office is the door of escape from hell. Day after day the stream of people press in. Today, for example, some of the Austrian Rothschilds (escaped from a concentration camp) are trying to pass their medical examination to go to Canada. Would I arrange a financial guarantee for them? The wife of one of the wealthiest men in England is trying to get out of the country. Her husband is a Jew and a leading anti-Nazi. Will I get her a letter to prove (on very flimsy grounds) that she is a Canadian? Lady B, looking radiant, comes to ask if I would arrange for her son's prep-school to be affiliated with a boys' boarding school in Canada and to migrate there *en masse*. The Marchioness of C, in the uniform of the Women's Naval Auxiliary Unit, wants to get three children out to Canada at once. Two Canadian journalists want to get their wives out but there is a mysterious delay in getting their exit permits. The

Spanish Ambassador wants us to get accommodation for his daughter, his mother and a troop of maids and governesses on board the next ship. They are going to Canada for a little rest from the nervous tension of the war. He knows he is slipping with his own Government and may be in exile himself any day. The Polish Ambassador wants us to take the wives and daughters of one hundred high Polish political and diplomatic dignitaries. Count X, the anti-fascist with a price on his head must leave for Canada at once on a mission of great importance. I have only touched the edge of one day's work. I do not mention my own friends and relatives who want to get out. Here we have a whole social system on the run, wave after wave after wave of refugees and these are only the people at the top, people who can by titles, letters of introduction, or the ruling manner force their way into Government offices and oblige one to give them an interview. What of the massed misery that cannot escape?

The sense of the dissolution of civilised society is overpowering.

7 July 1940.

Mr. Massey says there will be no revolution in England – if socialism comes it will be a gradual kindly English socialism. There will still be country houses but only the smaller ones. Chatsworth[9] will go. He foresees an early German attempt at invasion and the early establishment of martial law in England.

16 July 1940.

Lord Cromer, the former Lord Chamberlain, came in to see me today to explain some complicated business about the Suez Canal Company which boiled down, as usual, to our taking another refugee into Canada, this time a French Jewish financier. Lord Cromer was very deliberate, very formal, very detailed and conducted the whole negotiation with the leisurely flourishes proper to the transaction of business between gentlemen in the reign of Queen Victoria. It always amuses me to see how much these old boys enjoy getting what they set out to get and how much charm, manner, and wiliness they are willing to expend; sometimes on objectives which only remotely concern them. But such negotiations are the breath of life to them.

I have a hankering to get the Hutterite Brotherhood out to Canada. They are a sect of pacifist community-livers – many of them Germans at present residing in the Cotswolds where their life is being made impossible by the suspicions of the country folk. My weakness for obscure and unpopular religious sects of a pacifist or quietist complexion makes me susceptible to them. Their leader, a man called Arnold, looks an Oberammergau Christ with beard, smock and knee-breeches. He seems somewhat sly and smooth. The Canadian Government do not want them.

Lunched with Mrs. Andreae and the wife of the British Minister to Sofia. Mrs. Andreae says she has it on good authority that a French refugee approaching the cliffs of Dover on his way to escape from France saw a cloud of angels armed with spears hanging in the heavens over England. She firmly believes we are protected by God or the stars or something – I cannot quite make out what – as she alternates so much between Christianity and astrology. There is even a suggestion there was more than meets the eye in the British escape from Dunkirk – meaning that it was arranged for our special benefit by God. The latter idea is quite widely spread with the corollary that it was the response to our National Day of Prayer. It is not only old women who believe this but at least one contemporary of my own – a naval officer now in charge of a destroyer. However, naval officers do have strange beliefs.

I now hear that the ferocious internees whom the British Government begged us on bended knees to take to Canada to save this country from their nefarious activities are mostly entirely inoffensive anti-Nazi refugees who have been shovelled out to Canada at a moment's notice where they may have a disagreeable time, as our authorities have no files about them and will not know whom or what to believe. Part of the trouble is due to the fact that the Home Office and the War Office seem barely to be on speaking terms.

5 August 1940.

The intermingling of various ingredients of English social life is proceeding apace. War is stirring up the mixture. English men and women of different classes, localities, sets and tastes are for the first time talking to each other. This appeared to be an impossibility in England. The weather was previously the one subject upon which everyone had fixed for conversations with strangers.

15 August 1940.

Garnons, Hereford, the country house taken by the Masseys as a convalescent hospital for Canadian officers – big rambling house – early Gothic revival about 1820 – battlements and a great tower. Looks its best by moonlight (like all imitations of the Gothic). A nice house – big rooms full of chintz-covered sofas and bad Italian paintings collected by an eighteenth-century ancestor on the Grand Tour. Some beautiful mirrors – Lelys, Romneys and Laszlos in the dining-room. The view from my room was like the background of an eighteenth-century hunting print. The house was on a hill with a prospect over a valley and the Black Mountains as a back-drop – a lovely stretch of skyscape across which the aeroplanes pass and return on their way to intercept German bombers over Bristol. We live a country-house life – croquet, conversation, billiards and flirtation, while a few miles away the air battles go on which are to decide our fate. When one of these noisy monsters zooms across our neat, snug valley it is as though it had flown straight back into the old England of port and leisure in which we are incongruously living.

A terrifying night. There are old and evil spirits in this part of the world. A friend who spent his childhood in just such an old house as this set in a lush and misty park, told me that all this Welsh border country is haunted. Here one believes in the fears of peasants and one prays their ancient prayers.

I was led in a dream of circles through my private hell and all the images which congeal my blood and scarify my soul. My daytime self was abolished, I looked out from my window at the quiet moonlit valley and hoped for an air raid to break the silence and deliver me back in the world where courage and intelligence could still avail me.

As the days went by, one after another of those staying here let slip that they had been unable to sleep and nervously laughing asked, 'Is this house haunted?' All day the sun glows steadily through the mist. The heat haze lingers like smoke over the clumps of oak trees in the park and the aeroplanes pass and return across the slumbrous valley.

In the game book which goes back to 1860 I see that this week in August has always been oppressively hot here with the birds lying close. I like to turn the pages of this record with its thumbnail sketches of days' shooting kept by the successive squires of Garnons – of days when it was 'wild and wet' and 'I never remember to have seen the birds behave so badly' and the days when all went well and the score of the day's bag tells its own story.

Our nerves have been too long taut and this sudden relaxation, this enchanted castle, these long idle days – it is all somehow too much. Today's was only a small incident but for an hour it filled the sky. We were motoring to the Black Mountains and Mrs. Massey decided just as we were climbing the mountain road to Llantony through the close green lanes, to turn back. The rest of us had wanted to go on – impossible to describe the spell of dumb rage that seized us – the heavy clash of her will against our silent resistance. We motored back down from the cool mist-soaked mountain air into the summer languor of the valley. No one in the car spoke all the way back. When we reached the front door we separated to our rooms as if frightened to face each other and to reveal how strongly we had been shaken for no reason.

17 August 1940.

Complete change of atmosphere. The rest of the party have arrived from London. Most successful expedition to Llantony Abbey where the monks kept a Christian oasis during the Dark Ages of the Norse raids. The ruins are deep in a valley buried in the recesses of the Black Mountains, almost inaccessible most of the year as the roads are a morass. Now part of the Abbey is farm buildings, washing hangs in the ruined nave, chickens step delicately among the cowpats in the roofless lady chapel. I am glad the attempt to restore it in the 1900s by a Roman Catholic monastic order was a failure. Modern Roman Catholic priests would have ruined it with their atrocious taste in buildings and they would have given it a horrid, preserved, or worse still, 'revived' air.

Came back and read David Cecil's[10] description of eighteenth-century country-house life in an eighteenth-century country-house library – cream and gilt with classical busts and blue and white china urns over the bookcases. Mr. Massey and I are both bitten with this place. We cannot escape the charms of the past. Their institutions were made for men and women human in scale. Now everything is over life-size. We are no good for the future. It is not our picnic. I tell myself it will be exciting to be alive in an age of change after the war, but it would only be exciting if we could rebuild the human scale.

26 August 1940. London.

There go the sirens again! I do not know what will be left of our nerves after a winter of this. First the wail announcing impending doom. Then the city holds its breath as the last dying sound of the siren fades and we wait. Of course everyone is calm enough on the surface, but one gets jumpy at sudden noises. At first raids were exciting and frightening. Now they are getting unpleasant, risky and tiring.

3 September 1940.

Week-end with the Bessboroughs who are living on in the middle of the glorious Le Nôtre-style park which is now in the direct line of the German bombers attacking Portsmouth. During the night six bombs landed in the park. On Sunday morning we set out in a little procession to examine the damage. Lord Bessborough, wearing a panama hat, led the way. He prodded the bomb craters with his walking-stick and chatted with magnificent and old-fashioned condescension to the local farmers. Once this insidious process is under way, affability on the one side and an answering feeling of proud gratification are established, the silken cord binds all parties in their respective places in the social order.

5 September 1940.

Visit to the Canadian Headquarters installed in an ugly country house surrounded by repulsive yew-hedges. General McNaughton[11] holds forth surrounded by a Greek chorus of red-faced generals and brigadiers whose inertia (dating from the close of the last war) is troubled by his incessant darting vitality. They dare not meet that eye. He may or may not be a great man. He is a prima donna. The star of the party was R. B. Bennett, in a ponderously playful vein. Conversation was not brilliant – food none too good – atmosphere creaking with military courtesies enough to make the hackles rise on the back of any good civilian like myself.

6 September 1940.

Lunched with Sir J. M., Scotland Yard, to talk about internees.[12] He is 'liberal-minded', slightly malicious, a rather donnish sort of elderly civil servant with a passion for the science of finger printing. Very nice to me – rather stern with the Club's temporary waitresses.

Met that ballet dancer in the street. I wonder? She has magnificent pools of greenish eyes in a naïve, shrewd, American face – slight golden down on her cheek bones and the strong neck of her craft. She adopts a sort of little-girl trustful posture towards me and wears a small white bow in her hair.

7 September 1940.

Dinner with R. B. McCallum, my former tutor at Oxford, at the National Liberal Club, a portentous place, vast and gloomy with walls of dark green and brown tiles. The dining-room is like the main hall of a railway station with an enormous marble statue of Gladstone at one end of it. The whole place is the morgue where the remains of the Liberal Party might be laid out. Our conversation was appropriate. He began by saying that he had that day been motoring through the industrial suburbs off the Great West Road. 'A cheering sight,' he said. I suppose I may have winced at this description of that nondescript waste of dreary characterless little houses. 'You,' he went on, 'and other lovers of the picturesque may lament the green fields and pretty villages which once stretched about London, but remember that those villages housed a desperately poor population of agricultural labourers. You may say that the factory workers' houses which now stand there are ugly and depressing, but remember that the fathers and grandfathers of these workers lived four or five in a room in some filthy slum where misery, dirt, gin and incest flourished. Now these people have attained respectability, the dearest craving of the working classes. That is a great achievement. You with your apocalyptic talk of the spiritual deadness of the babbitry ignore all this, but it is the triumph of our civilisation, and we are too slow to praise it. You talk to me of our failure to turn the Industrial Revolution to good account in human terms, but when war broke out we were busily engaged in doing just that, although I admit that the pace was slow and that there was still a great deal of slack to be taken up.'

13 September 1940.

A week of air raids. Our ears have grown sharp for the sounds of danger – the humming menace that sweeps from the sky, the long whistle like an indrawn breath as the bomb falls. We are as continually alive to danger as animals in the jungle.

During a raid the silent empty streets wait for the shock like 'a patient etherised upon a table'. The taxis race along carrying their fares to the shelters. A few pedestrians caught out in the streets make their way with as much restraint as possible to the nearest shelter, keeping an eye open for protection – for friendly archways. They try to saunter but long to run.

In the parks the fallen leaves lie thick upon the paths. No one has time to collect them into bonfires and burn them. The paint is beginning to peel off the great cream coloured houses in Carlton House Terrace and the grand London squares. The owners will do nothing about it until 'after the war'. London is beginning to look down-at-heel and a bit battered. Every now and then one comes upon a gap in a row of houses or a façade of shops. In the gap is a pile of rubble where the bomb has hit. I suppose gradually there will be more and more such gaps until the face of London is pitted and furrowed with them.

The other night I was caught on my way home from Chelsea in a heavy barrage with falling shrapnel and turned into a public shelter to wait until things were quieter. There were half a dozen old women of the Belcher charwoman variety, two conversational old men in battered bowlers and a drunken Irish maid-servant who kept mocking the English for their credulity and stupidity, 'You English, sure you're the dumbest nation on earth. Now do you believe all this you read in the papers about how many German planes were shot down. Don't you see it is all propaganda now.' Her harangues were greeted with sardonic amusement. These people were all cold and all sleepless. They had spent three nights in this shelter and outside was the recurrent roar of the barrage. Their homes in Chelsea have been badly pasted. The shelter itself was a feeble affair giving no protection from bombs. But their stolidity was unshaken. Their retort was the Englishman's immemorial reply to danger – irony. The kind of joke which hinges on the thought, 'Well it ain't the Ritz exactly.' They were not afraid but they did want one thing – 'a cup of tea'.

14 September 1940.

The attacks on London have only been going on for ten days. So far people are steady, there has been no panic. But they are depressed. Everyone is suffering from lack of sleep and nervous tension. There is some feeling that the poor are taking it the hardest and many complaints about lack of shelters. The ideal thing from Hitler's point of view would be to continue this all winter and then to attack in the spring. Is he strong enough to wait? That is the question hanging over us. His raids certainly have not been a spectacular success, but they are making a dent all right.

My new girl is a ballet dancer. She is an American girl who studied ballet in Paris and is now dancing with a Polish company in London. She seems very dumb. We were walking along Jermyn Street the other day and by way of conversation I said, 'This is a great street for tarts.' 'What are tarts?' I nearly fell flat on my face in the street and then I explained it was an English term for prostitutes. She clucked her tongue disapprovingly. She has been in England six months and she does not know what a tart is. Sometimes she seems almost half-witted. She looks exactly like all ballet dancers. She has ivory, pale skin and a hard body like an athletic boy. The extraordinary thing about her are her eyes which are enormous – the eyes of a tragedy queen. She herself says she feels her eyes 'do not seem to belong to her'. She seems very truthful and quite without artifices.

15 September 1940.

The luxury restaurants of the West End are dying on their feet. I went into the Apéritif the other night for dinner. It was completely empty. Groups of tired-looking waiters muttering together in corners, the bartender brooding over his deserted bar. Miss Lily who does the accounts was listlessly turning over the pages of *The Tatler*. 'My gawd – what freaks!' she observed studying the wedding groups. She too looked tired and strained, and there was an edge of excitement and irritability beneath her carefully casual Mayfair manner.

16 September 1940.

It has come to a state where none of us can be sure that we shall meet each other the next day and we begin to look for a gap in the party. Bombs have been raining around here, Berkeley Square, Park Lane and Regent Street. So far none in St. James's Street or Pall Mall,[13] but this must be pure luck, and there is more than a chance that we shall get it in the next week. Life is 'nasty, brutish and short'.

I went to the lunch-time ballet. It was wonderful to see *Les Sylphides* and the meticulous attention that went to each movement and step. The permanent importance of an art compared with the noisy, accidental crashing of tons of high explosives. Aesthetic standards are the only ones that stand up in these times. They are not mixed up with the current political-moral mess – not mouthed by Hitler nor by the Archbishop of Canterbury – not understood by either, although the first knows enough of them to hate them. In this world there is still an escape – not away from reality – but back to reality.

Drove home through the endless mean streets around the Battersea Power Station – glass out of all the shop windows – gaps and piles of rubble in every street – signs saying 'Police Warning – Unexploded Bomb' at almost every street corner, but still women coming out of pubs with mugs of beer. Children still playing in the streets and a patriarchal old man with a beard sitting serenely on a porch looking at the sunset. Yet this thing is beginning to get people down. There are desperate faces of fatigue, not so much the danger as the sleeplessness and the dreary discomfort, the long Russian-style queues waiting for the buses, waiting to get into the shelters.

In the Dorchester the sweepings of the Riviera have been washed up – pot-bellied, sallow, sleek-haired nervous gentlemen with loose mouths and wobbly chins, wearing suede shoes and checked suits, and thin painted women with fox capes and long silk legs and small artificial curls clustering around their bony, sheeplike heads.

This is one of those stimulating nights on which I feel a complete immunity from fear. I put it down to brandy – a blessed drink which the war has made me discover. I walked home down St. James's Street under a brilliant moon to the usual orchestra of guns. There were autumn leaves thick on the street, leaves on the pavements on St. James's Street! It is like the Fall of Rome! These minor symptoms of dissolution make one sad. No tarts anywhere. If I had met one I should have been compelled to go home with her. The barrage seems lighter tonight and the bombs more frequent.

22 September 1940.

The moment I stepped out of the station I smelt the familiar smell of Oxford. What nonsense the woman was talking the other day when she said that it did not matter if a city were destroyed physically, if its soul lived. Cities are nothing without their bodies. When you have destroyed Paris and Oxford what happens to their souls? Oxford rebuilt in this age! It would be easy to see what it would be like by looking at the new Bodleian Extension – that blankly commonplace hulk which they have dared to plant in the face of the Sheldonian. *That* is the most distressing thing about Oxford – for the rest the changes are temporary. The streets surge with people – air force pilots and mechanics, soldiers, civil servants, evacuees from the East End and from the West End too, refugees from Europe – French, Austrian, Polish.

In the George Restaurant where aesthetes willowed and whinneyed, where hearties roared and roistered, the tables are taken by heavy-bottomed foreign women or local tradesmen turned majors (Oxford restaurant proprietors must be in seventh heaven). Occasionally one sees a few undergraduates up here on some kind of course edging their way with a self-consciously aloof air among this rabble. Absurdly enough one's own face instinctively takes on this same expression of superiority.

I walked back today part of the way from Marston under a rainy grey sky appropriate to an Oxford Sunday (indeed in my experience rain and Sunday are inseparable in Oxford). In the village street a group of little girls were collected under an umbrella held by the tallest of them. Two ancient dames dressed alike in black with touches of mauve at the throat and clutching prayer books and ebony walking-sticks trundled timidly to church, glancing up and down for fear of cyclists. Earlier I had met the vicar bicycling along a country lane with his black straw hat pushed on the back of his head. All this made me remember that life in England has not been touched – that the raids are only superficial wounds. I stood waiting for my bus in Marston churchyard. I could hear the organ grinding out the music for the evening service and could see lights in the church windows. Outside in the churchyard was a modest war memorial 'Lest We Forget' and lower down 'Their names are recorded within the Church'. The bus lolled slowly up the hill.

That night after dinner I went for a short walk passing the gate of Christ Church – went in – Tom Quad was deserted and I walked through to Peckwater. Mist hung thickly over the buildings, and the damp smell of the Thames valley filled my nostrils. There were chinks of light at a few windows where the blackout curtains were not tightly drawn and the rickety music of a gramophone came from one corner of the Quad where a family of evacuees were living. Inevitably I thought of that night at Oxford when I penetrated the Quad for the first time. I felt at once sad and quite unsentimental – sad and impersonal.

These two days in Oxford have passed in a trance-like state of convalescence. The absence of noise makes me feel as though I were in a dream. The misty atmosphere, the grey sky, the slight persistent rain and the ghost-like familiar notes of the clock in Tom Tower have induced a state of mild hypnosis. I have been passively suspended without will or desire. The hope of happiness and the wish for gratification seem memories as if I were already in some dim Lethe.

25 September 1940.

Two Poles and a Hungarian journalist for whom I got visas to go to Canada have been drowned in the *City of Benares* by enemy action on their way to Canada. One of the Poles, the Manager of the Gdynia Shipping Line, was a pleasant, pale man with spectacles who looked like a young professor. His wife and family had gone to Canada and he was going out to pay them a visit. The Hungarian was a very unattractive individual with whom I had had 'words' before he left. Tony Balásy says, 'There was a man moving heaven and earth to get out of the country because he was in such a panic of fear and then he meets with this dreadful end. That is fate.' Tony has no use for cowards or, as he calls them, 'people who do not control their nerves'. He is a very nervous person but totally disciplined. He is rather proud that he has never been in an air-raid shelter and always sleeps in his own bed. He does this from conviction and on principle. I do the same from laziness. If we were both caught in our beds by a bomb no one would know how much more praiseworthy Tony's motives were than mine.

28 September 1940.

This new American girl of mine is a starry-eyed little number from Portland, Oregon. She tells me that she comes from a fine family in Portland and that they have a lovely home there and she has a brother called Bugs because he is interested in the study of insects. She has taken a course on flower arrangement and says that in her opinion 'simplicity is more elegant than anything else'. She says she could not bear to marry a man she could not look up to and respect and he must be in a good position. She despises everything to do with ballet (she is a ballet dancer by occupation) because it is not respectable and the men she meets there she treats with scorn because they have not a good position by Portland standards.

Week-end with Ted Achilles of the United States Embassy. In the party was Colonel Lee, U.S. Military Attaché, with old-fashioned bristling moustache, the sort who I am sure likes a woman with a figure – 'none of your new-fangled ideas'. Very optimistic about English victory – thinks the war is going along very satisfactorily; a Secretary of the United States Embassy, a bullet-headed obstinate type with the habit of lowering platitudes into the conversation which really make one pause and look in embarrassment at one's boots. The Air Attaché described the new flying Fortresses – four-engined planes – ten times the size of the Hurricane and Spitfire. They think the Germans are making a poor showing in the air war.

6 October 1940.

Week-end with H.L. at his house on the slope of

Hog's Back. You could not have a more perfect example of the eccentric, comfortable, self-absorbed bachelor. Everything in the house has its own story. Nothing can be moved from its place without upsetting the owner. His taste is his own. It includes baroque, wooden, gilt candelabra, varnished copies of Italian primitives, small plaster figures of St. Francis of Assisi and the Christ Child and (the *clou* of the collection and of the collector) a painting in oils of a very handsome young American man. H. by occupation fills a prosaic job, but once at home he lives a life of play-acting and dressing-up. He came down to breakfast this morning in a pair of impossibly tight riding-breeches, a tweed coat and a kind of silk stock arrangement. He was not going to ride – it was just his idea of a 'costume'. With pride he showed me a silk and velvet dressing-gown which he had made for him at the cost of two hundred dollars; it was given to him as he says 'by a man with more money than sense'. Portly and priestly in appearance, ecclesiastical in taste, exuberant in dress, he is a slave of food and comfort. These are provided for him by a Scottish housekeeper who rules him by her concentrated attention on his stomach. A man of a dozen fads, he is a medievalist, an authority on local history, a believer in herbal pills, an ardent anglo-catholic, and a student of yoga. If you open a drawer anywhere in the house you are likely to find a crucifix or a string of beads. In the bathroom every kind of unguent cream and bath salts flourishes exuberantly. There are even glass pots of powders and creams. A bath becomes a minor sensuality. His beds (by a special bed-maker) are so vast and deep that, as he says, 'You have to be rescued from them in the morning.' In the end this concentration upon his manias, this obsession with comfort, this minute regulation of time and food and sleep are oppressive and even frightening. One smells the sexual repression through all the smokescreen of his whims. One scents the possessive tyrant in the genial host. He swells in one's eye by the very force of his obsessions into a sort of magician in whom kindliness and malice are mingled, but who has long since lost all real connection with the world of men in which he moves with such false affability.

9-11 October 1940.

How much does this continual danger to our lives make us forget our smaller fears? Do we still suffer from shyness, or feel that a cold in the throat may turn into pneumonia? If we do, I think it is more by habit than by conviction. We are accustomed to our familiar fears; in the same way even in the midst of a bombardment with planes droning overhead and the noise of the barrage I can sleep quite comfortably, but if through this monstrous uproar I hear the still, small voice of a dripping tap, I get out of bed unable to sleep until the sound is stopped.

Places I hope will not be destroyed – the unregenerate streets of Soho, the chilly splendours of Carlton House Terrace. But I would rather see them bombed than torn down to make way for blocks of flats. My fury against the German bomber is not nearly so great as the rage I feel against the speculative builder and his supine accomplices – the local authorities and the bovine public. We are at least doing everything possible to prevent the destruction of historic London from the air. I wrote just now of fury against the German bomber, but I feel none. The random bombing of central London is like an act of nature, like a volcano erupting nightly. The bombers are like the agents of some blindly destructive force. Their bombs fall, like rain, on the just and the unjust. They do not hate me nor I hate them. We are caught in a fated mechanistic duel of forces which maims and kills bombers and bombed. This is a war fought in cold blood. That is my feeling about it, but I often hear people say, 'Why don't we give them hell in Berlin?' I sense a lack of conviction, a sort of nervous irritability in this question as though those who asked it knew the futility of the query. But I may be reflecting in others my own feelings.

Sometimes I feel brave for no good reason and then I wish for danger. Why should one always be brave twenty-four hours a day any more than one is always amorous. The rest of the time one has to act courage or love because it is not admitted to say 'Today I am feeling cowardly' or 'Tonight I do not want you.'

12 October 1940.

Hart (Massey) and I went to an American movie –
a saga of a small town in America. We sat there
lapped in a feeling of false security while the cinema
shook from the explosion of bombs outside. As we
came out it seemed as though all Piccadilly were on
fire. Tongues of flames were licking the colonnade at
the top of the London Pavilion. We drove to the
Dorchester Hotel through bombs and shrapnel –
there seemed to be fire everywhere. For once London
had a catastrophic appearance worthy of American
newspaper accounts. At the Dorchester we found the
Masseys pacing the floor nervously. In our elation
Hart and I seemed childishly excited in telling them
what was going on. Mr. Massey lost his temper, and,
his voice rising to a peak of exasperation, he said,
'You seem to be pleased at what is happening. I do
not understand you. These places that are being
destroyed are irreplaceable – to me it is like a personal loss.' We looked somewhat shamefaced. Then he
led the way on to the Dorchester roof. We could see
fires in all directions. A bomb came whistling down
and we all ran for shelter except Hart, who remained
standing where he was – an obstinate figure. I was
annoyed with myself for taking shelter not because I
was afraid but because the others had run for shelter
and I had instinctively imitated them instead of waiting as Hart did to see if it was necessary. I noticed
that when Mr. Massey came down from the roof he
was in the same exalted state that we had been in

when we arrived. There is an exhilaration in this orgy of destruction and in the danger, but next day was the morning after the debauch. I was awakened by the sound of shovelling glass.

16 October 1940.

Dined at the Dorchester Hotel which is like a luxury liner on which the remnants of London society have embarked in the midst of this storm. Through the thick walls and above the music of the band one could hear the noise of the barrage and at intervals the building shook like a vibrating ship with the shock of an exploding bomb falling nearby. Meanwhile there was N. coming swaying into the dining-room, his hands resting affectionately – reminiscently – on his buttocks, with the pale, grey face of a tired but impudent and dishonest waiter. He stopped at several tables on his way to join a bird of gleaming and immaculate plumage whose habitat might be Cannes, Newport, Le Touquet or Mayfair. She wore in her hair a little velvet bow which by its irrelevancy pointed up the polished chic of her person. At another table was Lady Diana Cooper – the postcard beauty of the First Great War whom every officer in those days carried in his eye. I remember as a boy having her pointed out to me walking in Bond Street. 'There,' said my aunt, 'is Lady Diana, the Great Beauty.' In my anxiety to see what was meant by a Great Beauty I left my aunt's side and hurried to the other end of the street and walked down it again so that I could pass her once more. I caught a confused glimpse of a marble white arm and a glance from those azure eyes so often described and still so magical.

18 October 1940.

I went with Mary[14] to Bath to visit her mother, Mrs. Adlington. I have hardly seen Mary since she joined the A.T.S. at the beginning of the war. We have been swept apart – she out of London. Yet at once it was as if we had never been separated. Will it always be like this, this deep underlying feeling between us? Dear Mrs. Adlington, now very old and very small, sits up erect with her knitting, her jokes, her prejudices and her cast-iron loyalties. I love her. She has kept a kind of innocence through eighty years and like Mary she is true-hearted.

26 October 1940.

The Pheasantry is a new underground eating club for the new, classless, Americanized English who before the war had grapefruit for breakfast and pre-ferred the *New Yorker* to *Punch*. So far as I know they are limited to London, Maidenhead and week-end cottages in the home counties. The men are apt to be subject to ulcers. The women wear 'simple' black dresses with diamond clips and have an arrogant manner which follows the third gin. In politics they are against the 'Old Gang', whom they think slow-witted and blimpish, but an instinct of self-preservation makes them distrust 'parlour-pinks'. Connected with no tradition and with no part of the country they are a floating population financed on the money made during and after the last war.

Margery, Frank[15] and I went after dinner at this club off the King's Road to their house in Blantyre Street; they are still living in this dangerous outpost near Lot's Road Power Station. It is the only street in World's End which has not yet been bombed. Their house, like the others, is a little square box of bricks of the type that falls down when a bomb comes anywhere near it. On this occasion the bomb fell in the next street. We all rushed out and I found myself helping to remove the people from the remains of three bombed houses. There was a large crater where one house had been, and in the centre of the crater were Margery and a doctor, trying by the aid of a torch to see who was injured and how badly. People were being pulled and pushed up the sides of the crater, to be taken off to the nearest pub to wait for the ambulance to come. These were the 'shock' cases – an old man who let them make an injection in his tattooed arm without question or even tension of the muscles – an old distraught mother gasping for breath and trying to collect what had happened to her – a tall, scraggy daughter, her cheeks blackened with smoke powder and her hair wisping wildly about her head. Margery called in imperious tones from her crater, 'Hot water.' I rushed panting through the dark and empty streets to the nearest police station then to the nearest public house in search of water. By now the sky was an ugly 'fire pink' glow from a row of houses burning noisily in a street nearby. Bombs were steadily falling and the members of the Air Raid Precautions and Rescue Squad whom I encountered in the streets cowered in carefully restrained attitudes against walls as the bombs came down. In the end when I came back with the hot water it was only to find that full supplies had been brought up already. It was the same with everything I tried to do. I helped shock cases to walk to the First Aid station when it was plain that they needed no help. Frank and some men in tin helmets emerged from the crater carrying a wounded woman stretched out on one of the doors of her house. We carried the stretcher Frank calling, 'Go easy there,' 'Gently now.' When we put the woman down on the pavement a man came out of the mobile ambulance, felt her pulse and heart and said, 'She is dead.' Frank contradicted in a pettish tone, 'The other doctor found a pulse.' 'No she is dead.' 'Do not cover her face up,' said Frank as we walked away. We all went to a pub where a fat landlady, her hair in papers, was offering cups of strong sweet tea, while her husband with a conspiratorial air offered to break the law and give us beer or 'take-away ports' although it was two a.m.

We all went back to Blantyre Street and slept on the floor in the basement passage.

29 October 1940.

I was thinking today of the last time I was in Halifax, Nova Scotia, and went for a walk to my old home, The Bower.

That day I was trying to look outward from an introspective bout of indigestion by reconstructing the road as it used to be. Only it was more a question of destruction than construction. First of all that row of white clapboard bungalows would have to be swept away and replaced by scrub and pine trees. Then over the stone wall of Gorsebrook – green fields must stretch to woods beyond where now hulked St. Mary's newly-built Catholic College in a monumental freestone, priests pacing its cement-filled paths. Where that stone wall ran my eye could detect the gap built in of new stones where had been a gate on which Peter and I had leaned on a summer afternoon, undirected sex driving us clumsy and breathless. In the Gorsebrook fields I had walked in my new beige Oxford bags reciting Rupert Brooke and trying to keep my pace steady when the small boys from the village catching sight of me through the gap called names after me.

The wall ended at the turn into The Bower drive. Here I was thrown back on memory with no stick or stone to help me – gone the gateposts, gone the lodge, gone the woods on either side of the drive and the tall trees that cast a green gloom until you came out on the slope which curved between rough lawns towards the house. I turned into the cul-de-sac of new houses which with their gardens had obliterated the former drive and woods. My walk was becoming an archaeological expedition but instead of being buried under this new layer of living the old had vanished without a trace, swept off into space and time existing only in my memory.

There seemed to be an excessive number of dogs about. From each porch or garden gate of the new houses a barking dog bounded out sniffing my ankles. Children on bicycles circled the end of the cul-de-sac where The Bower house stood – for it still stood though crowded into a corner by the new houses so that it hardly had room to breathe. Shorn of its approaches it was at an awkward angle to the street. Altogether the house looked sheepish and out of place among its brisk new neighbours – too large – but without giving any impression of grandeur. They had painted it a musty pale yellow and torn down the vine from the front wall. All that was left of the lawns was a wedge of grass on which still stood the big oak tree. The house would, as they say, have been 'better dead'. Its physical presence there stopped the power of my imagination like a leaden block. I could not go into the house in my memory while that solid door stood facing me. Yet in that room above the porch on the left I was born. In that room I had shivered and sweated out my adolescence. From that window I had watched for Katherine coming up the curve of the drive from under the summer green of the trees into the sunlight in her pink cotton dress swinging her straw hat in her hand. But it was no use – these memories were manufactured.

6 November 1940.

Things one will forget when this is over – fumbling in the dark of the black-out for one's front door key while bits of shrapnel fall on the pavement beside one – the way the shrapnel seems to drift almost like snow-flakes through the air in an aimless, leisurely way and the clink of it landing on the pavement.

9 November 1940.

Dined alone at Brooks's off silver plate among the prints of eighteenth-century Whig lords to the sound of German bombers overhead. At the next table the Duke of St. Albans, an old boy in battledress who had spent the day on guard at the Admiralty Arch was saying. 'I hate all the Europeans, except Scandinavians. I have always been for the Scandinavians – of course I loathe all dagoes.'

16 November 1940.

I came back from spending the night at Aldershot to find my flat a heap of rubble from a direct hit, and I have lost everything I own. That is no tragedy but a bore – and doubtless a cash loss, as the Department of External Affairs will never approve replacing suits from Sackville Street at twenty pounds per suit. I am most annoyed at losing my new 'woodsy' tweed suit, the picture of the Rose that Anne gave me, volume two of the book I am reading, my edition of Rimbaud and the little green book of my own chosen quotations. I do not much regret all the pigskin which used to jar on her so much.

I am enjoying the publicity attendant on this disaster, particularly the idea which I have put abroad that if it had not been for a chance decision to go to Aldershot for the night I should have been killed. I should probably only have been cut about or bruised. The rest of the people living in the flats were in the cellar and escaped unhurt. Hart and I went to see the ruins, and the youth next door was full of the fact that Lord A and Lady A too had had to be pulled out of the débris – so had fourteen other people, but what struck him was that even a lord had not been spared by the bomb. A further fascinating detail was that Lord A's naval uniform was still hanging on the hook on the open surviving wall for all the world to see. Now I know that the *Evening Standard* is right when it prints those items 'Baronet's kinswoman in a bus smash' etc.

I feel like a tramp having only one suit and shirt and in particular only *one pair of shoes*.

Last week when I wrote this diary I was sitting on my sofa in front of my electric fire in my perfectly real and solid flat with my books at arm's length – the furniture had that false air of permanence which chairs and tables take on so readily – the drawn curtains shut out the weather. Now all that is a pile of dirty rubble, with bits of my suits, wet and blackened, visible among the bricks.

On top of the pile my sofa is perched (quite the most uncomfortable and useless article in the flat but it has survived) – this violent, meaningless gesture like a slap from a drunken giant has smashed my shell of living into a heap.

17 November 1940. Dorchester Hotel.

It certainly feels safe in this enormous hotel. I simply cannot believe that bombs would dare to penetrate this privileged enclosure or that they could touch all these rich people. Cabinet Ministers and Jewish lords are not killed in air-raids – that is the inevitable illusion that this place creates. It is a fortress propped up with money-bags. It will be an effort to go back to an ordinary house which can be blotted out by one bomb.

I went for a walk in the park with my ballerina. I am trying to talk her into coming to live with me, but am getting nowhere. She says her brothers back in Portland always told her it cheapened a girl in a man's eyes – he never would want to marry a girl who had done that. We walked round and round the equestrian statue of William of Orange in St. James's Square arguing the point until an elderly gentleman called out to us, 'I do not want to interrupt you but I feel I should tell you, just in case you did not notice, that there is a police warning on the railings saying that there is an unexploded bomb in the garden!'

17 November 1940.

The ballerina is ridiculous, but I must not begin to think that she is pathetic because she is really very well able to look after herself, and what is more she has succeeded in making me a little bit in love with her.

18 November 1940.

I could have strangled her today while she was eating her chocolate cake, but I was so disagreeable that I do not think she enjoyed it much. Poor little devil – I am sorry for her. She looked so gay and pretty today with her little coloured umbrella in the rainy after-luncheon Jermyn Street. It is rather touching the way she sticks to her American small-town gods in the midst of this London. When I first knew her only a few weeks ago she was excited at being taken to a smart restaurant. Now she thinks it fashionable to complain – 'The smoked-salmon here is not as good as at the Ritz' – 'I like the way they pull the table out for you here' (if the waiter has not pulled the table aside for her to pass).

27 November 1940.

I am living at Brooks's Club, a combination of discomfort and old-fashioned comfort. Magnificent coal fires in the living-rooms, icy bedrooms, the kind of confidential valeting that you get in a good country house, the superb bath towels, yards of them, impossible to manoeuvre – the only thing to do is to wrap yourself up in one and sit down until you dry.

As I write I hear the ever-menacing throb of a bomber coming out of the fog. Tonight there is an old-fashioned London fog. Fumbling my way along Piccadilly I could hardly – as they say – 'see my hand before me'. I hear the hall porter saying in a grieved tone, 'There is no air-raid warning gone.' This is one of the nights when I feel interested in life, when I should much resent a bomb removing me from the scene. There are other nights when I feel it could not matter less.

Came back last night in the tube from Earl's Court. I hear that the drunks quite often fight it out by throwing each other on to the live wire, which contrary to superstition does not always kill you. If the toughs in the shelter tube do not like a chap they wait for him and throw him on to the wire. I must say that I saw nothing of this – just people sleeping, and not the poorest of the poor. They were all fully dressed and looked clean and quite prosperous, some pretty girls who might be serving in a big store, quite a lot of men and children. I have never seen so many different ages and types of people asleep before. Their sprawled attitudes, arms flung out, etc. made me think of photographs of the dead in battlefields – their stark and simplified faces. What one misses in the sleeping and the dead are the facial posturings prompted by perpetual vanity.

I am off the ballerina – she is rude to waiters who cannot answer back.

3 December 1940.

If that bloody ballerina does not come across tomorrow I am through with her. She gave me a model of Our Lady of Lourdes today, but she seems positively to be getting colder the fonder she gets of me.

6 December 1940.

Week-end with the Sacheverell Sitwells. He is charming with a sort of gentleness, which is most attractive, and manners that show his delicacy and sensibility. He would disappear after tea with, 'I am going to my room to scribble for a little while' or 'I will withdraw to my apartment.' It was exciting to feel that up there he was distilling another of those magic potions of his. He thinks it is all up with Europe, its culture and vitality exhausted. There I think he is mistaken, although certainly his European tradition – that of the civilised aristocrat – is hard hit. His wife Georgia is a Canadian – a beauty – tall with pale skin and dark eyes. She is amused and amusing and impulsively warm-hearted. I came down on the train with Princess Callimachi (Anne-Marie), a lively little Romanian with the look of a lizard, who lives with the Sitwells at present.

21 December 1940.

Evening with the ballerina – some progress to report. We dined, thank God without music and away from the frowsy hotel atmosphere at a small but expensive restaurant in Shepherd Market. She felt, I think, that we were rather slumming. As usual she talked an immense amount about 'Mommy and Daddy', and at one stage of dinner I was sunk in such a stupor of boredom that even she noticed it and I had to pull myself together and begin talking rapidly, desperately and at random. The night was cold and starry outside, with quite a heavy blitz. We walked back to the flat. She has more sense and feeling than one would give her credit for at first. What is shocking about her is the contrast between her romantic looks and her flat commonplace mind. Her mainspring in life appears to be an intense desire to show that she comes from the right side of the railroad tracks. Like many completely uninhibited bores she wins in the end by sheer persistence. She has talked to me so much about people I do not know or care about, her family, the members of the ballet company, etc., that I am beginning to feel I do know them and find myself taking an interest in their doings. Later in the evening we went out to Lyons' Corner House where we were joined by two R.A.F. pilots, both D.F.C.s, one drunk, Irish and very funny. The R.A.F. have a line laid down for them – the gay, brave, young pilot with a joke on his lips, irresponsible, living to the full because they may die any day.

22 December 1940.

Dined with Alastair Buchan at Pratt's Club – the best sole in London, that is to say in the world. I always enjoy Pratt's, the atmosphere of open fires and easy unbuttoned chat, the equality where cabinet ministers sit around the table and argue with subalterns – the décor of red curtains and the stuffed salmon caught by His Royal Highness the Duke of Edinburgh in 1886. The other night a rather tight, junior lieutenant back from the Middle East was dining there. Anthony Eden began holding forth at length on the Mediterranean situation. This youth, after listening for some time, turned to a friend and said, 'I do not know who that man is but he is talking awful balls.' Immense satisfaction of all members.

25 December 1940.

Spent Christmas Eve in the country, came back on the morning train to London on Christmas Day – waited of course for nearly an hour at Horsley Station for the train. How well I know those English country stations in the morning after a week-end when you have tipped the chauffeur and told him not to wait and you walk up and down the station platform in the raw air that smells of babies' diapers, with a little view of the railway line and fields and a couple of cows, fields rough-surfaced and untidy seen at close range, although a billiard board of green if you flashed over them in a plane; or a flooded meadow, mist hanging about the trees. Two porters whistling and stamping, a lady in a fur coat taking leave of her rosy-cheeked niece, who wears tweeds and no hat – 'My dear, remember when you come to London there is always a roof.' Then the soldiers – bold-eyed Canadians with a slouch and a swagger, New Zealanders with overcoats hanging untidily, Australians often with girls, and English soldiers going back to London saying good-bye to plain, sensible, loyal wives wearing spectacles and sometimes carrying babies. The soldiers from the Dominions are invading armies of irresponsible younger brothers. The English soldiers look at them not unkindly but with a sober ironic air – puppies and old hound dogs. London was deserted.

29 December 1940.

Walked home tonight by the pink light of an enormous fire somewhere in the City. Heavy blitz. I dined alone at Brooks's. Read R. G. Collingwood's book on Roman Britain – sandy but with oases. I also tried unsuccessfully to put into despatch form some intuitions of how things may develop in this country after the war, provided, of course, that we win it. Funny, though reason may tell me that that is open to doubt, I never really contemplate our not winning. It is eerie tonight, the streets are so light from the fires and so completely deserted and silent now that the planes seem to have passed. Was that a distant barrage or somebody moving furniture upstairs? No, the only sound is the tinkle of ambulance bells in the empty street. This is not very pleasant. I think I will have a whisky and soda. Supposing that some day one of these days I just was not there to meet Billy for lunch at the R.A.C. The others were there – Billy and Margery and Hart but not me. *Now* – that was the barrage, and I can hear a plane right overhead. The man at the Club said that a lot of our fighters were up tonight. That was a bomb that time. When the building shakes from the floor upwards it is a bomb.

Spent last night at Stansted. We went to church this morning. Lord Bessborough reading the lessons – 'The flesh is as grass and like grass shall wither away.' He read it well – the rustic choir boys piped up 'Come All Ye Faithful' – clear voices like a running stream. The clergyman ranged from arrangements for the local paper chase to God's purpose. An iconoclast – he announced that God had other preoccupations in addition to the defence of the British Empire. We should will victory – call on the power of thought – pause for a minute every day before the B.B.C. announced the news. It bothers me this talk about calling on the power of thought and willing things to happen to our advantage, as if we were trying to force a lock when, had we the key, it would open itself.

1941

10 January 1941.

The ballerina was rather sweet really. We had breakfast in the Mayfair Hotel – rashers of bacon and great cups of American coffee. She did look beautiful this morning. People turned around in the street to look at her.

12 January 1941.

Reading Gide – the best antidote possible to the triumphant commonplace of an English Sunday. Not even the Blitzkrieg has been able to break the spell which the Sabbath casts over the land. One could not fail by just putting one's head out of the window and smelling and looking and listening for two minutes to recognise that this is Sunday. In my mind's eye I can see the weary wastes of the Cromwell Road beneath a sullen sky where a few depressed pedestrians straggle as though lost in an endless desert. One's soul shrinks from the spectacle.

Symptoms of Sexual Happiness

1. I look at people, men and women, from the physical point of view, not by class or taste but in terms of the senses. Which ones are out of the stream of sex? (How easy it is to see these!) And why? 2. I am temporarily cured of my mania for seeing things in a straight line. I admit and enjoy confusion. The relief is enormous. 3. Time no longer seems to be slipping away from me. I am happy to spend it carelessly. 4. Other people do not seem worth the usual effort. I cannot help treating them casually, often interrupting them and not listening to what they say. 5. I definitely am very much less amusing. The ballerina leaves today with the ballet company on tour. I am looking forward to early and varied infidelities during her absence.

12 January 1941.

Walked across Grosvenor Square to dine with Lady Malcolm at Claridge's. A London evening – damp air and mist. The guns in Hyde Park reverberated above the square and further away the guns in St. James's Park replied. Clouds slid past a full silver moon.

Lady Malcolm is really only interested in the work she is doing at the canteen at the Beaver Club and in her struggle for power with the other women workers. 'We are gettin' along very nicely.' (She is Edwardian about her g's.)

Her son-in-law, Basil Bartlett, was there, the playwright now in Military Intelligence, clever and amusing, and Thesiger, the actor – looking at him Lady Malcolm murmured to me, 'Cooks perfect *petits pois à la française* and always wears a pearl necklace under its shirt – rather sweet – don't you think?' He was too, with his cosy humour. You felt – there is a talented old creature who does not give a damn one way or the other but will not be bullied. (That was when Basil was trying to force us all to drink white wine because he was eating salmon, although the rest of us obviously wanted red with our fillet of beef.) 'I am for red,' said Thesiger, with a light flick in his tone, and red it was. He told us about the time in London about 1900 when it used to be the fashion to go down after dinner and sing patriotic songs outside Buckingham Palace to cheer Queen Victoria up. (It must have been during the South African War.) People would give dinner parties to go on to Buckingham Palace. One night he was there among the crowd singing with some friends – a foggy, misty London night with the front of the Palace (not the present façade – that was added later) lit up by gas jets. Suddenly there was a light in one of the windows, then the window opened and onto the balcony stepped two huge footmen bearing each in his hands vast lighted candelabra – 'and between them,' said Thesiger with feeling, 'and between them a little black figure of a woman'.

Then Lady Malcolm told us how when she was a little girl King Edward VII came one afternoon to see her mother (Lily Langtry). When she was brought into the drawing-room by her nurse he said to her, 'Would you like to go for a drive, my dear, in the Park?' He did not ask her nurse if she could go – he asked her and she was sent out in his carriage with his monogram on the door. People in the streets took off their hats as she drove by alone in his carriage. She had to make up her mind whether to acknowledge their bows – as though she were a little princess – or whether to stare at the horizon. She decided on the latter. Thus began a career of doing the right thing.

14 January 1941.

Lunched with Tony Balásy, who told me that he resigned from the Hungarian Diplomatic Service when Hungary joined the Axis in November. It must have taken more guts than I gave him credit for to break the chain of twenty years' habit, especially for such a cautious creature of habits. Now he is going back to his beloved United States without a job and with the somewhat dreary prospect of perhaps doing some writing on political subjects to earn himself a living. He quoted to me a sentence from Roosevelt's speech, 'Those who prefer security to liberty deserve to lose both.' He says he could not go on any longer without his heart in it. What makes it harder is that he was to have been appointed Hungarian Minister to Washington. I asked him if some people in his Foreign Office would sympathise with him. 'The consensus of opinion in Budapest will be the fellow is a damn fool, but maybe in 1943 they will say that Balásy is a shrewd fellow.' I admire him for what he has done and doubt if I would have had the nerve to do the same.

Last night was the Russian New Year. I took D. out to dinner and we walked home in brilliant moonlight – no blitz. Passing through Grosvenor Square we found the door to the square garden open and went in. There is a tennis court in the middle concealed by trees, very convenient for the square dwellers, but very disappointing to me. I had hoped for a little lake with even a few birds living on a miniature island. It would be impossible to explore a secret garden by moonlight with a woman like D. without a stirring of excitement. I kissed her. From the sensational point of view it was a sensation.

15 January 1941.

A routine day, worthy but not inspiring. This is the way my 'Better Self' would like me to behave all the time. Went to a War Office meeting in the afternoon. Waste of time. We all repeated what we had said a month ago about prisoners-of-war. It is so hard to resist the temptation to score at a meeting of this sort. One is giving a sort of performance, one has an audience, as one talks one becomes possessed by the wisdom of what one is saying and the folly or wickedness of those who oppose one. I find myself getting angry and aggrieved about something which does not matter a damn, when the only thing that does matter is to find the essential and stick to it.

The general in the chair, the 'tactful' type of soldier who thinks he is conciliating the touchy susceptibilities of the 'colonials', and wears a soothing smile while he is determined to get his own way. The only technique with such a man is to flatter him in his own coin and never give an inch.

29 January 1941.

I am ashamed of the despatches we send to Ottawa. They give an officialese picture of England at war without conveying any sense of the crosscurrents. Above all they leave out any pictures of the social changes stirring just under the surface. Mr. Massey does not want the Government at home to glimpse these abysses lest they should be disturbed in their belief that they are fighting for the survival of political democracy, liberal ideas and human individualism side by side with the traditional England. He thinks that anything that disturbs this set-piece might weaken the war effort and distract our will. (He says that my despatches read like socialist speeches!)

I dined the other night with Anne-Marie, one of the largest landowners in Romania, now on the German blacklist and unable to get any money out of the country. She is clever, full of wit and disloyalty. In her spare time she has dabbled in the arts, gambled on the Black Bourse, and conducted a good many highly personal political intrigues and vendettas. I met her at the Ritz Bar where she holds court every day, surrounded by half a dozen cosmopolitan perverts, smooth young French success boys, professional photographers, English and White Russian interior decorators. Throughout the evening she was always tipping and ordering and changing tables and bullying the waiters. At intervals soft-spoken young men appeared at her table, kissed her hand, murmured a sentence of greeting in French and slid away again. Meanwhile she sat smoking cigarettes and darting her lizard head from side to side as she observed the company – *'Cherchée et pas trouvée,'* she remarked as a young woman came in wearing a dress more remarkable for elaborate effort than for effectiveness.

30 January 1941.

If we cannot be strong enough to make peace with Germany within two years, Europe will go communist when the Germans do break. Our only chance is to be so strong in planes and navy that with the assistance of the blockade German power will collapse. We cannot alone defeat Germany militarily on the continent of Europe.

The papers are full of butchery in Romania. Rivers of hate, flowing blood all over Europe. How difficult it is for us comfortable creatures to understand all this hate, all this will to cruelty – that people who have lived next door to each other in a street in some small town for years should – the minute the policeman's back is turned – fall on each other like hyenas and butcher each other. What years of bitter, suppressed loathing and fear must lie behind that.

1 February 1941.

It is a relief to plunge into the warmly-coloured, variegated women's world of Colette, whose novels I am reading, to turn one's back on this man-made time when duty and team spirit are the dreary necessities for survival. Never have I so thanked God for women as in these months. While they still care more about their clothes, their children and their lovers than about the war it is still possible to breathe even in this constricted atmosphere.

Anne-Marie received me in her bedroom at the Ritz – marble mantelpiece, red satin panelling, rose-shaded lamps and a big double bed standing high off the ground – a period piece cosmopolitan Ritz style 1912. It exactly suits her. We were joined by a young lieutenant who, talking of a friend of his, said, 'He has such an adorable sense of humour.' 'Now, there I do not agree', she said. 'Funny, yes, but no sense of humour, you cannot bully him.' Her equation – sense of humour equals niceness equals susceptibility to being bullied.

It is getting very hard to obtain matches. It becomes a game to see how long one can make a spill of paper last. I go to buy some shaving-cream

134

and the man at the hairdressers says, 'It is the pots for the cream that are our difficulty. The shop in the City that supplied them was burnt out in the last blitz.' It is the same with our office stationery – shops that kept it have been blitzed. At the Indian restaurant they give you curry without onions that tastes like hot mud. There is a shortage of French novels and French wines, of glass for spectacles, of rouge. I do not speak of necessities like butter and eggs. In fact there is a shortage of everything except potatoes, bread and fish, and I believe the last is too expensive for the poor.

7 February 1941.

This morning I had to leave her house early before the maid-of-all-work arrived. It meant staggering up, getting dressed and out into the dark rainy street, but I was happy. I could see and smell again after days of planning, of talk, of papers. I felt like a living creature not a sort of filing cabinet of resolutions and schemes.

It was impossible to do any serious work today. I went for a walk in St. James's Park. It was a day like early spring – one expected to see crocuses but there were ridges of dirty left-over snow. I was walking along purposefully in my black hat swinging my umbrella thinking damn the war, oh damn the bloody war. I only curse the war when I am happy. When I am miserable it suits me that the world should be sliding down into disaster. Then, realizing that I was happy, I thought that this must not be wasted, let me sit on this bench in the sun, and say to myself as I watch the ducks, 'At this moment happiness is right here at my elbow.'

I am every day hearing of some new and horrific gas which is to be used against us – soporific, made at Bayer's works in Germany which puts you to sleep all right but from which you awake paralysed, gas that makes you sick in your mask – you remove the mask and they send over the mustard gas. Certainly people are far more frightened of gas than of anything else, yet it is obvious to me that it can be effective only over a small area and will cause relatively few casualties. I think the worst would be physical, personal, direct bullying, the sort of intimate cruelties that go on in the concentration camps.

I have been reading Colette's *Chéri* – her style light as thistledown, without a pretentious phrase, full of wit, so effortlessly and brilliantly constructed that you never feel a bump of transition. Is it too facile? No, because when you come to think it over you find you have not been cheated anywhere along the line.

10 February 1941.

Week-end at Oxford – motored down with Alastair and went over to Elsfield to the christening of Billy Buchan's child. Lady Tweedsmuir, gentle, intelligent, loyal-hearted, a few friends and relatives, champagne, little pink marzipan sweets in a white Sèvres bonbonnière – little jokes in the library afterwards. Met Elizabeth Bowen, well-dressed, intelligent handsome face, watchful eyes. I had expected someone more Irish, more silent and brooding and at the same time more irresponsible. I was slightly surprised by her being so much 'on the spot'.

Oxford.

I walked with M. around Magdalen Park. The newer buildings looked decayed like obsolescent Palladian mansions. There are no deer left in the Park. Dined at Anderson's, the new restaurant next to the George. The Bullingdon Club members came pouring in – children they looked – pink cheeked with long hair and the look of being hot from their baths – innocent and insolent past belief. Then the aesthetes with dangling hands and signet rings, brushing back the locks from their foreheads and swaying on their feet.

M. was very defeatist. He is now serving in the Military Intelligence and doing a course at Oxford. He thinks the Germans will invade simultaneously at four or five different points at the same time. They will concentrate on small areas and cut off communications, and none of our officers will have any initiative to act on their own without orders from the centre. (Quite unconvincing to me, but he knows more about military possibilities than I do.) He foresees a Pétain government in England with Gauleiters for Wales and Scotland. He believes that the Germans would encourage separatist national movements in these countries and that they would find plenty of material to work on. He views the prospect with malicious satisfaction. Failing invasion he thinks a patched-up peace is the only hope of saving us all from another thirty years of war. He is convinced that only the Germans are capable of organising Europe, that Britain would never be able to do the job and we should turn our backs on Europe. Despite all this he is very anxious to get a chance of fighting and blames the Catholics who he says run the Military Intelligence and are preparing to sell out for a compromise peace. Consistency was never his long suit.

Dinner with my former tutor, Ronald McCallum. Long argument about his beloved 'succession states', Czechoslovakia, Romania, the Baltic Republics and Scandinavia, that promised land of modern liberalism, the country of sound architecture, cleanliness, sexual freedom and painless socialism. I asked him why, in all these model states, there has been no resistance to the Germans to compare to unpopular Poland.

12 February 1941.

On Tuesday I motored down with the Masseys to see the Canadian Neurological Hospital at Hackwood. The doctors who make up the Neurological Unit are the best Canadian surgeons from Montreal and Toronto. They specialise in brain surgery – Cohen and Penfield of Montreal are probably two of the best brain surgeons in the world. The hospital is full of both military and civilian cases. The doctors and nurses are of the highest standard technically and still seem to be human. They make most of their English opposite numbers seem old-fashioned amateurs. Also they are a great relief after the military – no fuss and flummery here, no prima donnas of generals, no bone-headed brigadiers swaggering in kilts. Quiet, sensible men with a scrupulous tradition. Their uniforms may not fit, but they understand their jobs and do not show off. What a change from politicians.

They are housed in Hackwood Park, Lord Camrose's house, and formerly the scene of Curzon's grandeur.

After our visit to this hospital we went on to the Canadian Army workshop. There again we saw technical men who knew their job. They are skilled workers from Canadian factories. Some of them earned ten dollars a day at home. Now they get seven shillings and sixpence a day. They were repairing tanks, making tunnelling equipment, medical instruments and doing general repairing. Some were working with acetylene blow-torches or melting iron in forges. Others were mending engines. They are proud of their high standard of skill. The men are said to be tough customers and heavy drinkers. They had the absorbed look of mechanics who are captured by their work. The younger men without much training who are drafted into the unit learn quickly. They have the North American flair for machinery. I asked their officer how they compared with English mechanics. 'The English,' he said, 'are not too bad if they are not hurried. They cannot get a move on.'

23 February 1941.

It is being dinned into my mind with persistence that after all we may be going to lose this war. No one admits the possibility publicly, but you could hardly expect us to do that.

It looks as if the Germans might defeat us within the next six months, but if we survive, we shall be embarked on a long struggle against Germany, Japan, Italy, backed by the U.S.S.R., and our success in carrying on would depend on the U.S.A. If we repel the German invasion, as I believe we shall, then we shall enter a new phase of the war – a deadlock, and after a year or so of this it is possible that both sides may come to a compromise peace. It is even just conceivable that an Anglo-German combine might result, but that would imply the disappearance of Hitler. On the other hand, if this country is invaded successfully there is the possibility of a Pétain government here whose names one can already guess plus, perhaps, an Anglo-German alliance. This is an ugly picture, but the other, the picture of Germany crushed, of England and America restoring democratic governments in Europe seems to me incredibly remote. All this

140

gloomy speculation goes on in the back of people's minds. They do not talk like this, they hardly allow themselves to think such things. Most are content to repeat that Britons never will be slaves and that Britain can take it. They do not think ahead of the next move, and this is doubtless very sensible. Also they are pretty well blanketed by propaganda.

25 February 1941.

Stayed with Mike Pearson. He has a general and a colonel living with him. The general thinks the solution after the war in Germany would be to shoot one in every four Germans. Why one in four? On that theory it would be logical to shoot the lot.

Read Sir Robert Vansittart's *The Black Record*, a compilation of his broadcasts and a violent attack on the Germans. It is the kind of propaganda that used to flow freely in the last war – full of inaccurate generalisations and written in a 'hot gospeller' style which one would hardly expect from a man of his education. Its thesis is that the Germans are an accursed race differentiated from the rest of Europe by their savagery. This in itself is dubious. We know how unpleasant they are, how cruel, and how treacherous, but are they more cruel than the Russians or the Turks, or the Spanish, more treacherous than the Japanese? It is a mistake for a member of a Foreign Office to take this line in propaganda (even if it were true in fact). This makes nonsense of our official line, i.e. the Germans are being misled by the

Nazi Party. That is the line to stick to in propaganda. It is a long-term investment which may pay off in the end. When the Germans have received some knocks in battle, when – or if – their morale is softened by setbacks, then propaganda of this kind could be very useful. It is obvious that if they think we intend to make mincemeat of them and that we lump them all together as a criminal nation they will fight with desperate obstinacy.

27 February 1941 .

Obviously the biggest influence on all our lives at present is Hitler – as he is in a position to change or terminate our lives. Also his phrases have got under our skins, affected our language, made it impossible to think without his shadow falling across our thoughts. Never has so much hung upon the life of one man, never has one man so dominated the imagination of the world. Even if the Nazis went on his death would be release from an evil spell. He is the incarnation of our own sense of guilt. When he attacks our civilisation we find him saying things that we have thought or said. In the 'burrows of the nightmare' such a figure is born, for as in a nightmare the thing that pursues us seems to have an uncanny and terrifying knowledge of our weakness. We spawned this horror; he is the byproduct of our civilisation; he is all the hatred, the envy, the guile which is in us – a surrealist figure sprung out of the depths of our own subconscious.

2 March 1941.

Lunched with the Dashwoods at West Wycombe Park – Helen Dashwood looking pretty and being amusing. The house is in a state of slight disrepair, peeling statues with their noses knocked off, holes on the drive. In the big saloon the furniture is under dustcovers, the tapestry room is full of bundles for the troops – there are packing cases in unexpected places. It is the home of the Dashwoods, and down the road at Medmenham Abbey the Hell-Fire Club celebrated their boring black masses. Staying there was one of these aesthetic intellectuals or intellectual aesthetes who leave their London flats, their left-wing politics and their rather common 'boyfriends' at the week-ends for the more decorative and well-heated English country houses. When one asks what becomes of the Oxford aesthetes in later life, this is the answer. They are peering at old family letters in pillared libraries or adjudicating the origin of rugs or china – or else they are simply sitting on the sofa before the fire with their legs curled up having a good gossip with the wife of their host.

Field-Marshal Sir Philip Chetwode was there too, and his wife, a solid hull of an old woman of intelligence who likes old houses and to know of skeletons in aristocratic cupboards. After lunch the men talked about the war. Those who might be susceptible to defeatist influences were mentioned. 'I do not trust the press,' said Johnnie Dashwood. Sir Philip says Archie Wavell[1] came to see him the other day. 'When I saw him come in I said to him, "What are you doing here – have you been given a bowler hat?" (I thought they must have sacked him), but he said he was home to report. The Prime Minister has no use for him – says, "There is one of your dumb generals." But it is because he does not know how to talk to politicians. Soldiers are not stupider than other men. They say what they mean and politicians think they must be damn fools for doing that.'

6 March 1941.

I walked to the office a new way across Berkeley Square. The rain was dripping from the trees. They have taken away the railings and laid bare the mystery of the garden. It is so sensible that people should be allowed to walk and sit in these gardens. The railings will never be put back again. It is impossible to argue that they should be, but I loved those shut-in secret gardens. These oases of privilege and mystery seem disappointingly commonplace now that they are exposed to view – just a little grass and a few trees. West-End London had been a place of railed gardens and non-committal Georgian façades – behind these defences in clubs and drawing-rooms shut away from the vulgar, the ladies and gentlemen of England have disposed of their affairs – and the affairs of the nation. Now bomber and builder have conspired to attack these well-bred squares. What looked so solid and seemed so eternal has vanished.

I was talking to the Masseys' chauffeur today about the bombings. 'What astonishes me,' he said, 'is the way those old houses fall down so easy. You take that big house on the corner of Berkeley Square – used to belong to Lord T. My mother used to work there when I was a lad. It always seemed such a fine well-built old house and now it's just a pile of rubble. I would have thought that they would have stood up better – some of these big houses.' Although his tone was practical I thought I could catch an undernote of dismay queerly mixed with relief. That great gloomy house may have hung on his memory since childhood. It must have seemed as permanent as a natural feature of the landscape and clothed in dim prestige. Now brutally it vanishes. This sudden destruction of the accustomed must shake people out of the grooves of their lives. This overnight disappearance of the brick and mortar framework of existence must send a shock deep into the imagination. These high explosions and incendiaries are like the falling stars and blazing comets – noted of old as foretelling great changes in the affairs of man.

10 March 1941.

I have just been losing my temper with Laurie Audrain, our Press Officer, in an argument over what the Americans are or are not doing to help us in the war. He was saying that if he were an

145

American he would turn his back on the whole thing and say, 'to hell with England and her war!' I suddenly found myself shouting that, 'My God, I hoped we would lose this war first to see the spot it would put the American isolationists in.' I felt ashamed of myself afterwards because I remembered a resolution I had made to myself when I was in the United States that whatever happened I would never be one of those who cursed the Americans for staying out of the war just because I was in England and it was getting too hot for me.

All the same I feel that I never shall forgive the Americans for not being in this war. It is a purely emotional state but we are all rather emotional at the moment. That bloody blitz on Saturday night partly accounts for it. They hit the Café de Paris and killed forty-seven people including most of the band. I was opposite at the 400 Club. Just afterwards I turned around when I heard a young girl say to her guardsman escort, 'Darling, it was *rather* awful when they brought out all those *black* men.' This couple had come on from the Café de Paris where they had been in the lounge waiting for a table when the bomb fell and had seen them bringing out the bodies of 'Snake-Hips' Johnson and his coloured band, who were all killed but two. Many young officers on leave and their girls were killed. It was a bad blitz because they got so much that I had been hoping would escape. Worst of all Garland's Hotel, which was the great meeting place for myself and all my friends. Miss

Clayton, the barmaid whom we all loved, was buried under the débris for six hours and was rescued because she managed to make herself heard and give directions to the men who were digging her out. Laurie and I were walking along Suffolk Street on Sunday afternoon; when we saw what had happened to Garland's we stopped on the street and said to each other, 'Bugger them, *bugger* them.' But that is about all there is to do – just curse and go home and wait to wake up the next morning to see what else is gone. There goes the siren. It is just like September all over again, and this will go on all spring and all summer and, as far as we can see, forever and ever. Amen. Having this interval of normality has spoiled us for raids. This diary tonight is whimpering – and war does make one callous too. We were making jokes yesterday about 'Snake-Hips' Johnson, the band leader, and his death. Jokes that none of us would have thought anything but pointless and disgusting a year ago, but then I never used to think that soldiers' jokes in the last war ('Ha! Ha! George got his blooming 'ead knocked off!') were very funny.

Meanwhile the Americans are getting their toes dug in in Newfoundland and Bermuda preparatory to inheriting what is left of the British Empire in the Western Hemisphere.

13 March 1941.

An American newspaper correspondent called Lake appeared. He was suffering from what he solemnly called acidosis and he spent the evening railing at the inefficiency of the British censorship and the superiority and maddening 'slowness' of British officialdom. Slowness! Why don't the Americans hurry up and convoy over to us the war materials we need to defend them and us, or at least get their industry keyed up to producing them in sufficient quantities. The truth is that we are living on a different planet from the Americans. Their observations from the world of commonsense seem irrelevant and irritating. For the neutral to talk to the belligerent is like a sober man talking to a drunk. The sober man's fear is that the drunk will knock over his best furniture, break his glasses, assault his wife – 'Go easy, be reasonable' is his cry. 'Don't seize Brazilian shipping for fear of the effect on South American shipping in general. Don't hold up wheat for France in case the children perish', say the Americans. But this is mixed up with a contra-dictory cry which is, 'Why don't you *do* more – be more ruthless. We will scream while you are doing it but admire you for it afterwards.' Let us never forget our friends among the Americans – Roosevelt, Bullitt, Dorothy Thompson, Lippmann or our enemies – La Follette, Lindbergh, Nye, Wheeler.

Dupuy[2] back from France – still optimistic. He says Pétain is as pro-British as ever, full of vigour and master of the situation. Pétain does not entirely trust Admiral Darlan, and he is making use of him for just as long as he may wish to. Then he will put someone else in his place and send out a new younger man to North Africa. Pétain is pleased with himself, 'N'est-ce-pas que je me suis bien débarrassé de Laval?' Dupuy says that what Pétain aims for now is an agreement – wheat for France under United States control against a promise for Vichy to guarantee no German infiltration into North Africa.

18 March 1941. Garnons.

There are about twenty Canadian officers here mostly recuperating from pneumonia or bronchitis. The place is presided over by a big-boned, big-bosomed old woman – a sort of a Hindenburg of a woman. Apparently she is proving somewhat stiff-necked and cantankerous. In perpetual attendance on her is a Canadian girl brought up here and on the continent. There does not seem to be much point about her. She is sulky and introspective but not enough to be *farouche*.

The masseur employed here was talking to me about the Canadian officers today. 'They are all the same, same opinions, same swear-words. They are not interesting men in themselves, but I have only met two since I have been here who I would not be quite happy to serve under in the front line. What I foresee in Canada is an aristocracy beginning to grow up there. You will have aristocrats – the grandsons of the Eatons, Masseys, Flavelles and the other millionaires.' Of course he is dead wrong.

There is no aristocratic principle alive in Canada and you will not make it by a few rich men mimicking English lords.

In 1815 Russia was in some ways in relation to Europe what Canada is now, a new country with a deep feeling that the future belonged to her. The Russian officers quartered in France during the occupation soaked up so much of the 'spirit of the age' that when they went home to Russia they kept the Secret Police busy for a generation with their dangerous new ideas. Now England is in the midst of a social revolution and the continent is in travail with new forms of political and economic organisation. How much of this penetrates to our Canadian officers? So far as I can see, nothing whatsoever; they still think in terms of the last war. To them this is just another war against Germany – Hitler instead of the Kaiser.

As for the Englishman, he looks upon the Canadians as an army of friendly barbarians who for some incomprehensible reason have come to protect him from his enemies.

The Royal Tour in Canada was the occasion for an overpowering manifestation on the part of at any rate some Canadians of a deep yearning towards the *mother* country. (England never thinks of herself as a mother country nor is the phrase ever heard here.) Above all the whole Tour was an example of the English genius for making use of people – a genius so highly developed in both their

150

political and private lives.

28 March 1941.

1. Plutodemocracy is finished as a form of government.
2. The small national sovereign state is finished.
3. American culture based on optimism and the perfectibility of man through technical progress and education has had the bottom of it knocked out.
4. It follows from all this that we are groping for a new organisation and a new expression for our faith in the dignity of our destiny. After this war there will be no let-down into materialism. There will be another Age of Faith.

29 March 1941.

I am sick of my present hectic life – the work, the miscellaneous loveless affairs and the mixed drinks. I wish I lived in a small provincial town and spent the evenings reading aloud the Victorian novelists to my wife and my adoring daughters.

1 April 1941.

The Queen came to tea with the Masseys the other day. Acute suspense among those invited (only seven or eight). Each was to be presented, each wished to show that this was not at all weighing on his spirits, each was hagridden by the thought that through some mischance he or she would not be presented. Mrs. Massey would forget them or the Queen would get tired and want to go home before it came to their turn. I was led in with the other Secretaries – we sat down in front of a blazing fire in a circle around her. She sat very upright and talked to us in her sweetly modulated gentle voice. Yes, the charm is there all right, fabulous charm! You wonder, 'Is it done with mirrors?' To see that familiar postage stamp face, those gestures of the hands known to millions, that smile that moves strong men to tears, and what is behind it all? Intelligence, enormous control. She was tired by the time she got to us, but the timing of her departure, the unhurried certainty of her going, the faint regret that tiresome things made it necessary not to go on talking forever to three Secretaries at Canada House. No, it was a perfect performance.

16 April 1941.

Tonight is, I think from the war point of view, a new low. There is another of these infernal, eternal blitzes going on. The sky is crimson again from another great fire, this time in the direction of Victoria – planes are overhead all the time. The Irish porter has just come in to tell me that there is light showing from my window and I have been up on the roof with him watching the flares – great clumps of them – 'They're beautiful,' he says, 'though for such a bad purpose, you have to admit they are beautiful. Why, the sky is lit up like a ballroom.' He is right

– they are like chandeliers suspended from heaven. All the same this raid has got me scared for the first time in months. I feel like going downstairs to the shelter, but that is a thing I have not done yet. There are guns firing next door in Grosvenor Square and bits of shrapnel crackling down into the wall of the courtyard outside my window.

I saw in the paper the other day a letter recovered from a bombed house from a girl to her sweetheart describing a raid play-by-play and ending, 'I am writing this under the table, the planes seem to be getting nearer and nearer. They seem almost in the room with us now...' There the letter stopped. It was found a few yards from the girl's body.

There were two explosions then which shook this building considerably – it swayed each time and the blast has made my eardrums feel as they do when one is going up fast in a lift. I do not suppose there is much point in my going downstairs – if the building collapsed it would collapse on top of us. Besides, shelter conversation is insufferable – everyone standing about nervously making jokes. It seems at moments as though the Battle of Britain were being fought just above my bedroom. Someone is whistling tranquilly in the street outside as though it were an ordinary spring evening and he was strolling back with his girl on his arm from an evening in the park or at the cinema. Will there ever be such evenings again? But when other people say that we cannot win the war I immediately begin to preach optimism and victory. Bathos – but the universal bathos of people in all countries at war.

Virginia Woolf's house – Bloomsbury – has been bombed.

Someone was describing it the other day – the frescoes by her sister Vanessa Bell, the book-lined sitting-room where Lytton Strachey and Virginia conducted conversation in the twenties. Now the house is gone, and she has committed suicide because she thought that a mental derangement she had suffered from before was coming back on her again. A fear far worse than the fear of any bombs. For she found it so insufferable that she drowned herself in the peaceful countryside while we in London cling hard to life among the bombs.

What is meant by the collapse of civilisation? It means that we are glad when we hear that Berlin is getting the same bombing we are. It means that when I said I was sorry that our bombers had hit Frederick the Great's palace at Potsdam, someone replied, 'I cannot say I share that sentiment. I should like all their beautiful and historic places to be destroyed.' It means the Italians being prepared (if that story is true) to bomb the Vatican themselves and then put the blame on us.

The unending tale of death and destruction goes on piling up all over the world. And it is *too* much. General Franco (the Christian Catholic knight) makes a speech saying there is no such thing as peace – all peace is simply the period of preparation for the next war. I should say that war-weariness will soon show itself among all the peoples of the world. That is a thing which has not yet happened. Perhaps it has not yet begun to happen in Germany. I do not know. It is a feeling that takes a long time to assert itself in practical or political form.

Perhaps we are entering a new phase in which war no longer seems a titanic struggle between rival systems and nations, no longer seems even tragic nor glorious, but just an intolerable burden, a bloody pointless waste.

The grass is green at last in St. James's Park, but the gates are locked and one is not allowed in because it is full of time-bombs. I look through the railings at the deserted paths and lawns. Even the ducks seem to have been moved away.

I think of those Australians in that hell in Greece being bombed by planes that outnumber them three to one and by tanks that outnumber them three to one and by armies that outnumber them God knows how many times. It is like the feeling we had last year over Dunkirk and again Norway – the feeling of waste and impotent rage, the feeling that one has no right and very little desire to be alive when better men are lying dead by the hundreds.

The above gloomy entries in my diary have done me some good. It is better that I should pour all this stuff out in a private diary than after a drink or two begin to talk like this to my friends or write it in letters. There is much self-pity here, mixed with the higher forms of gloom. My own vitality seems to have given out.

21 April 1941.

An Edwardian period piece is Maggie Greville whose luncheons in Charles Street have been famous for at least thirty years. She was the daughter of a Scottish millionaire and possessed by that energetic worldliness which pushes the lowland Scot so far up the English social ladder. Just as whenever in England you meet with a genuine interest in the arts you may suspect Jewish blood, so whenever you meet with respect for the human intelligence you may guess that there is a lowland Scot about. Mrs. Greville is very old, lame, half-blind, and has as she says, 'everything wrong with her except leprosy', but she still puts on a great act, and cabinet ministers still ring her up and ask if they may drop in and spend an evening with her in her room at the Mayfair Hotel. 'My husband,' she told us, 'was in the Grenadier Guards. We had been married two years and were very happy together, but I could not bear army society, so I said 'If you must stay in the regiment I'll have to go away with somebody else and begin over again. These people are intolerable.' He left the army and thus began her social career in London. She talked of her interviews with Hitler, who evidently had charmed her by taking the trouble to talk to her quietly and intelligibly. Someone asked, 'Didn't you find him appallingly – well – common?' 'Not at all – one doesn't notice that with a great man – now Mussolini, yes, the only great man I have ever known who was truly pompous.' I liked her story of Mrs. Cornelius Vanderbilt saying to her at the time when New York was talking about the dangers of communism, 'If the revolution comes in America, Neely (her husband) and I will go first – like Louis XVI and Mary Antoinette.'

How the English hate being rescued by the Americans. They know they must swallow it, but God how it sticks in their throats. The Americans are thoroughly justified in their suspicions of the English, and the English I think are justified in their belief that they are superior to the Americans. They have still the steadiness, stoicism and self-discipline that make for a ruling race, but what will these qualities avail them if the tide of history and economics has turned against them? How will the volatile, generous, imaginative, spoiled and impatient Americans manage city populations in the after-war world?

24 April 1941.

Mr. Massey has said to me that he would not like to think that the National Archives contained no account from this post of affairs in this country during the greatest war in history. I quite agree, but how is one to report anything which does not appear in the propaganda press when he exercises a censorship over everything which could be considered critical of England? He fears that anything critical might weaken the purpose of our people at home. But we are in too deep to get out, and surely our people have the right to know what is going on and read things which, if they were over here, they would hear from half the Englishmen they met in the clubs. He has an unrivalled opportunity to compile a secret history of the conduct of the war – to illustrate it with social anecdotes and personal impressions of men. But he is too patriotic ever to publish anything that could be considered critical, and what is worse he is too blinded by wishful thinking ever to face the conclusions even when he is alone with his confessional diary before him. Some day he will publish his memoirs. In fact he is looking forward to doing so – but they will be composed in the prose he loves best – that of a *Times* leading article. It is a pity, because he has in conversation the vivacity of phrase to produce a vivid, if superficial, account of the London scene. Alas, his reverence is too much for him.

28 April 1941.

I am thinking not in military terms but in social and historical terms. The ruling class in this country has nothing to gain from victory. The loyalty of the ruling class is not open to doubt. They will die for England and will let themselves be bled white for England. They are Englishmen before they are capitalists or landlords (unlike the same class in

France). But the fact remains that if the war continues for some years, as it must if we are to obtain the victory, they will be ruined financially and in the event of a British victory they face – not the return of the *status quo* – but the completion of a bloodless, social revolution which will deprive them of all their privileges and bring about the destruction of all the things they hold dear. The reverse is true in Germany where the leaders know that victory means not only the triumph of the Reich but their own continuance in power and ever-increasing spoils of victory. England's ruling class are committing suicide to save England from defeat – it shows the stuff of which they are made, but all the same no one commits suicide with élan, and élan is a valuable quality in time of war.

2 May 1941.

We are in danger of losing the war. This is the way things might go if Hitler has his way as he has had it up to now. The 'pincer movement' in Egypt may succeed. If it does, and the Germans reach the Suez Canal, Japan will move south, Spain will attack Gibraltar and French Morocco. The Germans will then be able – for who is to stop them? – once the British army in Egypt is eliminated, to drive through Africa to the Cape. South Africa has neither arms nor men to defend itself. A quisling government will be set up there, Germany can then cut our communications not only with

India but with Australia and New Zealand which will be threatened by Japan.

As for England she will be outflanked on a world scale and left like the Maginot Line, a graveyard of equipment and static armies with nothing to defend except herself. These possibilities were outlined by General Smuts in a memorandum addressed to the United Kingdom Government in July 1940. They now seem to me to represent the most likely objectives of German strategy. It is possible that when the Germans have reached Suez they will make another peace offer on the basis that we can keep our Empire (except of course that they will control it by establishing themselves on the main routes of communication) and let them run Europe. They might join this with the announcement that they propose to turn their attention to the U.S.S.R. thus appealing both to our wish to save the Empire and to our hope that they may get embroiled in a grapple with Russia. Needless to say they will not have finished with us nor with the U.S.A. but they may prefer to transfer the war temporarily back to the sphere of pressure politics and to avoid their biggest risk, a frontal invasion of the U.K.

3 May 1941.

Went to a concert with Anne-Marie. Bach, to which I am deaf – though Anne-Marie says, 'He is a god.' As she had said a few minutes before that what she liked in music was 'sex – the frisson'. I cannot think that she enjoys Bach much. Then Beethoven's piano concerto with Moiseiwitsch at the piano. The Beethoven was what I had come for, but Anne-Marie somewhat spoiled it for me by leaning her shoulder against mine and 'vibrating' during the more exciting passages, at the same time glancing at me with a 'faint smile of pleasure' to make sure that I was sharing her ecstasies in the appropriate manner. This technique disturbed me, as what I like to do is to shut my eyes and concentrate like hell.

I always enjoy it when Anne-Marie talks of her fabulous youth. 'When I was a girl,' she says. 'I was a very precious person. My father of a very old family in Romania going back to 1200 – pedigree perfect. My mother came from nothing, but she was very rich. She died when I was eighteen months old, and half her fortune went to my father and half to me – forty thousand pounds a year each – so you see I was an heiress – for those days in Romania before the war it was a lot of money.' She adds this last deprecatingly out of worldly convenance – knowing perfectly well that forty thousand pounds a year is a lot of money anywhere at any time. 'My father was a charming person, but good for nothing. He went through his share of the fortune in a year – every penny of it – and nothing was left but bills. Under the Romanian inheritance laws if I died before coming of age my money went to my father – so now you see why I was so precious. I was brought up by my grandfather and grandmother – my father's parents. They were always terrified in case anything should happen to me. I might be kidnapped by some of my father's creditors who, if I was out of the way, could collect their money, or I might die. So if I flew into a rage they did not dare to refuse me what I wanted in case it should turn to a fever, and upset my health. My grandfather I disliked, but he was a very intelligent man – to him I owe any taste or knowledge I may have. But I got on badly with him, first because he made my grandmother, who was a saint, miserable – but that is another story – then because he was after my money all the time. But they were all after my money, like sharks – he, my father, my uncle, – all of them.

'I never went to school, but I had all kinds of governesses – Swiss, English, German, Italian, French. It was that way that I learned languages. I have never studied a language in my life. I was allowed to read almost anything I liked. I was allowed to travel where I liked – Venice, Paris, Munich – anywhere so long as it was by land. My grandparents were frightened of sea travel in case anything should happen to me. I was too precious. My grandfather used to take me to the Salon Carré at the Louvre when I was twelve years old. In those days the pictures had not been divided into the schools. In the Salon Carré was the best of Rubens, Rembrandt, Titian – everything – 'Go and look for yourself,' he would say, 'and come back and tell me what you liked and try to explain to me why you liked it.'

'I was brought up to sit on top of the pyramid of my fortune. I was taught nothing practical, but after the war when it became necessary I turned into an excellent business woman. I must have had that from my mother's side – where the money came from. So you see I am a mixture of everything, only I have no Jewish blood.'

5 May 1941.

I have just got back from a day in the country lunching with Loelia, Duchess of Westminster. She is witty, worldly, and sensible. She lives in a house full of rococo white china and pretty little eighteenth-century chandeliers and lovely abundant flowers, and is herself opulently handsome, with dark eyes and an independent swing of the hips. If there was a revolution she would open an interior decorating establishment on Fifth Avenue and do handsomely out of it. People like her just cannot lose.

I spent last evening at Margery Ziegler's. I shall remember that funny little converted box of a house and her window-boxes of dust-laden pink carnations and blue front door and the little drawing-room full of flowers and the slum neighbours going to and from the pub with caps pulled down over their eyes, and the river at the end of the street. She loves the house and has stayed in it all through the blitz, although it is only a box of bricks, and it is just luck that it has not already collapsed about her ears with all the land-mines that have fallen around it – for it is almost under the shadow of Lot's Road Power Station, one of the principal German objectives. If there is an air raid I always think first of her sleeping on a mattress down in the passage below the level of the area railings, quite sure that she is not going to leave her own house to live anywhere else.

We are all publicly agreed that it would be better to be dead than to be defeated. On this principle anyone of us would risk his life tomorrow. Yet do we really feel this to be true? I do not. Yet if necessary I would act on it.

21 May 1941.

I do not know how to account for the extraordinary feeling of happiness and of completeness which I have felt in this past year in London. I have a premonition that it must mean that I have gone as far as I can go – that I am being shown happiness like a stretch of fair landscape that I have been in search of for a long time but that once having seen the promised land I must lose it. Tonight sitting in the park in a deck-chair, smoking a cigarette, watching the searchlights, smelling the lilacs, I felt – this is too much – retribution must follow.

I dined with the Masseys – if only their enemies could see them like that they could not help being touched. Their love for each other is the most attractive thing about both of them.

25 May 1941.

Dined with Lady Malcolm after the ballet –
Orpheus and Eurydice, music by Gluck – so unbeliev-
ably badly done that the only thing to do was to treat
it as a joke, and even as a joke it was too long, chore-
ography infantile, costumes ludicrous, dancers ugly,
graceless and amateurish – they do not even know
how to get across the stage, much less any technique –
practically no dancing in it and I must say it is music
which makes no impression on me at all. The only
interesting thing was Constant Lambert's face – he
was at the piano – a remarkable face – sensitive, highly
intelligent and, I think, repulsive.

Well, I got Jack Grant out to Canada today with
his wife and child. I have paid that debt in a way
certainly never expected. I remember this time last
year when he came reeling into my office. He was in
the Bomber Command and had been going up in
France six and seven times a day and making night
flights over Germany. In a few months he had aged
years from a boy into a tired man – so dizzy with
fatigue that he did not know if he was coming or
going. I wrote him off as one of the war's losses –
never thought somehow that he would come out of
it alive. Here he is a year later with a wife, a
superbly healthy son and a good job, on his way to
Canada out of the war – and what is more the desperate look which he has always had – the look of a
man who is gambling against himself – has gone.
He is a responsible husband and father. I thought of

him as a tragic figure, a man who cannot compromise successfully with the world or his fate and so butts his head against stone walls. He is going as a Training Instructor with the Air Force. Now he is safe unless, of course his ship is torpedoed on his way to Canada or he is killed in an accident.[3]

30 May 1941 .

I took the ballerina to lunch at the Ritz. She was a little nervous of the place and kept her checked mackintosh on in the bar because it was new and under it she was wearing an old tweed suit. I told her today that I was falling a little bit in love with her and so I am a *little* bit. She is my perennial type. When I die they will find some woman's name written on my heart – I do not know myself whose it will be!

1 June 1941.

I like to remember the mornings after I have spent a night out when I have got up very early to be away before the daily charwoman arrives and standing in the damp grey morning air waiting to get one of the first buses with the people starting out for their day's work coughing and gossiping and grousing and waiting stolidly – patiently – for the bus – working men with coat collars turned up and stout women going scrubbing who spent last night at the local. I am unshaven and drifting and happy and with all the pores open to physical sensation and the tight core of will melted. Then to get into my smart pseudo-New York flatlet that always smells of whatever they clean the carpets with, and I have a hot bath and sausages for breakfast to celebrate the fact that I feel fine.

Love affairs. In my youth (that is until this year, for my youth was one of the protracted kind) I used to be bewildered by my own lack of feeling in affairs of the heart. I felt that my love affairs were not up to scratch. I did not yearn or suffer enough – not nearly enough. I still feel that – I believe it to be a much more common state than people suppose. For to hear me talking of my loves you would think me to be a creature of burning passions and palpitating feelings, particularly if I am telling a woman of my ecstasies and sufferings in love's lists. This is just advertising one's own temperament by exaggerating what one is capable of feeling in love. Most other people knowingly or not must employ the same trick. It is true that promiscuous love-making knocks a lot of the nonsense out of one, and at the same time it 'hardens a' within and petrifies the feelings!'

2 June 1941.

The common people of England deserve a few breaks and if it is socialism they want they should have it. I would trust them to make any form of government into something tolerant and tolerable.

5 June 1941.

It has begun to thunder – *that* is what I have been

expecting all evening without knowing what it was. I walked alone in the park. It was hot for the first time this year and everything was in bloom at once – lilacs (white lilacs leaning over the garden wall at Apsley House) hawthorn everywhere and chestnut. The grass is long and shaggy – people have trodden paths across what used to be smooth preserved lawns. There are cigarette boxes and papers everywhere, but the trees are in full magnificence and there are lovers on the grass and solitary ladies reading lending library books in their deck-chairs, and old dirty human bundles of tramps, and everywhere soldiers. I think of last year walking in the parks after Dunkirk when they were full of the remnants of half the armies of Europe with foreign voices and tired strained faces. Again we are on the edge of something momentous. And next spring?

7 June 1941.

The mournfulness – more than that – the terror of being alone is upon me. I am really frightened of these walls. I do not like the way my self seems to expand and fill the whole room when I am alone like this. I am more frightened than I dare to write.

We have had a little Scottish factory manager here who has escaped from Lille telling us about conditions in the north of France, the extent of the sabotage and the decline in morale of the Germans stationed in France. This is all to the good and gives one the much-needed refreshment of realizing that the Germans have their own difficulties and the hope that if pressed they might crack under them, if only we had the power to press them. From what one can piece together from unoccupied France it is rather different there. The richer people are adapting themselves to the new life. They no doubt vastly prefer the socially safe Pétain regime to the Blum government – they have not, apparently, been ruined financially by the defeat of France. It is the same kind of situation in Romania and probably all through central and south-east Europe. The richer classes are not doing too badly – business is good. They are picking up the strings of their lives again and cushioned by cash are accepting the inevitable. There is greater freedom to travel in Europe and conditions are coming around to a new kind of normalcy. 'You cannot,' says Basil, 'get the rich down.' People who are adapting themselves like that must wish for German victory – a British success means continuation of the war indefinitely, more destruction and danger, more interruption of business, and finally the probability of a social upheaval. The lower classes and the city intelligentsia are pro-British. But this class line of sympathy is blurred in thousands of cases by other elements, patriotism, race (e.g. the Jews) and individual temperament and experience.

I was talking to an officer of the United States Embassy who has lately been transferred from Berlin. I detect in him what I find in most people who have lived on the Continent since the war began, an unexpressed but apparent acceptance of the invincibility of Germany. He has been in Berlin during our raids there and says they are nothing – nothing at all – compared with German raids on London – that of course one knew already. Some believe that the German crack up will come in the end through the lack of inner toughness of the German people – their nervosity. They picture the fat men sitting around the bar at the Adlon Hotel in Berlin wiping their brows with their handkerchiefs and saying, *'Ich bin nervös.'* I tried that picture of the German temperament on my American friend who said it applied to the older generation but not to the young men. He obviously feels that the Germans understand the nature of war much better than we do and says they throw themselves into it one hundred per cent because they want to get it over with and see that is the only way to do it.

With the Americans more than with most people nothing succeeds like success. If we are defeated in the Middle East this summer, if Germany then proposes peace and we have to turn to the United States and say, 'It is up to you – do we continue the struggle or come to terms?' that will be America's hour of testing. *We* went through the same test and after failing twice came through with the goods in the end.

12 June 1941.

Went with Vincent Massey to the Conference of

Allied Representatives[4] held at St. James's Palace in a long saloon panelled in rather worn green silk and hung with copies of royal portraits. Winston Churchill delivered a melodramatic and moving oration and made a historic occasion of what could so easily have been just a formal gathering of politicians and diplomats sitting around a green baize table ('quite like a meeting of the Council of the League of Nations' as Belinski, the Pole, said). The Prime Minister made one see it as the assembly of all the duly constituted governments of Europe who had sought refuge in the embattled fortress of England and who would in due course issue forth to deliver their oppressed lands from the heel of Hitler. He indulged in one of his usual diatribes against the Nazis with all his usual relish. These terrific castigations always make me feel a little uneasy. He so obviously enjoys piling into Hitler and the Nazis – and you feel it is just too easy for him. Also you wonder if he won't one of these days overdo it and reduce the whole thing to a music-hall level. He is very near the music-hall sometimes, but he always manages to get away with it. One of the secrets of the hold of his oratory over the English people is that he makes them feel that they are living their history, that they are taking part in a great pageant. He gives them his own feeling of the continuity of English history. All the same there are murmurs. Crete was a blow to his prestige, already one hears again that phrase which used to be ever on the lips of Tory back-benchers, 'Churchill, oh yes – but he lacks judgement.' The Tory wives are beginning to say that again now, and that shows that their husbands have begun to say it to them again, although they dare not say it in public – yet.

Mr. Massey was made a Privy Councillor today – it was Churchill's own idea and Mr. King concurred. The Masseys are so excited and happy about it. It is really touching the way Mr. Massey reacts to praise and recognition. He is so open about it like a schoolboy who just cannot resist ice-cream. Brendan Bracken wrote and told him that few men living had done more for the Empire.[5] Certainly the Empire has no more loyal servant. Bennett's peerage provides me with the headache of writing to him. Lord Stampede of Calgary is the best title suggested.

Crossing the park I took a minute or two off and sat in a deck-chair beneath two May trees of varying hues of pink – under a parasol of blossom. I thought that I would like to spend the day drifting through the parks without object and without personality, watching the lovers, looking at ducks and flowers, listening to the bands – neither imposing myself on other people nor receiving their imprint and above all not having to observe with precision, not making mental notes – just drifting – as if into a sunny impressionist picture where everything swims vaguely in light and colour.

16 June 1941.

It really is most interesting about Billy Coster[6] brought up in the smart Paris-American world of Ritz bars, promiscuity and snobbishness. He now finds the only real fun he gets out of life is serving behind the bar in a small pub in a poor street in Chelsea. The people he enjoys being with are Bill Epps, the local plumber and Millie Lighthouse, the barmaid at 'The Surprise'. Those social charms which he would not dream of displaying at Newport are lavished upon the working people who come in for a half-pint. They obviously love him, and I suppose it satisfies his need of affection. I think he would do well to marry his barmaid, but then I am all for experimental marriages – where other people are concerned. In my advice to others I notice that I scorn worldly considerations and always counsel them to take a chance – a chance that nothing would induce me to take myself. I was thinking tonight at dinner with Billy how much more difficult it is to talk freely to one's friends than it used to be when one was young. There was a time when I would have told Billy quite freely anything about my private life – and now – no. The things that one cannot talk about accumulate each year – each month there are more things that one suppresses. One grows more polite, more guarded – why? How I cling to the few people to whom I still speak freely, yet no doubt they despise me for it.

Mackenzie King has been putting on the most

remarkable display of panic – was invited to come to the get-together of Commonwealth Prime Ministers. He has cabled the longest apologies to Churchill. 1. He cannot leave the country because of the problem of unity. 2. Labour difficulties. 3. Conscription. 4. External Affairs. 5. Possibility of the United States coming into the war. 6. Needed to campaign the country. 7. Knows nothing about strategy. I do not know why he does not add that he cannot leave because he is having his front parlour repapered and is needed to choose the design. When he says that anyway he does not think the meeting would serve much purpose he is on surer ground – in fact he may be quite right on the whole position. But what maddens one is that it is such a demonstration of cowardice, personal and political. If the cables were published surely he would be dished politically.

As someone has said (General McNaughton) he must be a very brave man to refuse to take the risk of coming. He cuts such a figure. It has put Mr. Massey in a spot – although he thinks that King should come, he does not want to put himself on record as opposing or supporting or confirming King's line – lest he should be made the public scapegoat – and at the same time the ball has been thrown to him, and he is in trouble if he will not play. Personally I would feel very tempted to try to put King on the spot, but that would be short-sighted. 1. The issue is not important enough – it does not involve anything really essential to winning the war. 2. Much as one would enjoy putting a spoke in the old hypocrite's wheel, the fact remains that there is no one who could take his place with anything like the same chance of keeping the country together. He is easy to rail at but not easy to replace.

We had an interesting Canadian lunch the other day – Graham Spry and I, and three Conservative army officers, all imbued with contempt for Mr. King and all agreed that the Canadian war effort is nil compared with what it might and should be. Graham, an ex-socialist, agrees with them on the last point and in fact considers that Canada has relaxed its efforts since September of last year. Certainly, unless King's telegrams are entirely bluff the situation at home must be very tricky. Now we need a few victories or else some bombing blitzes on North America to make us know what we are up against.

X. was talking about Churchill yesterday and said that when he first met him he was not impressed. It was in Canada – he was recovering from his accident in New York and was drinking too much brandy. Then he met him again a few years ago at lunch. He dominated the table with his compelling monologue which fascinated everybody, although he did not agree with his argument which was a scathing attack on the lower classes – the plebs – for whom he had no use. In summing him up he said, 'He has plenty of spirit but no soul.' In fact he is an old pirate and if things go wrong people will find out and will turn on him and he will end in disgrace and they will forget that he is the only thing that kept England – so far – from a Vichy Government.

I had sandwiches with D. in the Park. It was not a great success. She had dressed for the Ritz and was not too pleased at my enthusiasm for the simple life. If women only knew how endearing it would be if they occasionally expressed a desire for a cheap, simple meal instead of always exacting their full pound of flesh. But they all act on the assumption that the price you pay for their dinner is the measure of your regard for them. Just to prove to D. that I loved her I took her afterwards to the Apéritif where we had peaches and white wine for the price that would keep a working woman for a week, and I must say that she was right in wanting a smart restaurant as a background. It suited her and made one feel that this was Page 1 Chapter 1 of a new and exciting story. Also it restored my lust for the things that money can buy – smart women, fashionable glitter, all the frivolities that charm the eye. What I really dread from the sober reasonable socialism of the future is the eclipse of style, the disappearance of distinction – for mixed and intermingled with the vulgarity of our age is the survival of pleasant, ornamental, amusing people and things – and one's soul shrinks from the austere prospect of cotton stockings. The intellectuals do not mind, because they despise the glitter and speciousness of rich life. But the aesthetes – like myself – have their misgivings.

23 June 1941.

Went down to the House of Commons. Eden spoke on Russia.[7] He is not impressive – he never sounds as if he really means what he says. It is not that he seems insincere, but there is a lack of conviction or temperamental failure in power to convey his convictions to others. And one feels his lack of intellectual power. A nonentity although not obstructionist nor actively harmful in any way. I walked through Westminster Hall – the sunlight coming through the gaps caused by the bombing above the rafters in the magnificent roof. The House met in the Lords[8] – sitting on very new red leather benches. Churchill spoke about the postponement of the Prime Ministers' Meeting – a most instructive episode the secret history of which will never – presumably – be revealed to the Canadian people.

Lunched with the Poles – Marlewski, rather boring and vulgar, and Belinski in cool grey flannels with his quiet, sympathetic manner and his cynicism. Poor buggers – the Russians are laying waste their homes as they retreat.

The modern Englishman does not seem to have any desire to impose his will on anyone or even to impose his view of life. I cannot imagine that, even if the war is won, these people are destined to reorganise the Continent of Europe. They have nothing to say to Europe. They do not even believe any longer in their own mission as empire builders. Yet it is nonsense to say that they are decadent any more than the Dutch are, or the Swedes. It is just that what they are principally interested in is improving living conditions and spreading the 'advantages' in this island. They are aiming straight for a moderate socialist state run on rational lines – 'a little England' of the type which English socialists and radicals have always preferred. People of that sort who may be expected (if we win) to rule England have no use for the Empire which they consider an embarrassment and a bore. They will never apply force to continental politics but will expect continental states to be reasonable – like the English.

The younger writers, painters and poets who congregate in London and dine in the Charlotte Street restaurants form very much of a club. Most of them are middle-class young men, sons of school-masters, civil servants, doctors, colonels and clergymen – that is to say they were brought up in the religion of snobbery. They are trying desperately hard but usually with incomplete success to escape from the strait-jacket of the English social hierarchy. But who buys their books, pictures and magazines? Is it the working man? Whom do they like to dine with and spend the week-ends with? Is it with the workers? If they prefer the manual workers to their own class, why have they not flocked to join the army? Instead they are, many of them, filling white-collar jobs in America.

4 July 1941.

This war between Germany and Russia has made things seem different all over again. We have entered into yet another phase of the war. This war is like a complicated piece of music – a great symphony in which motifs are started then disappear and reappear in many combinations. Now in a way it is like not being in the war any longer and yet it is not in the least like being at peace. We are back again in the 'phoney war' feeling of that first year before Dunkirk. Of course the situation is completely different but the feeling of it is rather the same. The German pressure has momentarily been removed. We are not in physical danger. Apart from this unreal and unnatural war in Syria between Australians, Arabs and the Foreign Legion our people are not engaged in fighting.

I still believe that this German attack on Russia was an act of madness on Hitler's part. All the experts here said that Germany would easily overwhelm the Russians, but then these same experts said that there would never be a Russo-German Pact and believed up to a week before the attack took place that Germany would not fight Russia. One thing seems at least likely and that is that even the German military machine will be in no condition to attack England for several months after the

Russian campaign even if they do succeed in conquering Russia. This means that the attack on England is off for the time being.

Meanwhile we go from one cloudless, high-summer day to another in a kind of daze. The parks are full of soldiers and girls in summer dresses. It is difficult to get a table in a restaurant. My friends indulge their love affairs and their vendettas. Cabinet ministers gossip in clubs and the press print daily jeremiads warning us to prepare lest a worse thing befall us. From the endless plains of Russia comes news of vast combats between alien hordes, between armies of tanks, and our lives may be being settled somewhere between the Dvina and the Dnieper. We know this but we cannot realise it. We seem to be moving in a trance towards the day when Hitler's tanks are lumbering past the Kremlin and he is ready to settle his score with us. We feel that day must come and may come soon but we cling to the hope – the wonderful, white hope – that the Russians may hold him – may even, though this would be too miraculous to be mentioned – defeat him.

18 July 1941.

I went to the Air Ministry meeting this morning. On one side of the table sat 'Chubby' Power, the Canadian Air Minister, and his staff. On the other side were the high officers of the Air Ministry. They are an attractive lot – low-voiced, sensible men without the stiffness or the affectations – and above all without the bloody breeziness – of the army. Our people, especially Power, were moderate, plainspoken and willing to waive their own proposals if it was made clear to them that they would impair the efficiency of the war effort.

There was an interesting question over the Canadian request that we should be allowed to publish in the Canadian press the names of individuals in the Air Force who had performed outstanding exploits. This violates the sacred R.A.F. tradition of anonymity for individuals. Power pointed out that it was necessary for recruiting in Canada. He said that the British might think it 'Hollywood ballyhoo', but in our country 'you must make things human and above all personal'. It was plain that the Air Ministry did think it 'Hollywood ballyhoo', and that no Englishman in the room knew what Power meant, yet all the Canadians, whatever their inner reservations on other points, agreed with Power on this one. The English could not bear the idea of individuals thinking themselves heroes. We could not understand the blank refusal to admit the human and popular approach – 'The home-town boy makes good' myth.

10 August 1941.

Weekend at Miriam Rothschild's. Waddesdon is another of these monstrous Rothschild houses scattered through the Chilterns, and is a copy of

Chambord. The state apartments are closed and the pictures (some I believe are magnificent) sent to Canada. The family are living in a wing and somewhere in the house tucked away are one hundred and fifty orphans and their attendants. It gives an idea of the scale of the house that never during my visit was I aware of their existence. The inhabited part of the house is furnished exactly as it was in the 1880s. It is decorated entirely in deep crimson – the carpets, curtains, even the leather sofas and chairs are crimson.

There are certain peculiarities about staying in a country house in wartime, one is the problem of the black-out. When you retire to your room for the night you find that it has been most thoroughly blacked out in several layers. First the extremely tall heavy windows have been securely closed and fastened (these can only be opened by pulling on two long cords with white bobbles attached to the ends of them). Then the shutters have been closed and fastened with mighty crossbars fitting into grooves. The black-out curtain hangs the whole length of the window and then come the long heavy curtains which also can only be made to come apart by pulling the correct pulleys, so that one gazes in dismay at the number of possible cords all twined around knobs. If you pull the wrong combination of pulleys (i.e. one of the curtain cords and *one* of the cords that open the window) you are involved in a breathless struggle which yields no results save frustration. It must be remembered that the business of opening the windows has to be done in the pitch dark as the light must be turned out before you begin playing about with curtains. One night staying at Stansted I was completely defeated by the combination of obstacles and panting with exhaustion after wrenching at shutters and pulling at cords I took to my bed and tossed all night, in breathless confinement. But at Waddesdon I triumphed, and what a relief to hear the wind sighing in the trees and to feel the soft night air! Then, of course, fumbling your way by the light of a small hand-torch along black corridors filled with unfamiliar furniture to the W.C. (which one had failed to mark by daylight) or alternatively to the bedroom of your girl-friend is another country-house hazard. At Waddesdon the valet asked me what I would like for breakfast. 'Coffee,' he suggested, 'toast or anything cooked, sir?' What a question in any English country house! But I stood out for an egg – felt the Rothschilds should be able to manage it – somehow!

2 September 1941.

The first time I saw Elizabeth Bowen I thought she looked more like a bridge-player than a poet. Yet without having read a word of her writing would not one have felt that something mysterious, passionate and poetic was behind that worldly exterior?

17 September 1941.

The night porter said to me, 'I don't want my daughter to be in domestic service – to be a servant. When she is three years old I am going to buy her a typewriter so that it will be second nature to her. I waited until I was fifty to have her, not like some young people who have children right away like animals.

'I look upon you as a friend, not like some of them who look down on me. I have an encyclopaedia – the latest one – *Pears Cyclopaedia*. What I like about it is it always settles an argument. There is one man on the staff who says to me "I don't care what the book says." Now that can only be ignorance or else he envies me and my knowledge.'

I lunched today with de Selliers of the Belgian Embassy and another Belgian, a civil servant, and Berkeley Gage of the Foreign Office. We discussed the settlement after the war in a muddled way. What was chiefly shown up was the great divide which separates the Englishman from everyone else on earth. Gage said that it would be fatal to have another peace of bitterness. He would like the peace conference to take place in Peking. In that atmosphere the delegates would take their time and get to know each other. It would take them months to reach the final solution but so much the better – a peace that was made amid the passions of war would never be any good. Peking was the place – and then he typically added, 'I am afraid I am not being absolutely serious about this.' The two Belgians protested – so did I. De Selliers said, 'We Belgians – like all Continentals – would want to have things reduced to writing.' 'Oh,' said Gage, 'if only you Continentals could get tight with an Englishman we would understand one another and trust one another and it would not be necessary to put everything in writing. The English have never been in favour of writing everything down.' De Selliers said, 'When you say you do not want a peace made until the passions of war have cooled you mean let us give the Germans another chance – that you will begin your old policy of equilibrium in Europe, playing off one power against another. We want peace made while you are still angry. The work of Bismarck must be undone. Germany must be split up – Bavaria, the Rhineland, Saxony, etc., must be revived as separate states. We in Europe will take the Anglo-Saxon lead – but you must use your power.'

18 September 1941.

There is only one question of any real importance at this moment. Everyone is asking 'Why can't we make a landing in France or Italy or Greece, anywhere provided it is in time to divert some German troops and planes from the Eastern Front before it is too late?' The Russians are on the verge of being pushed right out of the war, and still we do not move. And to think that there are still people in the

Foreign Office and elsewhere who want to be sure that Russian strength is annihilated and that G. of the Foreign Office said at lunch the other day before two foreign diplomats, 'After this is over I suppose we shall have to fight the Russians.' 'Whom the gods would destroy they first make mad.'

24 September 1941.

Dinner with Elizabeth Bowen and her husband Alan Cameron and a few writers and critics. So far in my excursions into High Bloomsbury I have not encountered, except for Elizabeth, any striking originality of thought, phrase or personality but rather a group of cultivated, agreeable people who think and feel very much alike.

Inter-Allied Conference all morning and most of the afternoon pious speeches in English and French from case-hardened exiled continental politicians who abjure all aggression, talk of the rights of man and the territorial integrity and self-determination of nations. At least Hitler uses a new vocabulary and not this Genevese jargon.

25 September 1941.

Dinner at a dining club got up by Berkeley Gage of the Foreign Office. I sat between Archduke Robert of Austria and de Selliers of the Belgian Embassy, the former rather like someone seen in a distorted mirror. His head seems preternaturally shallow, his neck elongated. He has the romantic

Austrian charm which springs from an inveterate superficiality. He never asserts himself, but he is a Hapsburg and one cannot help knowing it. His mother, Empress Zita, and younger children are living near Quebec.

29 September 1941.

'Take it from one of the best living novelists that people's personalities are not interesting,' Elizabeth said in a dry voice; 'except,' she added, 'when you are in love with them.' Her books show much that you would expect if you knew her only as an acquaintance, her intelligence, her penetrating eye, her love of houses and flowers. These things you would have gathered from talking to her in her drawing-room. But there are certain passages in which her peculiar intensity, her genius, come out, which would be hard to reconcile with this cultivated hostess. That purity of perception and compassion seem to come from another part of her nature of which she is perhaps not completely aware.

This afternoon, Elizabeth and I went to see the roses in Regent's Park. For days we had been talking of those roses, but I could never get away from the office before nightfall, and it seemed as if we should never go together to see them. Then one perfect September afternoon she telephoned to say that if we did not go today it would be too late – they were almost over. So I put away the Foreign Office boxes in the safe, locked up the files and took a taxi to

Regent's Park. As we walked together I seemed to see the flowers through the lens of her sensibility. The whole scene, the misty river, the Regency villas with their walled gardens and damp lawns and the late September afternoon weather blended into a dream – a dream in which these were all symbols soaked with a mysterious associative power – Regent's Park – a landscape of love. A black swan floating downstream in the evening light – the dark purplish-red roses whose petals already lay scattered – the deserted Nash house with its flaking stucco colonnade and overgrown gardens – all were symbols speaking a language which by some miracle we could understand together.

Week-end staying with Miriam Rothschild. She is a remarkably handsome woman, heavy dark eyebrows, dark eyes which nothing escapes, a slow deliberately cockney voice and a free-ranging bold experimental intelligence which is beautiful to watch, an antiseptic wit which can puncture a pretension or exorcise a neurosis, a glorious capacity for gossip and fantastic invention. Add to these endearing qualities that she is a respected research scientist, is keenly interested in problems of aeroplane construction, is an authority on plant and animal life, buys and looks at modern pictures, runs her own business affairs, sits on Jewish welfare committees, and manages a large agricultural estate, and one has some idea what her energies must be. With all of this she has the most generous good heart for people in trouble, and is the most loyal friend and the most ruthless critic. People are frightened of her because her intelligence is free and she does not bother with English circumlocutions.

1 October 1941.

Old men in clubs are puzzled by the Russians' successful resistance. 'My nephew who was in the Navy was out there after the last war, time that Denikin was fighting in the Crimea, he used to tell me, "You can never organise the Russians to do anything. They are feckless, absolutely feckless." Everyone said the same thing – now how are they managing all the organisation of a modern war?'

'Well,' says another old boy, 'scratch a Russian and you find a Tartar – you know they are slow to rouse but once roused – why at Tannenberg five divisions of them marched unarmed straight at the Germans.' 'What beats me,' says a third club member, 'is that the Orthodox Church is praying for the success of the Soviet Union.' The attitude of officialdom about the U.S.S.R. is 'Necessity makes strange bedfellows.' When at one moment optimists were proclaiming the possibility of a Russian counter-offensive which would drive the Germans back across the borders, people in London were already getting very exercised about the possibility of the Russians being the ones to liberate the Poles, Czechs, etc., instead of the English. The idea of a smashing Russian victory and communism in Central and south-eastern Europe appalled them.

What would suit them best would be a stalemate in the East with the Russians holding the Germans, and if by any – as it now seems – remote chance the Russians did seem to have the Germans on the run – they no doubt would do their (probably successful) best to stop any more aid to Russia. As it seems unlikely that we shall ever have a land army big enough to finish off the Germans ourselves that seems a somewhat dog-in-the-mangerish attitude. It is worth noticing that the argument which you hear quite freely expressed now that maintenance of the Russian army in the field is the only way of defeating Germany on the European continent implies that if Germany had not attacked Russia we ourselves would never have been able to defeat Germany, which is true enough but used to be hushed up.

Meanwhile the Russians do not trust us any further than they can see us. The present accusation that certain members of the British Merchant Marine have been expressing anti-Soviet views is not surprising. Sailors have a habit of saying what they think.

Anne-Marie says that the Germans are physically frightened by the Russians and are terrified of the country itself with its immense empty spaces. This may well be so – if it is, it is another proof of the courage of the German soldier as well as of the vaulting boldness of conception which has inspired them – probably the most ambitious offensive in the history of war.

18 October 1941.

The gloom of these times is inescapable. It is a grey Sunday with a warm, restless, futile wind blowing London leaves about streets and squares. There are even dead leaves on the red carpet of the Ritz vestibule blown in through the swinging door.

19 October 1941.

I cannot get away from the dilemma that Sachie Sitwell put to me last week-end. If we cannot land an army on the Continent now while the Russian army is still in existence and holding the mass of German power in the East, how are we ever to defeat the German army? Why not give up the Continent to its fate and withdraw into isolation just defending our own if it is attacked? Of course we all know that such a programme is an impossibility, that we must go on until the Germans' will or our own is broken.

22 October 1941.

I was thinking this morning about that time in Boston when we went there as boys with Mother and Aunt M. We had a furnished apartment at the wrong end of Commonwealth Avenue. They thought it would be a relief to have a winter away from The Bower – not to have a house to bother about, and of course it would save money too. But it was not a success – the flat was too small – we were always falling over each other, and there was a horrid little gate-legged table in the sitting-room on which we had our meals. It was so low that we always had to stoop down, to eat. There was always a wind in Commonwealth Avenue and dust blowing and glare on the pavements. One day I went out to the bus in my patent-leather shoes and without a hat. Two girls in the street turned around and made some sort of crack. I felt ridiculous and humiliated. When I think of my youth it makes me angry even now. I feel that I ought to have my own back at someone for all that that vain, timid, harmless dreamer had to put up with. Now I have the weapons – then I was unarmed.

Elizabeth was saying the other day that a sense of guilt seems to be specifically a middle-class complaint – not enough humility and sense of limitations.

23 October 1941.

They were beginning to hold a meeting in Trafalgar Square for more aid to Russia. I thought of staying to see what it was like, but it was so cold. There were a lot of scrubby men in dirty mackintoshes with packages of red leaflets. They looked like the sweepings of the Communist Party hoping to stir something up. Charlie Hébert (a Canadian officer friend of mine) was with me – solid, military, well fed. They seemed to look at him with envious, hating sidelong looks as if they longed to be strong enough to pull him down.

I should like to have seen the Masseys standing

next to Maisky (the Soviet Ambassador) and singing the Internationale at the private viewing of the Soviet films. It is quite a long step from 'dear Alba'(the Spanish Ambassador) 'the last great gentleman in Europe' and Lord Halifax and 'all of us'. When I came here two and a half years ago there was no more devoted adherent of Chamberlain than Mr. Massey. Churchill, of course, in those days had 'no judgement'. I could never get Mr. Massey to accept an invitation to Maisky's ('I feel uncomfortable with that little man') but the Masseys have followed the English ruling class in the most spectacular somersault in all recorded history and never have they felt consciously insincere except perhaps now they do feel their conversion to the U.S.S.R. a little – shall we say – sudden. The more candid just go on hating communism as much as ever – 'Anything to save our bacon.' But they will not feel comfortable for long in this open cynicism. Already the Archbishop of Canterbury has found that communism contains the seeds of Christianity – even if the Russians wear their religion with a difference. A few really consistent Tories are in danger of being locked up in Brixton jail. They are guilty of the unpardonable sin of putting ideas before the interests of England. The English always said they were not interested in an ideological war. Mind you, I think they are quite right, but what does a little appal me is that when the storm is past they will bring back the old prejudices and what is much worse – the 'old principles'.

27 October 1941.

The sights – the long tree-lined avenue in Hyde Park at dusk echoing with the noise of soldiers' boots as they come strolling, swinging, whistling, singing, or alone looking for a girl, and the girls plain – most of them – little working girls in short skirts and sweaters with fancy handkerchiefs around their necks. They know they are wanted – they twist and turn as they walk and break into sudden gusts of giggles and cling to each other's arms. The whole length of the avenue is alive with desires. There are satyrs behind every tree. Silhouetted against the half-light soldiers with their girls sit on the deck-chairs on the grassy stretches that border the avenue. The flicker of a cigarette lighter reveals for a long second – the pose of a head – the movements of hands. Near the park gates the Military Police in their rose-topped caps stand in groups of twos and threes hoping for trouble, longing to exercise summary justice.

In the expensive restaurants at this hour pink, well-scrubbed schoolboys masquerading in guards uniforms are drinking bad martinis with girl-friends in short fur capes and Fortnum and Mason shoes, who have spent the day driving generals to the War Office or handing cups of tea and back-chat to soldiers in canteens. Grass widows in black with diamond clips or pearls are finding the conversation of Polish officers refreshingly different from that of English husbands. Ugly vivacious A.T.S. are ordering *vin rosé* at the Coquille. A film actress (making the best of a patriotic part at present) is just going through the swinging door of the Apéritif with David Niven at her elbow. Ageing Edwardian hostesses whose big houses are now shuttered and silent are taking little naps in their hideouts on the third floor ('so much the safest floor, darling') at Claridge's or the Dorchester. Cedric (in a yachtsman's jacket) and Nigel are hipping their way through the crowd of pansies in the Ritz bar (they all have the most madly peculiar jobs in the Ministry of Information or the B.B.C.). At the Travellers' Club Harold Nicolson in his fruity voice is embellishing a story as he settles on the leather sofa. Anne-Marie is sitting on the side of her bed at the Ritz making eyes at herself in the mirror and trumpeting down the telephone in Romanian French. It is a world of hotels and bars and little pubs that have become the fashion overnight – of small drinking clubs run by gangsters who make a nice profit out of prostitutes and the dope racket – packed with R.A.F. pilots, Canadian officers, blondes and slot-machines and perhaps a baccarat table in the upstairs rooms.

And along Piccadilly from the Circus to Hyde Park Corner is an incessant parade of prostitutes, and out of the black-out an acquisitive hand on your arm and 'Feeling lonely, dearie?' 'Hello, my sweet,' (in a Nöel Coward voice) or *'Chéri.'* In Berkeley Square the railings are down. An old man is making a bonfire of dead leaves beside the little pavilion in the centre of the garden.

28 October 1941.

Until this war began I never felt that I was a member of a community and that I had an obligation to others. The idea of 'doing my bit' had always seemed to me a piece of schoolboy morality, not applicable to me. I was still the bullied schoolboy who gets his own back in the end. Now this attitude seems to me not so much wicked as childish and dangerous too. It was because so many of us thought that 'the world' was something alien to ourselves which owed us the plunder of a living and as many privileges as we could lay our hands on that we are in our present spot. That lonely but pleasurable anarchism we shall never enjoy again in my lifetime. We shall never be safe enough to afford it. We are bound together now either in brotherhood or in fraternal hate. After this we either have a state based on human relationships or we have civil war.

2 November 1941.

I suppose I ought to cultivate the society of solid civil servants instead of rococo Romanian princesses and baroque dilettantes.

8 November 1941.

I have been reading with singularly little pleasure some modern poetry in *Horizon* magazine. What can you expect of poets who keep on thinking about 'the happiness of the common people', as if happiness could be an 'ideal'. They remind me of those thick-headed Babbitts who drew up the American Declaration of Independence and who announced 'the pursuit of happiness' as a political aim. The poets' contemporary left-wing opinions have no real political significance; they have not faced up to the fact that the new world for which they are rooting will be just as immoral and selfish as the old. They still believe in Santa Claus. To me that makes all that they have to hint about the future childish and silly. The only hope for the future is that more political intelligence will be applied to our problems so that the machine will not break down again. It is first of all a *technical* problem. But that it will be a better world for poetry to flourish in is poisonous nonsense.

10 November 1941.

I used sometimes during last autumn's air raids to say to myself in a stupid bewildered way, 'I wonder if those people in Berlin ever think of the hell we are going through.' Now I feel quite sure that they never did. We never stop to think that they are now having just the same terrifying experience. We shut our eyes to that fact and only think how many bombers we have lost. The capacity for sympathising with other people's troubles seems to have completely dried up. Do we ever think of the thousands of starving people in Europe? Do we sympathise

197

with the sufferings of the Russians? I doubt it. Think of our sympathy for the persecution of the Jews in the early days of Hitler. It seems that now the response to suffering is dead. Peter Quennell was saying the other day that he was surprised at the apathy of the people over the Russian war news on which, after all, our skins depend and that the fall of Moscow would hardly make people buy an 'extra'. We have long ceased to find the war thrilling – any excitement in the movement of historic events is gone. There is a vague but persistent worry in people's minds about the coming air raids this winter, but like everything else this is accepted as inevitable. The truth is that the war has become as much a part of our lives as the weather, the endless winter, and when the ice does break there will be no cheering in the streets.

So far as I know we have only one fascist poet in England – Roy Campbell – and his poetry is worth reading not only as poetry but as fascism. It is full of vitality, blazing with heat and colour. He is a Catholic and a romantic. He rides a high horse and takes you for some splendid gallops although he comes some bad croppers. The croppers in taste and feeling are mostly the result of showing off for the poet rams his legend down the reader's throat. He is the gay and spirited cowboy herding on the plains of Castile with a rose between his teeth and a song in his heart and cocking snooks the while at the suburban 'Charlies' as they trot obediently to their city offices. Such uninhibited posturing takes us back to the early days of the Romantic movement when every man was his own Byron. All the same it is rather refreshing to find someone with the spirit to cut such capers, and if Campbell has a touch of Byronic silliness he has a touch of Byronic fire too. For the man is a poet and his poetry strikes sparks. It is easy to see his faults, his damn 'picturesqueness', his blatancies, and his lack of discrimination. The first poems in the series called *Mithraic Emblems* are his most careful works and some of them are magnificent. In the second poem 'The Solar Enemy' he sweeps into his stride.

> Enemy of my inward night
> And victor of its bestial signs
> Whose arm against the Bull designs
> The red veronicas of light:
> Your cape a roaring gale of gold
> The scarlet of its outward fold
> Is of a dawn beyond the world.

24 November 1941.

Visited by my familiar devils which I fondly thought I had exorcised. I do not know what brings on these attacks when I am reduced almost to idiocy by ridiculous nervous compulsions, tics, obsessions and all manner of foolishness. I used to think they were brought on by living 'too chaste' but that can hardly be the case at the moment. Or it may be discovered when they have my brain in a bucket that there has been some recurrent form of pressure on it.

My finances are in a bad way which means dining alone in clubs and missing good chances. Now is the time for culture to come to the rescue and fill up the void. She seems to come on lame feet.

Went with Miriam to a party given by Lady Victor Paget for Bea Lillie.[9] Nöel Coward sang 'London Pride' in a manner which I found all the more revolting for being sincere. There was a gathering of pansies and theatrical blondes interspersed with Lord S. and latest girl-friend and Hore-Belisha[10] – an obscene spectacle. Old Lady Crewe[11] having a 'diplomatic' conversation with the Counsellor of the Washington Embassy. David Herbert[12] looking more *racé* than he knew. General atmosphere: a réchauffé of a gay twenties party with everyone looking that much older and trying to get back something which is not there any more.

29 November 1941.

Week-end at Miriam Rothschild's at Ashton. Miriam is becoming a friend – she certainly has no time for me in any other capacity.

She was talking about her cousin Baron Louis's imprisonment by the Nazis in Vienna. He was kept in solitary confinement in a space four feet by six feet. His glasses were taken away from him and he was not given anything to read. He was not ill-treated physically. Almost every day some neighbouring prisoner was taken away and shot, and he was continually expecting to be the next. One thing that worried him was that he was never able to make out how the Germans' minds worked. For instance, they legalised every step they took to deprive him of his fortune in the most tortuous manner instead of just grabbing it. One day a whole string of lawyers came into his cell laden with account books. He thought, 'Now it has come – they want me to sign something which will show that I have been swindling the shareholders.' The lawyers said, 'We regret to inform you that there has been a swindle in your affairs.' 'Yes,' he replied, 'I know. Who have I swindled?' 'No, Baron, it is you who have been robbed.' Then they explained to him in detail how one of his agents in Germany had been cheating him. The lawyers then went away leaving him baffled that when they were robbing him they should take the trouble to show him that someone else had been cheating him.

One day Himmler was announced in the cell. He came in, sat down and after a few platitudes said, looking around at the absolutely bare cell with nothing in it but a palliasse and a chair, 'Now is there anything you want?' 'No,' said Baron Louis, 'but what I should like to know is why I am here.' Himmler's face clouded looking at him coldly he left the room without a word of reply. Three or four days later a parcel arrived for Baron Louis from Himmler. It contained a pink satin eiderdown for his bed. (This is pure surrealism.)

There was a Belgian Jewish banker staying at Ashton. He and Miriam talked about their connections and friends on the Continent. They have cousins in every capital in Europe. I got an impression as they talked of the international *haute juiverie* of the days before the Nazis – energetic, experimental, cultivated, sensual people, fond of sport and pleasure and by far the best educated aristocracy the world has ever seen. He struck me as an almost sentimental idealist who would change once he got into his bank into a steely intelligence. He is now serving in the Belgian army. There was also a young Hungarian who was in the Pioneer Corps. He said bitterly, 'I am not allowed to have the honour to fight the Nazis although I hate them worse than any Englishman.' I do not like what I hear about the Pioneer Corps. It seems to be officered by a poor type of English officer who has been a flop in his own regiment. Half the N.C.O.s are English – half are foreign. He says the English N.C.O.s are the bad lot who have been got rid of out of their own regiments.

4 December 1941.

Elizabeth has been telling me how she goes about writing a novel. She talked about *The Death of the Heart*. I see the two women in *The Death of the Heart* as the two halves of Elizabeth. Portia has the naïveté of childhood – or genius. She is the hidden Elizabeth. The other woman is Elizabeth as an outside hostile person might see her. But all this is my own surmise and not what she told me. She said that besides this Eddie-Portia theme there was a second situation – that of the poor unworldly girl who comes lonely with her pathetic trunk containing all the things she owns to live in the house of grand relations. Portia is in the position of the governess in *Jane Eyre*.

Baudelaire quotes Edgar Allan Poe who said that no one would dare write a book called *My Heart Laid Bare* which was true to its title because 'the paper would shrivel and blaze at every touch of the fiery pen'. That is not quite what I am afraid of. My pen is not, alas, fiery. I am afraid to face my own smallness.

Elizabeth says that T. S. Eliot told her that without alcohol he could never have got in the mood for his poems. That is good news!

George Ignatieff[13] was talking today about the 'German smell'. He remembers that smell in the changing room at Amsterdam when he was playing hockey against a German team. He says it comes from their gross eating of coarse heavy meats.

4 December 1941.

Thinking over what I have written. What a pack of lies intimate journals are, particularly if one tries too hard to be truthful.

This autumn has been curiously characterless. After being the centre of the world's stage London has become unexciting. As soon as Russia was invaded and the direct threat diverted the temperature of the town went down. We are not as heroic, desperate and gay as we were last winter. London seems drab. The tension is removed – the anxiety remains.

7 December 1941.

The attack on Pearl Harbour has caused very human sardonic satisfaction to everyone I have happened to see today. This will take the Americans by the scruff of the neck and bounce them into the war. The picture is that of an over-cautious boy balancing on the edge of a diving-board running forward two steps and back three and then a tough bully comes along and gives him a kick in the backside right into the water! And only yesterday they were still hovering, saying they felt almost sure they might back us up if the Japanese attacked the Kra Peninsula, but they would feel happier if we could give a guarantee of the territorial integrity of Thailand before we invaded its territories. The President had a hot tip that the Japanese objective was Rangoon – but, lo and behold! it was Pearl Harbour. For years I have seen movies of United States reconnaissance planes ('the eyes and ears of the U.S. Navy', as the announcers portentously described them) circling away from the U.S. base at Pearl Harbour to spy out the Pacific for just such an attempt as this. What were they doing when those five aircraft carriers sneaked up close enough to disgorge those planes? Mr. Massey says, 'They have been living in a Hollywood world of unreality.' We listened to Roosevelt's address to Congress on the wireless in Mr. Massey's big office at Canada House under the great glass chandelier – the room where he told us of the declaration of war on Germany. Roosevelt was moving and had dropped his mannerisms. He sounded profoundly shocked and bitterly angry. His speech was exactly right.

At the Admiralty they suggest, 'Why not a British naval adviser on every American battleship.' At first the news of American unpreparedness and its results was an immense *soulagement* of a longstored, carefully restrained grudge in this country, but when the number of U.S. battleships sunk began to come in an Admiralty official said, 'This is getting past a joke.' I have not heard one word of sympathy for the United States here. The note of outraged American indignation at the treachery of which the U.S.A. has been a victim meets with no real echo here. It is like a hardened old tart who hears a girl crying because a man has deceived her for the first time. We have become very much accustomed to treachery – now let the Americans learn the facts of life and see how they like them.

We Canadians feel all the same that once the Americans have got over the initial shock they will get on the band-wagon and will get into the war one hundred per cent and be producing tanks, planes, etc., by the million when the Japs are finished. The English have no real faith in the United States. Now it is our business to begin boosting the Americans here.

17 December 1941.

Reading Peter Quennell's *Byron in Italy*. This is the irresistible Byron of the letters and of the early cantos of *Don Juan*. I can hardly imagine any man, certainly any young man, reading Byron's letters from Italy to Hobhouse and Kinnaird without loving the writer. I do not know if a woman would be so delighted with them. I doubt it. One could hardly blame them, for no man can read about Byron without having his own egoism reinforced and without experiencing a frantic desire to show off and to find a woman to show off before. This deleterious influence at one time swept the entire European continent. But alas, what puny creatures we all are beside the Great Originals. Hamlet and Byron – the modern world is unthinkable without them.

I enjoy my walks to the office in the mornings – the elegance of Grosvenor Street, the Maisons de Haute Couture, behind their ageing façades, Jacqmar's interior seen through the long plate-glass windows with the soignées salesgirls drifting about among the lengths of patterned silk. It looks as a temple of fashion should look – dimly lit and solemn, but luxurious – a proper place to stir the imagination of the passing woman. Oh God, leave us our luxuries even if we must do without our necessities. Let Cartiers and the Ritz be restored to their former glories. Let houseparties burgeon once more in the stately homes in England. Restore the vintage port to the clubs and the old brown sherry to the colleges. Let us have pomp and luxury, painted jezebels and scarlet guardsmen, – rags and riches rubbing shoulders. Give us back our bad, old world.

21 December 1941.

Stayed in bed in my new flannel pyjamas reading Byron's letters with a Christmas fog outside. I had not the will-power even to change the water in which Elizabeth's flowers were dying. I liked the picture of Byron's life at Ravenna playing with his animals writing to his friends, or sitting before the fire remembering the past which weighed heavily on him with Proustian power. I like the sketch of him yawning in the fog in Bennet Street on just such a day as this. I walked down Bennet Street today past where his lodgings used to be before they were destroyed in the last reprisal blitz.

Elizabeth came to tea in her smart black coat with a pink flower in her buttonhole. She lay on the sofa as she likes to do in an oddly elegant and relaxed pose. She never sprawls – mentally or physically.

Her long, high-bred, handsome face was pink from the outside damp. She had on her gold chains and bangles.

On the way home tonight Raymond Mortimer said to me, 'Oh Elizabeth, she has such charm and is so kind and makes most of one's friends seem irremediably vulgar.'

28 December 1941.

Just back from Christmas – the Sitwells' at Weston – my favourite house – fire in the bedroom with a view of a piece of lawn with conifer-shaped shrubs. White frost on Christmas day. We sang carols in the family pew in the stone, stone cold of the little church. It was only the family – Sachie, Georgia and their son, Reresby, at home from Eton. At the moment I am happier with them than anybody. My sadness and staleness went away. Sachie is sensitive, lovable and very funny – an ageless creature. He does not seem any older than his fourteen-year-old son. He has altogether escaped pomposity and has no desire to impress. The boy looks seventeen but he seems, too, no particular age and can talk about anything that comes along, but yet is a spontaneous, excitable child. Georgia sparks all talk with her wit and warmth and looks a young beauty. There is a magic about the place that must be distilled in some mysterious manner by Sachie.

1942

11 January 1942.

Elizabeth came to see me in the morning and brought me a cyclamen.

She talked about women's friendships, apropos of Virginia Woolf and her niece and Jane Austen and her niece, Fanny Knight. She says that every young woman has such friendships and that the older woman puts into them all the lyrical, poetic side of her nature and that she lives her youth again. The girl finds so much pleasure in being seen through the eyes of love and admiration that she may have a flirtation with a man simply for the pleasure of telling the other woman about it. This is all quite apart from Lesbianism.

The river in the park was frozen today, and the gulls slid on the ice, looking as if they were doing it for fun, although it probably annoyed them. There was a wintry sun, what, for the lack of a nearer word for the colour, is called an orange sun.

I had an embarrassing dinner with the Masseys.

She was irritable and he was making Balliol answers to her haphazard remarks and beginning his sentences with, 'But, my dear'. I did not know what to say or where to look, as my unfortunate face always gives me away. She said, 'You have a very guilty look this evening.' I should have answered, 'I always look guilty when anything unpleasant is said, even if I am in no way responsible for it.' It is an idiotic characteristic, but I cannot help it.

13 January 1942.

Miriam and I were talking about love. I said that the words 'Do you love me?' said earnestly had a putting-off effect. Miriam said that on the contrary – this repetitious earnestness is a very good line for women. I said, 'But it is such a bore.' She said, 'Look how often it works with a man.'

The sheets are cold and I have just drunk two glasses of ice-cold barley water – emblem of chastity.

20 January 1942.

I am reading *Tristan et Iseult,* the story reconstructed by Joseph Bédier from twelfth-century sources. It is giving me as much pleasure as it used to give the inhabitants of draughty, medieval castles when it was recited or sung to them by passing troubadours. It has the same variety of incident and lack of proportion as the scenes in old tapestries in which some detail in the foreground – a dog or a group of flowers – has interested the artist so much that it crowds out the knights and the castle. It is certainly one of the most enjoyable books I have come across.

They have taken my chairs and sofa away to have them covered in 'off-white' (as the manageress calls it). Meanwhile I have a temporary sofa which looks as if it belonged in an undergraduate's room at Oxford.

Elizabeth and I dined at Claridge's. She was in an easy and cheerful mood. She said, 'I would like to put you in a novel,' looking at me through half-closed eyes in a suddenly detached way like a painter looking at a model. 'You probably would not recognise yourself.' 'I am sure I wouldn't,' I lied.

A red-haired young man came up to me in Claridge's and said, 'I have met you somewhere before.' Neither of us could think where or how. He kept on coming back to our table while we were dining and suggesting clues which led nowhere. 'Was it playing tennis in Surrey or dining with mutual friends in Cambridge?' In the end I remembered it was on a Sunday afternoon when I was staying with the Fullertons. He played Chopin in the drawing-room while we all sat around on chairs draped in dust-covers. There was a thick mist outside – we sat listening to him until dinner-time and after dinner he did ingenious and boring parlour tricks. Since then he has been shot down in an aeroplane, lost a lung and gets six pounds and six shillings a week disability allowance. I think he must have landed on his head. He has a wild look in his eye.

22 January 1942.

Dined with Elizabeth at her house. She always manages to have unheard-of quantities of smoked salmon. The house was so cold that we put the electric heater on a chair so as to have it on a level with our bodies. Elizabeth was wearing a necklace and bracelet of gold and red of the kind of glass that Christmas tree ornaments are made of. Some woman friend had given them to her – she considered Elizabeth to be 'a Byzantine type'. She had on a white silk jacket over a black dress. We sat on the sofa and talked.

23 January 1942.

I feel that this country cannot – in the end – escape the European civil war. My friends seem to me to be waiting offstage to take up their parts. James Peel is going to be the out-of-work ex-officer trained in methods of violence (and yet the most kindly creature), an adventurer and a patriot. There are other friends of mine of the same stamp mostly now employed in Military Intelligence who might qualify for a post-war secret police. My role is indicated – the diplomat who hangs on until the last moment, feeling it his duty to defend his country's actions right or wrong, reluctant to give up his career.

26 January 1942.

Fascinated by the Tristan and Iseult legend, I have been reading Swinburne's 'Tristan in Lyonesse'. It is much too heavily upholstered, the passion is stifled in ninetyish verbiage. Occasionally a line strikes – Laurence Binyon is better with the same subject. But his last dialogue between Tristan and Iseult is flat. Nothing so far touches the twelfth-century French legend.

27 January 1942.

Heard the Prime Minister defend the Government's conduct of the war in the House. It was the greatest speech I have ever heard. For an hour and a half he developed the central theme of the grand strategy of the war and at recurrent intervals sounded the note of his own desire for a vote of confidence from the House. It was an orchestral performance, lesser motifs interspersed were all handled with the same easy strength. To read it would be to lose half of it – the implications in his slightest side-glance were significant.

One small thing that struck me before the Prime Minister got up to speak was the reception given to a question asked by a Labour M.P. as to why certain people were still allowed to have three or four domestic servants in their employ. The question was greeted with ironical laughter from Conservative M.P.s, the implication of the laughter being that there were no such persons. The Cabinet

Minister who answered the question pooh-poohed it and said that he could not accept that such a situation existed. 'Of course not,' laughed the Conservative M.P.s scornfully. Yet they must have known as well as I do (better, since most of them no doubt have still got three or four domestic servants of their own) that in any country house you choose to go into there are still domestic servants in threes and fours. A small thing but typical.

George Ignatieff is shocked that behind closed doors in the War Office the M.I. boys express the hope that the Russians will be defeated and that *three days* later the German army itself will collapse. It is and has been all along the ideal British solution. The Russians know this as well as we do. It is the obvious reason for the so-called 'mysterious peasant suspicions' of our Soviet allies. But it is not a state of opinion peculiar to this country. You would get just the same reaction in Ankara, Vichy, Rome, Madrid, Stockholm, in the State Department and in Wall Street.

29 January 1942.

Dined last night in the Guardroom at St. James's Palace, a pleasant eighteenth-century white-panelled small dining-room. The lights were turned out during the whole of dinner. Candlelight from heavy Victorian candelabra and firelight. A perfect example of a Guards colonel passing the port says, 'Will you try some of this Grocer's Blood?' It was port of a kind you never taste these days. Politics consisted of railing at Hore-Belisha (of course, they say his real name is Horeb-Elisha). 'If they put him back at the War Office I personally would lead a meeting at the head of the regiment and go and kick the little bugger out.' Around the table the young subalterns, a nice crowd most of them lately from Oxford, more interested and intelligent than the peacetime Guards officer. One of them when the subject of genealogy was being discussed (his name was Cayzer) said something about his family's claim to be descended from Julius Caesar, and in quite an inoffensive boyish way he said, 'I believe the descent was quite well established.' 'Nonsense,' said the colonel, 'Your uncle paid the College of Heralds five hundred pounds to say so.' A very English evening.

5 February 1942.

Mr. Massey signed the Agreement for Exchange of Consuls between Canada and the U.S.S.R. at the Soviet Embassy. I had forgotten to provide for a seal so we had nothing to seal with on behalf of Canada. Otherwise everything went well. I feel I have played some part in getting this Agreement safely signed. Did my best to get into the press photographs. Actual signing was in the drawing-room full of yellow silk-covered chairs, with daffodils in a vase in the embrasure of the window and snow outside. Talked with S. of the Tass Agency and he said the war could be over this year if

(a) We and the United States gave the Russians enough tanks and planes so that they could finish the job themselves, or

(b) We would start an offensive in Europe.

What was happening in the Far East was tragic but it did not matter in the long run if Germany could be knocked out. We must go for the weakest link in the chain. Afterwards we and 'perhaps my country' (i.e. the U.S.S.R.) could go for Japan and finish her off.

Elizabeth has gone to Ireland. Miss her even more than last time. I am getting dependent on her.

10 February 1942.

Lunch at the Royal Empire Society for a leading lady of the A.T.S. She made a speech afterwards about A.T.S. work. I thought her a detestable woman, a hard-bitten clever careerist. Reminds me of the manageress of these flats. She has a soft voice and a piquant manner calculated to go over big with cabinet ministers and generals.

Dined at the Conservative Club. Gossip about Stalin – they say he wishes Cripps would not come and bore him by talking communism to him.[1] Stalin hates bores but takes a great interest in the Windsor-Simpson story. He cannot understand why Mrs. Simpson was not liquidated.

16 February 1942.

Maisky, the Soviet Ambassador, to lunch – very

amiable with an amusing attractive face. Madame Maisky won the Masseys' heart by taking an interest in the claret and talking about the days of her courtship in Omsk. When they left the Masseys subscribed to the opinion that they were 'a dear little couple'.

17 February 1942.

A cold wind blowing all the dust in the streets. I went down to the House of Commons to hear the Prime Minister make his speech on the escape of the *Gneisenau* and *Scharnhorst*.[2] The House in an agitated and restive mood, a series of short speeches and questions. A fumbling about for a voice in which to express the wish for a new deal. A fag-endish, nervous, inconclusive semi-debate, the rattling together of dry twigs that only wanted a flaming voice to stir them into a blaze of public indignation. The Prime Minister, strained and tired, keeping his voice low and being very patient and restrained in a perfectly obvious manner like a parent dealing with naughty children and determined not to lose his temper. The control snapped when he spoke of the House being in a mood of 'anger and panic'. At the word panic an angry wave of protests spread through the House.

27 February 1942.

Dinner with George Ignatieff and a friend of his, an instructor from Harvard. If the Russians win and Europe is Sovietised, at least to the Rhine, the

English socialists will want a socialist England to join up in some sort of federal union with the countries of the 'New Europe'. On the other hand, the governing class here pin their hopes more and more on the United States. Which way will England go? If history and geography can be relied on, I should say with Europe, and what about Canada? Probably under the United States' umbrella, where some of our professors of economics have been telling us for years we ought to be. I cannot imagine going back to the old small-town Canada with its narrow, intense, local interests and sitting down under it again.

My brother Roley's mess is a depressing place.[3] They live in slum conditions – they have taken over an ugly, characterless country house in Sussex. The mess is beaver-boarded – I suppose to protect the panelling – not a picture on the walls, just dirty beaver-board. Three uncovered dirty old sofas, each adorned with the person of a pot-bellied, bored, senior Canadian officer in a recumbent position, with a glass of brassy whisky in hand. A few hard wooden chairs with younger and equally bored officers seated on them.

Politics have caught up with me at last. Here I am reading G. D. H. Cole in preference to Rimbaud. (Rimbaud's phrases are time-fuse bombs – I read them without understanding and their meaning explodes later in my mind.)

3 March 1942.

Elizabeth was discussing her method of writing the other night. She says that when she is writing a scene for the first time she always throws in all the descriptive words that come to her mind. She overdoes the situation, puts in everything which will heighten the effect she wants to get, like, as she says, someone doing clay modelling, who smacks on handfuls of clay before beginning to cut away and doing fine modelling. Then afterwards she cuts down and discards and whittles away. The neurotic part of writing, she says, is the temptation to stop for the exact word or the most deliberate analysis of the situation when one should hurry, get the general effect and then come back and write over, but sometimes one gets stuck like a needle in the groove of a gramophone record and cannot stop going over and over one point.

She says that characters must not be made to say things which fit into situations intellectually conceived beforehand. The best writers of dialogue in English, she thinks, are Jane Austen and E.M. Forster in *Howard's End*.

Sat with Miriam in her room at Claridge's while her maid curled and brushed her hair – felt like a French abbé in an eighteenth-century boudoir print.

I wish I could get a job for Mrs. Elliott Smith – poor old girl. I think one should do one's best to provide for one's friends if one is in office. I cannot bear the assumption of impersonality by civil servants. I am all for nepotism and jobs arranged over the luncheon table by feminine influence, etc., etc. – provided it is not at my expense. Still I would take a chance on that.

7 March 1942.

For some time now I seem to be getting more and more greedy about food. It may be partly due to having considerably less to eat, but the way I wolfed my food at the Masseys' tonight was rather too much. What a curious and fascinating character Mr. Massey has – that blend of acuteness and superficiality. He has enormous susceptibility to more phoney forms of charm. What he loves in life is delicatezza – the pleasant surface style. He is a puzzling person because behind his London *Times* leading article official views and his carefully polished manner there lurks an ironic appreciation of things as they are and of himself as he is. When he has a decision to make – disappointingly – he always decides in favour of the conventional. His charm is remarkable. It springs, as charm so often does, from his own insecurity. He is painfully easy to hurt or ruffle and full of *prévenances* for the feelings of others if he happens to like them. If not, he is ruthless. Sometimes I have been stifled by the too strong atmosphere of the Masseys' love of power, but I am very fond of them and diverted by them. Their relationship to each other is the most admirable thing about them. I never expect to have another chief who is so personally sympathetic – after all, I share so many of his weaknesses. His critics may have a great deal on their side, but he is so much more interesting as a personality than they are.

6 April 1942.

Week-end in the country. Nancy Mitford staying there – witty in a high-pitched, restless way, clever, and giving off that impression of courage which some people convey even when making small talk around a tea-table. She belongs to the world of Evelyn Waugh's novels and to the set of which Evelyn Waugh is a member. They have a definite tone of their own. They are all now in their thirties or early forties and were the bright young things of the 1920s. Except for one or two who have become Roman Catholic or Communist they are as bored by religion as they ever were. In the arts they admire Baroque and Regency (in architecture cathedrals and Tudor beams are their aversion), Mozart in music, in literature anything that shows style and exuberance – nothing that is soulful, formless or introspective. In love as in conversation a flavour of insolence is appreciated. With both sexes the thing admired is to do what you want just as long as you want to and not a moment longer. Hence the speed with which people change partners in this game, which requires a good eye, a cool nerve and a capacity to take punishment as in any other kind of sport. Toughness is the favourite virtue. Any form of cry-babyishness (wistful yearnings, hopeless passions, plain self-pity) is taboo except among pansies, in whom it is recognised as an innate characteristic which does not affect their essential toughness. In this little world almost none are stupid. Some have 'dumb' husbands or wives whose excuse for existence is that they are rich, good-looking or superlatively bed-worthy. There are also a few 'holy idiots' tolerated who are 'rather sweet' and who are often rich and sometimes American and who pay the bill. Their gossip is so frank, so abundant and so detailed it is a wonder that their lives are not even more complicated than they are. Discretion is looked upon as a paltry virtue like thrift. Their closest friends' reputations are ripped to pieces at the tops of their voices usually in a restaurant. Among themselves they practise a mixture of delicate sympathy and charming attention, alternating with dive-bombing attacks of brutal frankness. Rows are frequent but seldom lasting. They stick by each other in misfortune with the loyalty the English usually show to their friends.

13 April 1942.

I am reading *Barometer Rising*, Hugh MacLennan's book about the Halifax Explosion.[4] It is the first time that anyone has succeeded in giving the feeling of the town and the poetry peculiar to the place, the dreariness and yet the fascination of those fogbound days when the town is smothered and shut in, half asleep, half in a slow trance, snow running in the gutters, horses on the cobblestones of Water Street, the sound of trams whining over the uneven rails, the recurrent melancholy of the foghorn, the feeling of the sea – February in Halifax, Nova Scotia.

In the afternoon I went with Elizabeth to Hampstead. On the way back, walking through Keats Grove and the quiet French provincial streets full of flowering shrubs, Elizabeth talked about Virginia Woolf, saying how tall and graceful she looked wearing some flowing dress of mauve or grey. Elizabeth said she had a sort of 'fairy cruelty' but she did not know how much she could hurt. There were many forms of being hurt about which she knew nothing. She had never been humiliated herself although she used half-jokingly to say how shy she was and that she could never go into a room full of strange people without feeling that they thought her odd. In fact, she had always lived in a sort of Chinese world of intelligent, complicated people who had made a cult of her. From that world she never issued – she led a guarded life.

Elizabeth met a female admirer last night at dinner who said to her, 'To meet you is like meeting Christ.'

14 April 1942.

Dined with the Masseys – Margot Asquith was the big attraction. I was amazed – I had expected her to be pretty gaga and to have the depressing job of trying to reconstruct the original from among the ruins, instead of which I am inclined to agree with Mr. Massey that she is still the best woman or perhaps man conversationalist in England. What put her on her form was the presence of Sir Andrew Duncan, the Minister of Supply, who was there. She arrived in full war-paint, crossed swords with him at the close of the fish course and carried on a duel all evening. Her enjoyment of her own skill is still infectious. Her vanity is stridently insistent, but she has a streak of humility - a sort of refreshing honesty running through all her boasting. I believe she is considered an old nuisance, but I think she is a phenomenon. She brought with her a protégé, a boring German Jew editor. She said she brought him because he was such a remarkable man that she wanted the Masseys to meet him, but he hardly got a word in and looked, I thought, slightly bitter about it. He has probably had a good dose of Margot, who is obviously like all these entertaining Edwardian relics an impossible woman at close quarters.

I must add that we each had a filet mignon for dinner – one week's meat ration for three people! How?

16 April 1942.

David Cecil had dinner at Elizabeth's. I was charmed by him, his quick responsive flicks of attention, his irony and his wit, his contempt for the middle-brow, the snob and the inflated personality. At one point in talk he said, 'One does not often have to put one's foot down, but I feel it is useful to have a Foot to Put Down.' I like him and Cyril Connolly best of Elizabeth's literary friends.

Later in the evening Stephen Tennant came in. He and David had a lovely little conversation - effusive, sprightly and prickly.

Lunched with Anne-Marie at Claridge's. She looked pure Paris. When I asked her how she did it she replied that first, she always dressed her age (forty-nine), never a year younger and that gave her an extra five years' margin, second, she always wore black, and thirdly, she attended to detail. She said that every Englishwoman should be presented with three more clothes-brushes than she has at present and told how to use them. Her territory at the country house where she is living with rich friends has been invaded by a parasitic bugger called Mr. Midge. Anne-Marie says that he has 'cried his way out of the army'.

30 April 1942.

Dined with the Masseys off salmon-trout and asparagus. Mrs. Ronnie Greville was there – sitting up in a bath chair with her feet dangling on to a footstool. Her small hands covered with diamonds, and with her painted face – she looked like a monstrous baby – something in *grand guignol.* This was also the impression given by her having only one eye – the other is dead and blind – and that one eye raked the table round – illuminated by intelligent malice. The conversation was on a royal plane during a great deal of dinner, highly aristocratic titbits of scandal (Lady Y. who has run away with the groom. Lord X who has eloped with his stepmother.) Resigned prophecy that Cripps will be the next Prime Minister. The old girl is kept alive by her sleepless snobbery, her still unquenchable zest for the great world. She is a lowland Scot, and the lowland Scot from Boswell on is the most insatiable animal on earth when it comes to worldly glitter and bustle. I should know – I am one.

10 May 1942.

Yesterday was a day of flowers. The tulips are out in St. James's Park – they are at their time of perfection – not one has fallen out of the ranks. Three unattractive little girls were picking the faded bluebells that grew on the bank above me and stuffing them into a shabby leather handbag that must have belonged to one of their mothers. It irritates me that since the railings have gone people pick the flowers and trample the grass in the parks until it becomes hard dry earth. The lilac is out. It gives me a feeling of urgency – its time is so short – only about a fortnight.

Something of the panic of middle age is coming over me. It is the bald spot beginning on the back of my head. This morning I combed the longer hair from the sides back over the place where it is thin. I felt as if I were adjusting a wig which the wind might blow out of place. I seem surrounded by nice but ugly girls.

19 May 1942.

Went to the House to hear Attlee on the war situation. He treated the House to an insulting meagre string of platitudes. The Members were impatient and rather badly behaved like schoolboys when the headmaster is away and a weak under-master is temporarily in charge. L., who is in the Dominions Office says, 'I now serve under Attlee who would be ideally suited as an assistant manager of a bank in a small town in the south of England.'

Margot Asquith waylaid me in the passage outside the gallery wearing a green tulle dress and a brown fur hat, her make-up dashed on with a careless hand, rather gaga – but only when the wind blows nor'-nor'-west.

24 May 1942.

A perfect May day. Elizabeth and I went to Kew. It is hardly worth my while to describe the scene or dwell upon the dreamlike state in which we drifted among ravines of rhododendrons and azaleas. It was a day like a page from one of her books, the involved relationship between the two people who are wandering among the flower beds. They sit together on a bench to look across the narrow muddy Thames at the set-piece of Syon House and discuss projects of happiness, voyages they may never take, childhood, but never Love. There is sun and then a shower – they take shelter under the green tent of a weeping willow and go together through the modest, white-panelled rooms of Kew Palace where hang the framed embroideries of dead princesses. Then tea among the devitalised inhabitants of Kew in a room full of small tables each with its white tablecloth and its groups of whispering, mumbling people who are bound by some spell not to raise their voices, not to laugh and not to gesticulate. At moments I could see Elizabeth peering about her – her head a little back, her eyes half closed (how affected it sounds – how utterly unaffected the gesture was) focusing on the memories of the place.

Elizabeth has been going to an Austrian psychoanalyst to be cured of her stammer (which is so much part of her). So far it seems to me that she has told him nothing while he has told her the story of his life. This hardly surprises me.

25 May 1942.

My feelings are mixed when I read speeches like that of Wallace in the United States – 'this is the century of the common man'. Apparently we are to devote ourselves after the war to bringing the blessings of mass production, hygienic American civilisation and American uniformity and materialism to the world.

26 May 1942.

I had lunch with Nancy Mitford. She fluted away in her light, modish voice, being amusing and looking so distinguished with her beautiful head and thin arms. She says there is no use speculating on what will come out of Europe after the war because no one dreamt of fascism twenty years ago and something equally unexpected is brewing now. Yet one ought to have anticipated fascism – all the signposts were there and had been for the previous one hundred years. I had drinks with Billy Coster – his politics are wonderful. He blames everything on 'Mr. Morrison, the Duke of Bedford and the Archbishop of Canterbury'⁵ and thinks it would be possible with the scientific use of gas and the R.A.F. to exterminate at least fifty per cent of the German people.

2 June 1942.

I went to see Elizabeth this afternoon and found her standing on the balcony of her sitting-room that looks over Regent's Park. The tall, cool room is full of mirrors and flowers and books. She wants to dedicate her next novel to me. I hope she will, and that it will be her best.

Later we walked out into Regent's Park. It was a blazing June day – we sat on the bank by the canal watching the swans 'in slow indignation', as she says, go by.

Of what is her magic made? What is the spell that she has cast on me? At first I was wary of her –

'*méfiant*' – I feared that I should expose my small shifts and stratagems to her eye which misses nothing. Her uncanny intuitions, her flashes of insight like summer lightning at once fascinated and disturbed me. Now day by day I have been discovering more and more of her generous nature, her wit and funniness, the stammering flow of her enthralling talk, the idiosyncrasies, vagaries of her temperament. I now know that this attachment is nothing transient but will bind me as long as I live.

5 June 1942.

Some slightly drunk and defiantly cheerful American soldiers were piling into a taxi tonight in Berkeley Square shouting and in general throwing their weight about. Surprised looks on the faces of two elderly English gentlemen of military bearing who were waiting to cross the square – an 'old-fashioned look' – contempt concealed by policy.

11 June 1942.

Dined at Nesta's – J. was there. I drew him out to see what his line is at the moment and he gave me my money's worth. He says that Russia will be defeated this summer which he thinks is highly desirable. After that we and America will defeat an exhausted Germany. He thinks that is the secret plan of the War Cabinet. There would be two stages in Germany's defeat, the first will be that the German General Staff will get rid of Hitler and offer peace and to liberate the occupied countries. He says that the masses in the occupied countries do not hate the Germans – it is only the intellectuals. Hatred of the Germans would disappear if their troops were actually withdrawn, etc. His immediate concern is that the British people should be warned of the approaching collapse of Russia. He asked me what my reaction to the fall of Moscow would be. I said, 'Blank dismay and discouragement but not despair.' 'Ah,' he said, 'that is what I am afraid people's reaction would be,' I might have asked him if he expected me to hang out flags in the street. I do not say the man is a German agent but his line of talk, though a farrago of nonsense, is about the best a German agent in England could produce at the present time. I do not think it would be at all a bad thing to lock him up. I think it is monstrous that he should still be printing his bloody pamphlet. He gave me a lift home in his ostentatious Rolls-Royce, which must be the only one of its kind left in London and which is usually parked outside Claridge's or the Ritz.

13 June 1942.

Worked all afternoon on my despatch about the future organisation of Europe, application of the Atlantic Charter, the treatment of Germany after the war, etc. I have almost decided not to send this despatch at all. I think it would be too vague to be useful or interesting.

Dined with Elizabeth. Drank a lot of red wine. Who could help becoming attached to her?

23 June 1942.

This morning was interesting because the work was about something that really may matter – the control of trans-Atlantic airways now and after the war and the part that Canada should play. Had lunch with the new Dominions Office appointee to Canada. He must be as sick of meeting me at lunch as I am certainly sick of meeting him. Mentally and socially he is a permanent pre-last-war subaltern in a not too good line regiment. What a man to send to Ottawa to cope with that little group of bristling professional Canadian nationalists who would welcome him as a heaven-sent confirmation of all they have ever said about the Old School Tie! The anti-British members of the Canadian intelligentsia will never be happy until they have pulled down the Old England of Tradition and can dance on its grave. He is the sort of Englishman who makes one understand why.

28 June 1942.

Pierre Dupuy came to pay me a visit. What an enjoyable war that little man is having! He exudes high politics and dark diplomacy. He is intelligent – yes – but nine-tenths of it is his capacity to put himself across. From being a dim little diplomat he has become an international figure – the only Canadian except for the Prime Minister whose name is known in Paris and Berlin political circles and in the inner circle in London.

Dined with the Masseys. Mrs. Greville rang up in the middle of dinner to say, 'Winston must go – some of our friends are here with me and we all agree – go he must. I have known him for fifty years and he has never been right yet.' Just the sort of party I should have thought would be sitting there in Claridge's spinning trivial but not harmless gossip.

10 August 1942.

Although there are no indications that we are winning the war, I feel that the Germans are committing suicide, that even if they won they would be incapable of profiting by their victory. They have not got what it takes to organise Europe and rule it as the British ruled India. They are not healthy in themselves. Perhaps they have too much imagination. The rebound from their tensed up national effort must be towards materialism, individualism and a wish for the cosy and pleasurable. Once beaten they may not prove so hard to handle for the time being. People talk of the Dark Ages, of a reversion to semi-barbarism, but is that really possible? The dream of the masses everywhere is comfort – the American standard of living. It will be the same for the Germans. Once out of the iron circle of fear, hate, slaughter and revenge they will turn passionately to materialism.

Dined at the St. James's Club among the remnants of the Diplomatic Corps. It was pleasant for a change to be back among the *chers collègues* – not an atmosphere in which ideas are encouraged certainly, but of anecdote, amiability and polite enquiries about 'so and so who was at Teheran or Washington at the same time I was'. A feeling of complicity in belonging to a class or craft which has its own mysteries – although the initiates know these to be trivial. Outside the narrow windows a November-like gale tossed the trees in Green Park. From the walls the blank frames stared eyeless forth. The Club sent its pictures into retirement in the days of the Blitz. They have moved their funniest marble nymph from the foot of the stairs to the lavatory where she shares pride of place with a steel engraving of Paolo and Francesca whirling through space in their endless loves.

Talking of endless loves makes me think of Saturday night which was a grand catharsis – getting drunk, making love, spending more money than one can afford – things one should never regret. How innocent in comparison with the poisoned pleasures of boasting, showing off, giving false impressions or phoney confidences, or the wicked glooms of sterile introspection.

10 August 1942.

The waiter in these flats is trying to get me to give him one of my suits. He talks to me as though the revolution had already come. If it ever does, God defend me from the city hotel servants and all hangers-on of the rich, spoiled and eaten up with envy, full of dirty tricks and cruelty to each other. Gorky in one of his books suggests that the revolution should protect itself by bumping off such people.

Reading Rebecca West's book about Yugoslavia.[6] What the Croats felt about the Serbs is (I hope in a minor degree) what the French Canadians feel about us. What the top-dogs cannot imagine or understand is the degree of resentment which the under-dogs feel. Because we know ourselves as Anglo-Canadians to be fairly mild and good-natured we feel injured that we can be so hardly thought of, but it is not only cruelty that people resent, it is unconsciousness, lack of insight, the bland shrug of incomprehension. The British are paying for this attitude now all over the world and we British-Canadians will pay for it with the French-Canadians in Canada before we are through.

19 August 1942.

Dined at the Allies' Club – afterwards a Polish exile played Chopin and jazz in the former Rothschild drawing-room. I sat next to a Polish Countess, a county family type (Polish version) – her country house has been burned down by the Germans, and her brother and his wife have been murdered by the Bolsheviks. As the pianist played a Polish peasant dance she said, 'It is funny, but the last time I heard that tune was when I was dancing it over and over again with that Polish officer over there at home in Poland – and now we are both here.'

Lunched with Anne-Marie by the open window at The Etoile in Charlotte Street. She arrived in a new summer dress, saying, 'Imagine a Canadian soldier twenty-four years old but intelligent and a poet – he fell in love with me at first sight. Such a nice present on my fiftieth birthday. It has given me so much confidence.'

Street fighting in Stalingrad – I heard the news at the St. James's Club where I dined with Archduke Robert, who seems to have loosened up and become less careful in manner. He has a love of fun underneath the Hapsburg reserve and *calcul*.

29 August 1942.

There is summer lightning tonight. At first I thought it was guns. I dined alone at the St. James's Club among diplomats and old prints – rather dreary.

3 September 1942.

Anne-Marie's young soldier came to see me today about getting transferred from the army to something in which he could 'use his power to create'. He has written a poem about Canada 'in six movements'. I do not know what the hell I am supposed to do about it. Although he is an American with a Scottish name he looks like a half-breed

Filipino with large and lustrous dark eyes and a pale pink tongue. He came in trailing clouds of Anne-Marie's extremely cloying perfume after him. He gave me an oration in deep and thrilling tones about his own genius. I could see he had made up his mind to make the biggest possible impression on me. He is such a bounder and so humourless that the poem may be some good. I could see how an older woman might find him touching. When he left he said he would 'always be my slave' if I could get him transferred from the army.

Last night Margery and I started drinking at a pub with a drunk with whom I got into an argument because he said that no woman could be called beautiful if she had 'bad legs' and went on to say that he would never sleep with anyone who was not physically perfect – 'not if I fault them'. This infuriated me for some reason. Margery and I went back to her house and had rice and pickled walnuts and drank red wine and gin while the cat and Pekinese joined actively in our dinner-table conversation.

4 September 1942.

Staying with a Canadian friend, Anson McKim – a cold day like November. I have escaped to my room. The others are playing tennis. Even the park here is ugly – detestable fir trees and a tree with leaves the colour of a bloodstone. The wind is making a loud melancholy sound which suits my state of heavy sensual melancholy. The millionaire who built this dreary expensive barracks of a house came to tea today. A brisk air battle is going on overhead, rumbling anti-aircraft fire far off.

Four Montrealers, including Anson, staying here – all about thirty-three years old – one stockbroker, one businessman, one lawyer – all now in the army – all with that Montreal voice that echoes from the locker-rooms of good clubs, all coming from the solid homes of the Montreal merchant aristocracy. Good chaps and good company with a pleasant debunking humour, no side and a canny tendency to under-play their hand. Anything excessive, strange or alarming can be brushed aside in a tolerant bantering tone. They are far from stupid, though – without mannerisms yet they manage to establish a type.

A young Belgian named Moreau came to see me who had just escaped from a Nazi concentration camp, arriving with nothing but the suit he wore – having got across to France – then in a Spanish concentration camp and here via Gibraltar. These people who are working in illegal organisations on the continent come from another world. They stare at our food and our normal lives and still have something of the trapped animal about them.

14 September 1942.

Spent the day with dearest Elizabeth to whom I owe everything.

19 September 1942.

What is going to happen to Canada after the war? Then what is a Canadian? We are a new type among the nations of the world. As the British Empire becomes less able to protect us our future will need more statesmanship and more knowledge of the world. Our greatest enemy is the parish pump. How are we Anglo-Canadians and the French-Canadians to get on together in the future? We have never succeeded and indeed never seriously attempted to become a bilingual nation, and there is the feeling of the French-Canadians that they are being exploited, although that we also feel in the Maritime Provinces.

This war is digging deeper the gulf between Anglo-Canadians and French-Canadians – the fatal word 'conscription' may haunt us after the war. If the casualties are big and still there is no conscription, things will be worse. But supposing a Conservative government came in and introduced conscription, it would undo so much and gain so little. The uneasy but tolerable relationship between French and English Canadians has only been possible because we have used our strength sparingly. We owe much to Mackenzie King for not being panicked into throwing all that overboard. Where we have been the weakest is in making any effort to understand each other, and this is a two-way accusation – the French have been just as bad. But it is a disgrace that these Anglo-Montrealers do not speak French.

The Canadian war effort may be weak in spots, but if we ever get together to the same extent to achieve anything in peacetime Canada it would be a different country. Our social services are backward, our protection of the really poor from exploitation is nearly non-existent. We have done nothing to encourage the growth of civilised standards of taste, and we are harnessed with an absurdly old-fashioned and cumbrous Dominion-Provincial relationship which just must be overhauled. The Mackenzie King Government has not had the guts to tackle any of these questions. The Tories represent the business community plus some honest imperialists. The Liberals have no programme, they represent everybody and nothing. They stand for equilibrium which has to be preserved to keep the country from splitting seriously on any issue. It is a matter of papering over the cracks. The C.C.F. are old-fashioned socialists, but they do propose certain economic and social adjustments. Canada cannot go in for revolutionary constitutional and social changes in the middle of a war but she can and does tend in the direction of change. For example, the innumerable state controls introduced and efficiently worked during the war by youngish men with no strong party affiliations.

Canada will not go in for pure socialism but we do not want to develop into an unco-ordinated group of 'interests'. The war will make people impatient and ready for a change. The post-war period is our great opportunity.

I have a new feeling about my fellow Canadians – a feeling that there is good material among the young – idealism, energy, practical ability which somehow never gets a chance to express itself in the public life of the country. I feel that if we can break the crust on top we could make Canada a much better country to live in. What is stifling us is the system – social, economic and political.

20 October 1942.

I went to see Ernest – found him in his dressing-gown with a muffler around his neck in his large dark sitting-room furnished in Curzon Street Baroque. 'Bored,' he said. 'That is what I am. When I was eighteen years old I swore I would commit suicide on my thirty-first birthday. Now I am thirty-one and I have not committed suicide. I cannot get hold of a girl who attracts me, the old women cling like ivy.' He looked the spoilt fractious not-so-young Frenchman with a sensual mouth and bad teeth. We had a cold dinner, and I left immediately afterwards with the feeling that there was a wounded snake.

These days with their falling leaves and bland autumn weather make the shabby parks seem like Tuileries of memory. The waiter here has been wearing my suits, which I suppose is flattering of him. The confident voices of American girls at Claridge's make me feel that the past is still the present and that there is still a comfortable world safe for American humour.

26 October 1942.

I have been reading George Moore's *Memoirs of My Dead Life*. The mixture of sensuality, sentiment and cloying knowing caddishness is more than one's stomach can take, but the impressions of places in London and of a journey to Paris via Dieppe are nostalgic and remind one of the civilised silver age before the barbarians had broken through. I like the part about my favourite Soho. 'The smell of these dry faded streets is peculiar to London. There is something of the odour of the original marsh in the smell of these streets. It rises through the pavements and mingles with the smoke.' That smell is still there, and I have often caught it on my way to the office on autumn mornings.

I lunched with Mary Bartlett at the Etoile. She showed me the tongue motion that women make when they are cleaning lipstick off their front teeth and I feel that I have gained a valuable piece of information.

27 October 1942.

Tonight we had our first fog with a full moon. I walked home with a bunch of violets in one hand and *Mademoiselle de Maupin* in the other, thanking my stars that any attempt to move me from London has been frustrated and acknowledging to myself that what holds me is not duty or patriotism but London and the spectacle of its decay and the continuance of its fascination.

I was talking to a man who was telling me of his escape from a concentration camp in France – sawing his way through iron bars with a saw smuggled into the prison in a loaf of bread – 'Scarlet Pimpernel stuff' he calls it. He was in a camp composed of Englishmen caught on the continent – these ones were the most sordid type of pseudo-pimps and book-store agents-cum-pimps. When he had first proposed to escape the camp leaders put a guard of fellow prisoners on him to stop him in case his escape should bring reprisals on his fellow prisoners. He says that from the moment he arrived at the camp and witnessed the beating to death of a French prisoner his nervous reactions and sensitivity seemed dead – he was 'like an ox being led to the slaughter' and felt only dull fatalism. He has that same peculiar look as others who have escaped from a concentration camp – shifty, nervous and on the defensive – slightly mad by our standards, or is it just the contrast between the wild and the tame?

30 October 1942.

I thought I would have a look again at the New Testament and began reading St. John's Gospel. I wanted to see how much of a Christian I still might be. I was looking for some sort of copy-book tags to help one along. Instead I met a blazing fire so hot and dazzling that I shield my eyes from it. I read on for ten chapters without ever coming on a moral precept. All is a challenge to believe in the divinity of Christ – not even a challenge – an affirmation. This Christ is a comet miraculously lighting up the skies and He does not want our partial approval or our attempt to find that something can be salvaged from Christian doctrine.

23 November 1942.

Went to the 400 Club with Margery and stayed drinking there until 4 a.m. That place has become part of my life. It is the only place of pleasure left in London with any character that is not infested with middle-aged stout gentlemen and their blondes. At the 400 Club there is always the same background – nostalgic music, half-lighting, eternal youthfulness, guards officers and girls and myself – not so eternally youthful – always well in the foreground.

What will happen in Canada after the war? Both the state and our own nationalism are growing stronger. I suppose we shall attempt some kind of an egalitarian planned state, where the power is hidden. There will be a monstrous increase in the hypocrisies of government and a monstrous growth of peddling politicians of the lowest and most dangerous sort. The country will be run behind the scenes by powerful quiet men whether financiers or Treasury officials. It will in that way be different from our old-fashioned Canada but in no circumstances can the people have an effective voice in administering the modern state – it is far too big a machine.

27 November 1942.

Went to a party at Nancy Mitford's – I had a long conversation with Unity Mitford. She started the conversation by saying, 'I have just hit my left breast against a lamp-post as I was bicycling here.' She said, 'I tried to commit suicide when I was in Germany but now I am a Christian Scientist – not that I believe a word of it, but they saved my life so I feel I owe it to them to be one.' 'I hate the Czechs,' she said suddenly in a loud, emphatic voice, 'but that is natural – they tried to arrest me and I had not done anything. I did not even have the Führer's picture in my suitcase as they said I had.' She has just recently returned to England where her role as Hitler's English friend does not make her popular. I must say I liked her better than anyone else at the party. She has something hoydenish and rustic about her.

Great discussion with George Ignatieff about the future of Europe. He sees the great age of the Slav people dawning. I see our being drawn gradually into supporting every and any regime in Europe that offers a bulwark against communism, i.e., in terms of power politics against a triumphant Russia with overwhelming influence at least as far as the Rhine. Of course we shall try to get rid of the more stinking quislings and put in progressive governments, but above all, we must hold the *cordon sanitaire* against Bolshevism. Could there be two worlds after the war – the Atlantic and the Middle

European plus the Balkans – the former dominated by Anglo-Germany – the one democratic and semi-capitalist, the other communist?

What will our relations with Russia be after the war if they win against Germany? As long as they remain behind the Curzon Line and busy themselves with reconstruction we might get along all right, but Russia will inevitably be on the side of every revolutionary government in Europe. We shall become suspicious of her and will tend, for the sake of balance, to back anti-revolutionary forces. Thus a new war will be prepared. Indeed we can see the forces that are already preparing it.

23 December 1942.

Went down to spend last week-end – Elizabeth and I – with Stephen Tennant. It was a dreamlike and unrepeatable occasion. From the moment of coming out of the rainy December countryside into his apartment all was under a magician's spell. It was partly the sense of being picked up on a magic carpet out of the prosaic into the midst of everything that is extravagant and strange. In one wing of what was formerly his country-house and is now a Red Cross Hospital he has furnished a set of rooms to suit his own fantastic taste. Such huge white velvet sofas, piles of cushions and artificial flowers, chandeliers, such a disorder of perfumes, rouge pots and pomades, such orchid satin sheets and pink fur rugs, toy dogs and flounced silk curtains, mirrors at angles, shaded lights and scented fires. But the unreality of it attained to an intensity which was pure artistic illusion – too fantastic to be vulgar or funny and with a strange honesty as a natural mask for Stephen's highstrung, high-coloured but never vulgar nature.

On the train down we found ourselves sitting opposite Augustus John wearing a tweed cap which he removed to reveal that noble head of a moth-eaten lion. Fixing us with his unfocussed gaze he made an effort to assemble meaning and made charming light conversation, full of malice and fun. At intervals he dozed off – his beautiful hands in his lap.

At Salisbury Stephen met us coiffed in a blue knitted helmet – his too-golden hair arranged in a becoming crest. Through the driving rain under a gun-metal sky with sodden leaves piled high in the ditches we drove to Wilsford and were wafted up into the pink rococo of his apartment. 'Rich stains of former orgies,' he said giggling at the spots on the silver-satin cushion covers; but he is not a comic. His drawings are brilliant evocations of the Marseilles underworld. His note-books are full of them and all the same characters reappear – *matelots* and tarts, procurers and pimps – faces which have obsessed him. Perhaps he is too undisciplined to express his obsessions in terms of writing.

Elizabeth talked to Stephen of dialogue in the novel – of how every sentence must bear directly or indirectly on the theme – must be a clue or the counter-point to a clue. In that sense how 'every novel is a detective novel'. It does no harm to linger in places where one has pleasure in writing provided one makes it up by skimming quickly elsewhere so that the tempo of the whole is not slowed up. How a phrase should be written down when it occurs because it may be fruitful of unexpected developments; may contain seeds which would only come to life when it is on paper.

Then they talked about the sticky passages that haunt writers. Whether it was best to make a frontal attack on such difficulties and never rest until they were overcome or, as Elizabeth said, to sidestep the dragon in the path and to go on to what one wanted to write and return to the difficulty later, perhaps from a different angle or aspect. She told us how Virginia Woolf when writing her last book *Between the Acts* was heard to say, 'For six weeks I have been trying to get the characters from the dining-room into the drawing-room and they are still in the dining-room.'

Virginia Woolf haunts the lives of all who knew her. Almost every day something is added to my knowledge of her – that she was a snob – that she could be cruel, as when one lovely May evening a young, shy girl came into her drawing-room in Bloomsbury to be greeted with the overwhelming question from Virginia, 'What does it feel like to be young in May?' The girl stood shambling in silent consternation in the doorway. But how they revolved around Virginia Woolf, how much she must have done to liberate them all, to give them weapons of coolness and wit, and how often they say, 'Virginia would have enjoyed it' or 'she would have enhanced it'. But to me her reflected atmosphere is rather alarming – the exquisite politeness – but an eye that misses nothing and a power to puncture gracefully, opportunely and mercilessly if occasion arises or the mood changes.

28 December 1942.

To have heard (as I did the other night) T. S. Eliot on the subject of Charles Morgan[7] was to be entertained at a most delicate feast of malice – the sidelong, half-pitying, good-natured, kindly approach – ('Poor old Morgan, etc.') the closing in on the prey, the kill, so neat and so final and then the picking of the bones, the faint sound of licking of lips and the feast is over.

1943

1 January 1943.

Last night the end of the year with a wind howling down the steep gully of flats outside my window. I feel both sad and excited as though I were seventeen and in my bedroom at The Bower on some winter night in my youth. Christ! Why has it all happened?

3 January 1943.

Elizabeth has borne with all my attempts to play-act my life, although she has so little patience with histrionic characters, without ever making me feel a fool. She has shown me up to myself – good money to some extent has driven out bad.

People in Russian novels stand for hours – sometimes all night – gazing out of a window dreaming over a landscape or lost in a mood. I have never been able to stand at a window for more than a few minutes at any time in my life.

4 January 1943.

Now arises the question of whether or not I should join the army. Elizabeth thinks that I might make a 'useful soldier'. She says if I join the army she will join the A.T.S. I doubt if either of us will do either. I can see that this idea of joining the army is closing in on me unless I can prove to myself that it would be unfair to the service I am now in and just a piece of heroics. Unfortunately the work here has been so slack recently that I find it impossible to believe that I am pulling my weight in the war.

Walked alone in Regent's Park beside the grey waters of the canal, under a grey winter sky. I tried to get Elizabeth but she was out and the house was shuttered and looked as if it had been unoccupied for years. I felt as though I had come back years later to find her gone and the whole thing in the past.

What a joke it is – a cosy bachelor pried out of his shell and being drawn principally for reasons of face-saving into the horrid prospect of army life. What a short story for someone. By suggesting that I should become a soldier I have put myself in for stakes which I know I cannot afford to play, and depend on other people to get me out of the situation. Perhaps no one will be bothered to do so, and that in itself has a sort of attraction for me. I have now a card to play against myself.

30 January 1943.

I saw a Duncan Grant painting today that made

me want to go in and ask the price. I suppose it would have been about two hundred pounds. It was a picture of a small closed café with blue shutters by the sea-front somewhere not far from Wimereux – I should think painted in the early morning before opening time – before the patron had come down to give a perfunctory polish to the linoleum bar – on a morning of damp and shifting weather. The paint had the wetness of the weather and the indecisive cloud shiftings. This morning was just such a morning. I got up early with the idea of going to Holy Communion but decided while shaving that I was not fit to receive Communion – too selfish and sin-satisfied. So I went to the little Anglo-Catholic church and knelt facing the altar while the Service went on – 'It is meet, right and our bounden duty' etc. I was cut off and felt it.

I asked Elizabeth last night whether it was possible to regard oneself – not with violent disgust but with a steady cold distaste as one might feel towards an unattractive acquaintance whose character one knew all too well. She thought, 'Yes, if one had been over-praised for the wrong reasons.'

31 January 1943.

A day like a day at the seaside. You expected to hear the waves lapping and pictured rain-swept piers. In fact I was nowhere near the sea. I went to visit Roley in the hospital with jaundice at Horsham in the heart of the Canadian-occupied district.

Everywhere Canadian soldiers, often with local girls. I suppose somewhere under the surface a Sussex rustic life goes on. An occupying army irons out the character of a neighbourhood – everything looking down-at-the-heel as in London. The rich settled bloom has gone, the stripped naked country-houses are all barracks or hospitals, the avenues morasses of mud from military vehicles, the fences down, the gardens neglected – the little towns submerged in khaki.

6 February 1943.

A sunny, almost spring morning spent in solitary bachelor fashion like so many similar solitary mornings of self-soliloquising – in Oxford to the sound of bells – at Harvard a breakfast of waffles and maple syrup, the good and abundant coffee, Sunday papers, the North American sunlight – in Paris, in Ottawa, in Washington, and in Tregunter Road with the Salvation Army band in the street outside and even the cats and dogs oppressed by a London Sunday. All those Sunday mornings and now another with the wireless in the distance and the servants banging and whistling in the courtyard. Mornings when I have repaired the holes in my ego.

Shaftesbury Avenue was lined with American soldiers just standing there, very quiet and well-behaved, watching the crowds or waiting to pick up a girl. The American troops are everywhere in the West End. They make a curious impression, very different from the legend of the swashbuckling, boasting Yankees abroad. I wonder what they really think about it all. They are so negative that they arouse one's curiosity. They themselves seem completely incurious. They look as though they were among strange animals. The Canadian soldiers up against the British try at once to establish human contact – they make jokes, pick quarrels, make passes, get drunk and finally find friends.

13 October 1943.[1]

Conclusion of the Civil Aviation Talks. This is a test case for our post-war relations with the Empire. Unless Ottawa reacts strongly we shall have accepted in these talks the idea of a Commonwealth body presiding over an 'all-red route'. What functions and powers such a body would have is as yet by no means clear, but the precedent is interesting. It is the first post-war Empire body to be set up. The initiative came from Australia. The Australian concept of the future of the Commonwealth is in contradiction to the Canadian and South African. It obviously suits the British book to have projects for greater centralisation come from a Dominion. Australia has served notice that she will continue to be a member of the Club at her own price. I should be much surprised if there is not a fight from Ottawa.

6 November 1943.

Talked to Elizabeth about the way women seem,

however they purport to be employed, to have the leisure to spin a cocoon of imaginings and question-ings around their personal relationships so that when a man blunders into this area he so often finds it thoroughly mined beforehand.

16 November 1943.

Saw Archduke Robert of Austria at the St. James's Club. He surprised me by suddenly saying, 'I am the cat's whiskers.' He had just been week-ending with de Courcy who, he said, would embarrass him in the train coming up to London by addressing him in consciously loud tones as, 'Your Imperial Highness' before a carriageful of suburbanites.

4 December 1943.

Dined with Simon, the gold-haired pretty-faced son of a doting and strong-minded mother with a damp old country-house in the Shires and not enough money to keep the old name going. He went from Oxford into the Guards and has now married a Viscount's daughter. He reminds me of the young officers whom Litvinow happens on at their picnic near Baden in Turgenev's *Smoke*. He has a smattering of liberalism, a survival of Oxford days and a core of gentlemanly *arrivisme*. He was talking about the discussion groups that have now been instituted in the army. At the last group meet-ing he had put up for discussion the inevitable release of Mosley.[2] He found the soldiers solidly but incoherently against the release. Then they talked about the Hereford Birching case,[3] and there again the men were, as he put it 'silly and soft' and all against beating children – said it did no good. He explained to them about the merits of corporal punishment but refrained from quoting from his own experiences at public school because public schools are a 'tricky subject' with the men.

The night after the release of Mosley, Barrington-Ward, the editor of *The Times*, came to dinner at the Masseys'. He was cagey. He said it was a bad blunder, but he did not intend to publish any letters of protest yet until he had heard Mosley defend himself. In fact he never has published one. I think most Englishmen were disgusted at the release, but within the next day or two it was clear that the Extreme Left were making political capital out of it. 'All of us' closed their ranks. *The Times* published a guarded leader in support of Mosley. On the division the Tory Party went solidly into the lobbies to vote in defence of his release. The Liberal individualists rushed to the support of the Habeas Corpus.

20 December 1943.

Spent the entire day at the International Labour Organisation Conference and ended by being rather fascinated by the play of interests and personalities and absorbed by the family party atmosphere of an international conference. It has been interesting to watch the skilful old hands at this sort of game.

About the usefulness of our proceedings I am in some doubt. There is a good deal of mass self-hypnosis engendered at such gatherings and confirmed in this instance by visits from Mr. Eden, blessings from Ernest Bevin and a laudatory article in *The Times*. But the doubts persist. A code of labour legislation and social security for the liberated European countries? Splendid, but who is to apply it and in what conditions? In the chaos of a half-starved Europe ridden by class conflict? Are the Balkans ripe for such an utopia? Is Spain? Will Russian commissars order the rhythm of reconstruction by this measure? Will they agree to it in the parts of Germany they may occupy?

21 December 1943.

Lunched with Derek Patmore – he and Peter Quennell are editing Anne-Marie's memoirs and are bringing it out in a very *Almanach de Gotha* manner – I think quite wrongly. It ought to be given a full Romanian flavour – a sort of rococo Ritz 1912 affair. I am afraid they will make her a bore by treating her too seriously.

22 December 1943.

Dined with Elizabeth, Maurice Bowra and Raymond Mortimer[4] – a most unusually entertaining evening. Every now and then in London you have such an evening and feel at the end of it that this is what is described in memoirs as 'brilliant' conversation. Bowra fascinated me by his vitality, malice and wit. Although a very Oxford product he looks like a Midland businessman – stocky, bullet-headed with very small hands and feet. He has donnish tricks like 'that is a good point', if he is pleased with what you say. Raymond Mortimer seemed young and vulnerable beside him and was on the defensive throughout. At dinner Bowra made a dive bombing attack on him, 'Catholic! Conshie! Cagoulard!' Raymond seemed to love it.

25 December 1943.

In the morning Elizabeth and I went to the Christmas service at the Abbey. It was crowded. The procession had to make a path between the people as it wound its way through the nave and into the choir. One saw the banners moving unsteadily over the heads of the people – an immemorial lurching movement. Candles were blazing against the iron-black pillars. We came back to lunch with Alan, off cold duck and white Corton 1924.

I sat next to Margot Asquith at dinner. We talked about the place of the bed in marriage. She is too old and there is nothing left but senile vanity and play-acting. Once with a trace of her old verve she said, 'The man who never falls in love is filleted.' She horrified me by saying, 'I should like to live forever.' I was thinking at the very moment how tragic it must be for her not to have been able to die before now. She wore a black tricorne hat with a long black crêpe veil, a shrilly bright green silk jacket and a flaring skirt of black and white tartan silk. She looked like a witch – a surrealist witch – in a modern fairy tale.

1944

17 January 1944.

Just back from a week-end with Roley at Bournemouth where his regiment is stationed. He is a local legend in the regiment and he lives up to it. Dark, restless, warm-hearted, caustic and above all natural. He has captured the imagination of the men in his regiment by being more alive than any of them.

In the morning I went for a solitary walk down the steep Bournemouth streets full of soldiers and airmen. I think I was the only male civilian in Bournemouth under eighty. The whole atmosphere of the mess was like a school just before the holidays – high spirits, jokes and friendliness. They made the discomforts, most of which are avoidable, seem fun. With dozens of soldier servants they live in unimaginable squalor. Nowhere a picture or a curtain or even an armchair, but plenty to drink – cars right and left – the slipshod cheerful untidiness of bachelor life lived in common. An atmosphere in which even the most pompous, touchy or old-maidish get into the habit of taking jokes against themselves and resigning their privacies. Also like school – the photographs of wives and mothers and children beside every other bed. I think what has cheered them up so much is the consciousness that they will be joining in the coming invasion of Europe.

18 January 1944.

The news of Jock Colley's death – killed in the R.A.F. – a lamb to the slaughter.

19 January 1944.

Talked to George Ignatieff about this ghastly raid on Sofia where we have wiped out the whole centre of a town, which has no shelters, is built of wood and is inhabited by people most of whom seem to be pro-Ally. The horror of these destructive attacks on the cities of Europe! It is such a revolting way of waging warfare and no one seems to try to realise what we are doing. It may be necessary, but at least we should accept the guilt and not send out brave, callow youths as our scapegoats to bomb in our names while we treat the news like a cricket score. If the clergymen were worthy of their salt they would make themselves unpopular by voicing our inner doubts about this methodical slaughter.

19 January 1944.

Dined with dearest Elizabeth and Cyril Connolly. He was suffering from a sore throat, but he said when he began to say critical things about his friends his voice came back to him.

27 January 1944.

Our minds much occupied with the incident of Lord Halifax's speech in Toronto.[1] It was not a speech calculated in terms which could appeal in Canada. It was ineptly put and showed no understanding of our psychology. It ought to have been argued in terms of Canadian self-interest. Mr. Massey says that the Prime Minister told him, 'In peace-time I would have gone to the country on it.' Yet Halifax's general argument is hard to answer.

Might it not be more satisfactory if we gave up being in the Empire at all and concluded a self-respecting alliance with England? Of course that would not be practical politics – it would divide Canada. But it is important that the loyalty theme, making sacrifices for the Home Country, should not be stressed – they are preaching to the converted and enraging the unconverted. Also the combination of Lord Halifax, Tory Toronto and an Empire Club is so unfortunate as a starting point for a debate over the future of Canada.

2 February 1944.

Mr. King says that Empire conferences should be for consultation and co-operation but not for the formulation or preparation of policies.[2] Presumably he means that you have a talk but commit yourselves to nothing. While one can agree with him about the dangers of formal machinery, surely that does not mean a totally negative attitude, and how in hell can you co-operate unless you have something to co-operate about, and what can you co-operate in except in plans and policies? The question really is the spirit in which you approach Commonwealth problems. The proper approach it seems to me would be to try to arrive at common objectives towards which we can all work in our separate ways. Where some or all of us can co-operate closely and in detail over plans let us do so without trying to enforce policies on members to whom they do not appeal. Let us have in mind how best these Empire plans can be merged in the wider objectives which the U.N. will have set before them, but Mr. King does not want to work through the Empire towards broader affiliations. He mistrusts the whole thing.

9 February 1944.

I did not think I was still capable of the friend-ship I feel for George Ignatieff and I am touched by his demonstrativeness. He has a noble and generous nature.

18 February 1944.

Elizabeth says that she works around to getting what she wants like a cat trying to get out of a room, and like a cat forgets in the middle what it was she wanted and remains standing vaguely gaz-ing into space.

Victor Gordon-Ives[3] killed in Italy – he was looking forward to enjoying life if there was anything left for an Eton and Oxford young man to enjoy after this war. He used to say how much he envied us having lived in the gay twenties. He did not have a chance – only twenty-two – straight from school into the army. Oh hell!

2 April 1944.

Dined with Nancy Mitford. She is a queer mixture of county and sophistication – you never know which reaction you are going to strike. She talked about Chatsworth where she has just been staying – says that the wind in the corridors blows your hat off like in an underground and that the portraits are being ruined by the breaths of the evacuee orphans who are occupying the house – that they have fat legs in black stockings and are always charging about playing hockey in the state rooms.

20 April 1944.

On Sunday morning at six o'clock Mary Rose Thesiger and I were walking through Hyde Park. It was only four o'clock by the sun and had the desolating stillness of four a.m. We walked down to the bridge with the ground mist still rising. The Park guns looked forlorn and powerless like the débris of some long-forgotten war – débris resting in a deserted field yet still sinister like prehistoric remains.

When we got to the bridge we lit cigarettes and

looked out over the Serpentine stretching to dream-like mist-enshrouded distances grey and silent. The dawn wind came up – a woman passed with a small boy in a school cap. Why were they there in the Park before dawn on Easter morning, 1944?

22 April 1944.

Went down to the House of Lords and heard a pretty thin debate on the Empire. They just do not know much about the subject. There was one old bugger who made me feel like personally establishing a secession group in Canada – Lord W. who had had 'three hundred lads from the Dominions' stay with him since the war began. 'My imperial conferences, my friends call them.' Patronising old Pecksniff!

No one in the House showed any real understanding that Canada is a nation with a soul of its own. They all say it but none of them really understand it.

7 May 1944.

Lunched with Elizabeth in the downstairs grill in the Ritz. There were pink tulips on the table with pinkish lights. It was odd coming into it from the sunlight and wind. We talked as we did when we first got to know each other. It was one of those times which we shall both remember afterwards and say to each other, 'That fine, windy Sunday in spring when we lunched underground in the Ritz.'

12 May 1944.

Perhaps it is the invasion. We live for D-Day, and after D-Day I suppose we will settle down to some way of living – the same way but with everything shifted a bit. After each of these crises – September 1939, June 1940, September 1940, there has been an adjustment – like a building that has been just missed by a bomb. It 'settles' a little – one or two cracks appear. It is still standing the next day, and you are so surprised to see it there that you only notice later that a bit is gone off the cornice and the drawing-room ceiling is sagging badly.

I met my brother, Roley, last night. He appeared in his beret – the first time he has worn it. He said it was to impress me that he was a Commando now. We walked up the towpath from Richmond to Kew. It was a beautiful evening – the enormous chestnut trees in full bloom – the May-trees dusty with white. Before he came when I was sauntering among the people waiting for him I felt a premonition, 'That last time I saw him at Richmond.' When I met him in the hall of the Elephant and Castle Hotel it was like meeting him in a dream – just that touch of irrelevance, 'Why Richmond? What were we doing there? Why was he wearing a beret and looking so brown?' – the sort of questions one asks oneself when one wakes up.

28 May 1944.

Reading Lady Ottoline Morrell's[4] memoirs which should certainly be published. They have the same mixture of vitality and silliness as George Moore's memoirs of a young man, and for all her wild fumbling she has an artist's gift for describing people and places. At one point she brings in Henry James who said of Clive Bell, 'that little soiled piece of humanity', and on being invited to meet an ageing actress, said to his hostess, 'A tightrope, a banister, backstairs – anything to save me from meeting that battered mountebank, dear Lady.'

6 June 1944.

D-Day has come. It had become a hallucination – something like the Second Coming or the End of the World. Roley has not yet gone. He rang me on the telephone yesterday. I hope Peter[5] will be all right.

The soldiers who have been left behind in London look forlorn and subdued. The town seems empty. The gaiety and sense of pressure and excitement have gone. There is a morning after feeling abroad. The taxis have become plentiful again and the drivers are beginning to be quite polite now that the American debauch is over.

7 June 1944.

The relief of having got home from that party. Not Daniel escaping from the lions' den, not Marie Antoinette escaping from the Paris mob can have felt a more profound sense of deliverance than I do. The scene – a converted mews, a vast underground saloon – like the vestibule of a cinema or like the anteroom of Hades – light percolating only from the ceiling. In this 'luxurious interior' the most deadly effort at social gaiety ever perpetrated. In a space which could have held four hundred people was collected a handful of American officers mixed with a smattering of peculiarly snobbish women – endless dry martinis, interminable whisky. The final touch for me was added by a lame American with silver hair and dignified appearance who was a 'specialist on Russia' and who was in the last stages of gin-intoxication. He got it firmly into his head that I was a spy, and when I said that I could not understand Russian he said angrily, 'Don't you try to pretend with me.'

Mary Rose has a collection of Victorian Valentines thrust in the drawers of an old cabinet and a scrap book of her life. I understood more about her when I saw the photographs of her and her two sisters acting in the play that J. M. Barrie had written for them when they were children. Then I saw the connection with her 'little girl' dresses – the schoolgirl dresses that she wears to the 400 Club. She poses as a lost girl and she is one. She and Stephen Tennant are companion pieces – those exquisite children growing up in a world of taste and imagination, of green lawns, strawberries and cream, footmen and whimsicality – those last blooms from the hot-house. The photographs of the pre-war débutante with a half-boiled guardee-peer – the fashionable marriage and now this strange lost child – this cheerful little waif – and anyone – a waiter, a policeman, a man or woman – would come to her help if she needed them.

9 to 14 June 1944.

At this point I became unendurably restless and determined by hook or crook to get to the Normandy beach-head. This was strictly forbidden to all civilians, as the landing had only taken place on 6 June and troops were still landing. However, I had the inspiration to sell Mr. Massey the idea that a message of good wishes should be sent to the Canadian troops in Normandy from Mr. Mackenzie King. I then drafted the message in Mr. King's name and induced Mr. Massey to get the Prime Minister's approval. Admiral Nelles of the Royal Canadian Navy arranged a passage for me on a troopship, but said that I would have to arrange my own landing in Normandy as it was impossible to obtain permission for a civilian to land.

I left London on Wednesday, 14 June, in the company of Lieut.Commander B., Royal Canadian Navy, who had been told off by the Admiral to look after me. He was a tiresome little man, in appearance and also temperament not unlike Mr. Mackenzie King, a neurasthenic bachelor whose job was to look after the Canadian personnel on the large troop landing craft which are about two hundred and fifty tons and have eight diesel engines. There are about twenty of these manned by the Royal Canadian Navy and the Royal Canadian Naval Volunteer Reserve, who had been serving in combined operations with the Royal Navy. B. described these men as 'his children' and spoke feelingly of how they were neglected by the Canadian authorities and bullied by the Royal Navy, of how they had been given ships in bad repair and expected to keep them in order. The officers and crews were of an average age of nineteen. I was to get to know a good deal more about these landing craft and their crews.

B. and I took a train to Portsmouth that night and we repaired to a hotel on the front at Southsea which had been taken over by the Royal Navy – its lounge serving as an unofficial meeting place where officers newly arrived from 'the other side' sat in wicker chairs drinking beer and talking shop. B., who had a violent anti-English complex, on being asked for his identity number by the woman at the reception desk said, 'Canadians do not have identity numbers – you people know nothing about us do you? Except that our boys fight for you and we feed you.' The woman flushed and looked embarrassed. I did the same. My natural dislike for B. was tempered by my feeling that as he was my naval guide and I was completely off my own ground I must bear with him.

15 to 17 June, 1944.

Thursday, 15 June, was fine – we started off to join our troop-ship *Prince William*, going first by ferry to Ryde and thence by jeep to Cowes, which consisted of a narrow winding street packed with the Royal Navy. It was at this point that I first became conscious of my civilian clothes. (I was later to be the only male out of uniform to be seen anywhere in the course of my time in France, except for the Norman shopkeepers and peasants.) I was eyed with curiosity and – not quite – hostility. It was apparent to all that I must be some sort of a bloody nuisance, most probably a journalist. Not for the last time on the trip I longed for the protective colouring of khaki. We took off for the troopship in a small troop-carrying craft guided by a remarkably pert young R.C.N. officer who treated me in the slightly insolent manner common among junior officer to civilians until they have gauged by the behaviour of their seniors what their attitude should be. This cue was readily and warmly given by the Commanding Officer of the *Prince William*, Captain Godfrey, and in addition my old friend, Rastus Reid, now an Admiral, was on board.

The first day we went over to lunch with the Captain of the sister cruiser, the *Prince Henry* and I had my first insight into naval rivalries. The Captain of the *Prince Henry* was a six-foot Irish cop type called Kelly. He was Royal Canadian Naval Volunteer Reserve, not Royal Canadian Navy, not in fact a Straight Striper. I soon discovered that the R.C.N.V.R. hate the Royal Navy as being stuck-up, stuffy and superior. They also hate the Royal Canadian Navy whom they consider quite rightly to be an imitation of the Royal Navy. The Royal Canadian Navy for their part pride themselves on the accuracy of their naval tradition, admire, albeit slightly resent, the Royal Navy, and look down on the Royal Canadian Naval Volunteer Reserve. These and other naval mysteries have been revealed to me in the course of this visit.

That evening B. and I returned in a small landing craft to Portsmouth for me to obtain a landing pass. A tall florid officer with a calm naval manner received me with relaxed politeness but no actual enthusiasm. He remarked casually that he was not a Cook's Tourist Agency. It was not a promising beginning, and although he became exceedingly amiable when he had seen my papers he would not give me a pass. He said it would get him into trouble with the army authorities. I asked what would happen if I succeeded in landing without one. He painted a depressing picture of my being taken up by the Military Police and shot on sight as a spy. I must say that I was wearing just the sort of raincoat that a spy always seems to wear. It was a dirty old Burberry, but in each pocket I had placed a bottle of bourbon whisky for use as bribes. They clanked about a good deal in the course of the interminable jumping from one small craft to another during my travels. Depressed by the refusal of the pass, I repaired to the bar, where I ran into John R., a large young man, dark, with a look of Indian blood, in the R.C.N., and this was fortunate as his acquaintance was very useful to me. Later on that night I returned to spend the night on board the *Prince William*. The navy atmosphere was novel and cheerful – more fun than the army, suffering less from strain than the air force – in fact, not suffering from strain at all. That night they had a party on board – a formal dinner, then schoolboy jokes and horseplay. At the end the party got rough and the younger ones debagged B. It was then that I realised with satisfaction the dislike of B. was not restricted to myself but was shared by all his 'children' of the combined operations.

The next day, Friday the 16th, I got word to transfer at once to the *Prince Henry* our sister ship as she was sailing forthwith for France. We took on troops that night – infantrymen – four hundred and sixty of them – one after another coming up the ship's ladder until watching them coming made you dizzy. Stolid, cheerful, English faces – about half of them looked like boys in their teens. All were top-heavy with the weight of their equipment, staggering as they slid down the incline from the gangplank leading on to the ship's deck, blundering about helplessly like cows caught in a too narrow lane. Their tin helmets covered with camouflage to look like leaves were like some stylised headgear of the kind worn by peasants participating in a fertility festival. The troops were very quiet as we steamed out of Southampton Water. They lined the deck looking back at the pattern made by the masts and derricks against a luminous evening sky. It was one of those moments, common in the war, when everyone shares the same thought. As the sun set we were passing to starboard the white romantic castle on the Isle of Wight where it stands among its woods. No one seemed to know what it was called or who lived there, and indeed it looked like a mirage across the calm waters of the Solent.

Saturday, 17 June, I woke, looked out of the port-hole and was disappointed not to see the coast of France. I walked about rather miserably on deck feeling out of place and in people's way. The Captain asked me up to his cabin and talked to me about ways of cooking Peruvian fish. I listened politely. The only thing I was interested in was whether I was going to be able to land without my pass. About eleven a.m. we sighted the coast of Normandy and anchored about five miles off the coast opposite the port of Arromanches. The landing craft came alongside to take off the troops. The Captain sent me a message from the bridge that if I liked to take a chance I could go aboard the landing craft but that if there was any delay in landing the troops the ship could not wait for me – I would have to find my own way back to England. What I needed in order to land was a uniformed escort. I asked B. whether he would go with me. The miserable little man hedged. I asked a moustached Guards officer in charge of troop landing. At that moment my acquaintance John R. whom I had met that drunken evening in Southampton appeared on board the landing craft. I thought he might prove a friend in need and clambered down the ladder among the lines of descending troops, the bottles swaying in my mackintosh pockets.

It was my first experience of the machine-like precision of the landing arrangements about which we read in the newspapers. The troops in the end were landed but there was nothing very machine-like in the process. By hollering from the bridge at every passing small craft asking for aid and by an exchange of insults with those who refused it, some craft which should no doubt have been taking troops off another landing craft was pressed into our service. Eventually, however, in the midst of shouts, orders and counter-orders, we reached a pontoon bridge and remained stuck there until nighttime when we got free and tied up to the bridge.

There is no natural harbour at Arromanches. The artificial harbour which has been constructed is known as the Mulberry and was full of small shipping – the bigger ships ride at anchor outside. It was crowded with troopships, a variety of landing craft, tankers, munition and supply ships and small tugs in which are seated majors with megaphones who are supposed to have some control over the movements of the shipping. They dash about like sheep-dogs. The majors shout down their megaphones in gloomy authoritative tones at the small craft which crowd the Mulberry telling them they must move out of this berth or tie up to that ship and above all keep a safe distance from their precious pontoon bridge which is their chief concern. The captains and crews of the hounded small craft curse and protest but in the end do as they are told.

John R. very kindly asked me to stay on board a Canadian manned landing craft. Life on board is an intimate business. It has to be in a ship of two hundred and fifty tons – the three officers eat, sleep and live in a cabin about forty feet by twenty feet in size. The galley opens on to one end of the cabin and the conversation of the crew is clearly audible when the communication trap is open. Life at such close quarters could be hell, but, in fact, it was carefree and cheerful. It was an efficiently run ship, but not run on any orthodox Royal Navy lines but in a peculiarly Canadian way – the lack of fuss and feathers, the humour and the horse-sense with which the whole business is handled. This atmosphere was due in part to the officers. The Captain was a cool, reserved young man of perhaps twenty-three with serious tastes – Plato, *War and Peace*, Mill on *Liberty* were in the small bookcase beside technical books on navigation. He was an ideal Captain with a simple, rather dry sense of humour, conscientious to a fault, but with an easy direct way with the crew. The First Officer was a nonchalant youth, imperturbable in difficulties and dangers, easily amused and amusing. My friend, John, was the most unusual and most complex character of the three – a rich man's son, quick-witted, enterprising, exuberant and uncertain in temper. Between the three they knew how to run the ship and keep happy a crew of boys of nineteen, including a French-Canadian, a Dukhobor, a lumberjack, an ex-rumrunner, a Newfoundlander. They were a tough, good-natured lot who would have been impossible to manage by spit and polish. They enjoyed every incident and welcomed everything but monotony. It was an atmosphere of youth.

Details of Life on a Landing Craft

For breakfast pancakes the size of a large soup-plate with golden syrup. Drinking gin and eating chocolates in a high gale. Listening to German radio propaganda quoting Kipling's 'Tommy Atkins' to weaken our morale while German planes are overhead.

The perpetual booming of guns and falling of bombs from the mainland, the knowledge that the Germans are only sixteen miles away behind that cliff and yet here we might be in Canada.

The crew, 'Keep your fucking shirt-tails out of the spuds.'

The pictures of pin-up girls and John saying, 'if only they moved – it is having them suspended like that in one position that gets on one's nerves.'

Sunday, 18 June 1944.

It began to blow hard and gale warnings were out. A fine drizzle blew against the port-holes. We decided to go ashore and have a look at Arromanches, and walked the length of the rain-swept pontoon which was swaying and creaking in the high wind. No one stopped us at the shore end. No one asked me for a pass. I strolled ashore on to the beach-head in an oilskin coat – and was doubtless taken for a member of the crew. Arromanches looked like a stage-set that had been left out in the rain – a little cardboard back-drop of a French seaside resort, but badly battered about. Port authorities, town majors, naval officer in charge, have set up their quarters in the hotel de Ville and in the bigger houses of the town. We walked about among the closed and desolate little villas coloured grey and sand, or biscuit colour – coquettish little affairs – 'Mon Repos', 'Doux Séjour'. The gardens were overgrown with rain-sodden roses, red and white.

The few remaining inhabitants were occupied in salvaging bits and pieces of their possessions or walking about among the débris of the invasion to see if they could find anything which would serve some useful purpose. We went into the church – a big, grey, empty church with a shell hole in the roof above the altar – otherwise intact and the windows unbroken. Before the statue of the Virgin – the usual chocolate-box figure wearing a bright blue mantle – were piles of white roses. There was a Roll of Honour 'Mort Pour La France 1914-1918' – too long a roll for a village like Arromanches. No flowers before the statue of Joan of Arc, but St. Thérèse de Lisieux was popular.

Monday, 19 June 1944.

John and I departed by jeep for the headquarters of the Third Canadian Division. This represented a considerable achievement on his part. He had bluffed the local brigadier into appreciating the importance of my mission, and I found that wherever we went he had built me up to almost embarrassing heights and I was greeted like a visiting cabinet minister.

It was another day of wind and rain with low cloud. We drove along excellent, hard-surfaced roads from village to village looking for the headquarters. Along the roads went an unceasing stream of traffic, trucks, DUKWs, jeeps, tanks, and interfering with this traffic was the occasional peasant's cart. A red-faced old farm woman riding a bicycle appeared from behind a row of oncoming tanks. She had the same air of going – with a sort of desperate stubbornness – about her own business, which marked most of the local inhabitants. In this area the peasants did not seem to have been evacuated. The military say they are helpful and co-operative but not demonstrative. They did not seem much in favour of de Gaulle. In Bayeux two French officers have established themselves as representatives of the French Provisional Government. We saw their proclamations posted on the walls there side by side with those of General Eisenhower.

We went by car over a good portion of the bridgehead – a windswept country of high bare ridges and big fields studded with rough wooden poles, as protection against gliders. The German warning signs still left beside the roads, the skull and crossbones and the word *Minen*. There was hardly a field in which there were not either tents or supply dumps – soldiers naked to the waist washing in a wet field, hospitals marked with red crosses, petrol dumps and stores stacked in rows – one of 'our' airstrips thick with planes grounded by bad weather. Until the day before the country had been a dust bowl, now it was being transformed overnight into mud. Our road led through Bayeux and a dozen small Norman villages. I went into some of the shops in Bayeux. It was pleasant to be among French people again – so willing to make every small negotiation into a conversation. They seemed to have lots of food in the shops and luxury goods. The people were full of smiles, glad to see us but not emotional.

The main street was decorated with tricolours, but the demonstrative period, if there ever was one here, was over.

General Keller's headquarters were only a couple

of miles from the German lines and at one point we nearly took a wrong turning in our jeep which would have brought us out behind the German lines. There was little sign of enemy activity except for the almost casual booming of guns. The Headquarters are in the grounds of a château, not in the house itself – a small formal eighteenth-century stucco house – but in the park and gardens. The General who was living in a camouflaged truck concealed in a mound in the park emerged on my arrival looking ruddy and confident, just as a General should look, and clad in a khaki pullover and breeches. He talked like a General saying that his men were 'in good heart'. He summoned a circle of officers and some men standing in the damp park. I read them the Prime Minister's message of goodwill as drafted by me. The General expressed gratification and sent a message to our people at home. I thought his enthusiasm rather muted, and I do not think that the name Mackenzie King makes the military heart beat faster.

I asked one of the officers whether I could go along the line to see my cousins, Peter Smellie and John Rowley, who were with their regiment a mile or two away. He said that a moving vehicle on that road might attract enemy fire to their position and wondered sarcastically whether they would want to see me in these conditions. I said probably not.

A day or two later after my return to the beach-head at Arromanches I ran into Bill Wickwire who was in Roley's regiment and he told me that Roley had been very badly wounded. He had last seen him swathed in bandages from head to foot on a stretcher. He had been returned to a hospital in England as an emergency case. I was now desperately anxious to get back to England to see him, but for the remaining four days we were storm-bound tossing in a landing craft against the pontoon bridge or tied up to a larger ship in a storm-tossed mass of small shipping where a furious north-west gale blew incessantly. We could not cross the Channel by day because of the danger of enemy planes. To manoeuvre at night was difficult and dangerous. Next to us a destroyer out of control was beached. Two tank landing craft were broken up by the storm. All the time until the last day, apart from my worry about Roley, I thoroughly enjoyed myself. Outside – hostile coast, a sweeping gale, clouding skies; inside in the small wardroom we drank gins, told stories and listened to the wireless until four days later the weather became calm and we were able to return by night to England.

10 July 1944.

It is as if this had been not one war but half a dozen short wars with intervals of truce in between. The last truce ended about one month before D-Day. Since then we have been steadily on the stretch and one begins to add up the reckoning as the end of the war approaches. Roley, wounded, perhaps not beyond cure – Gavin Rainnie, so physically alive, so solid, so racy of health and vigour, blown up in his landing craft before he even reached the beaches – Enid Grant sitting in her farm at Oddington waiting with lessening hope to hear news of Jack who is missing. Jock Colley and Victor Gordon-Ives killed.

The buzz-bombs go on – that poor little Grosvenor girl has her face full of hundreds of fragments of glass from the shattered window in her flat.

Elizabeth and Margery have both had their houses blasted and are trying to think it worthwhile to start again.

13 July 1944.

Morale much improved – we are getting used to the buzz-bombs and also fewer are coming over. People are beginning to come to life again – to ring up their friends and to go out to restaurants. I heard my first fresh piece of scandal today – a healthy sign. Anne-Marie has returned to the Ritz with a new hat and a new admirer. Life marches on.

There goes an air-raid warning. I have been completely unmoved by these buzz-bombs – I was more scared by the early raids at the beginning of the war.

20 July 1944.

Elizabeth's house in Clarence Terrace has been hit by a blast for the third time. She has at last decided to move out now. All the ceilings are down and all the windows broken. She and Alan only escaped being killed by a chance. I hate the disappearance of Clarence Terrace – so will her other friends. It was the last house in London which still felt like a pre-war house. There was always good food, good talk and wine (as long as wine lasted) and a certain style. Then I liked the house itself with its tall, airy rooms and good, rather sparse furniture. I suppose they will re-open it after the war if it is not hit again. Elizabeth's nerves have been under a terrible strain, but she is resilient and if she can get away and get some rest she will be all right. In the midst of it all she is still trying frantically to write her novel.[6]

12 August 1944.

Fine weather, victories, the falling off of buzz-bombs (bugger bombs as Mrs. Corrigan innocently calls them) have improved everyone's spirits. There are bets that we shall be in Paris by the end of September. Meanwhile the casualty lists get longer, and we who need good men in Canada are losing some of our best.

Lunched today with Anne-Marie at the Ritz. She had on a little hat with a crêpe veil – a mockery of a widow's peak. I think she is mourning her lost love, although she hides her scars and her scars never seem more than skin deep.

Elizabeth has moved to Clarissa Churchill's[7] flat,

as her house has been blasted once too often. It is high up in a monstrous new block of flats overlooking Regent's Park. She likes the flat which is full of Clarissa's empire furniture, gilt and maroon velvet – too palatial for the size of the flat. Elizabeth is writing a short story, 'The Happy Autumn Fields', and told me about it in an excited way while I lay on a sofa looking out at the sea of green tree tops with here and there an isolated high building.

18 August 1944.

Dined with Michal Vyvyan. He says that to go on fighting the Germans is a waste of men and that people who continue a war after it has ceased to be necessary are as criminal as those who started it. We now dispose of superior power, therefore it is no longer necessary to deploy it militarily. We are like people who hold all the good cards in a bridge hand and insist on playing it out card by card instead of just throwing in the hand and writing down the results. He says we could have had a cessation of hostilities any time in the last six months.

19 August 1944.

The hatred of the more intelligent English upper classes for the age they live in is profoundly discouraging, though less irritating than the shallow optimism, perfectionism and venom of the Left.

I never seem to put a foot wrong with Jews. I feel at my ease with them. They are more human and more mentally honest than most Gentiles and their minds are alive. Beyond this in my own case there may be a blood connection. I wonder?

I was brought up in the tradition of gentlemanly English culture but it is not deep in my blood. I have not got the English love of things done in due order. Sometimes I think that the English do not care a pin about justice. What they like is seemliness.

2 October 1944. Ottawa.[8]

Drove out to the Fishing Club up the Gatineau Valley to which a small group of civil servants belong – younger men – some of them temporary wartime appointments – a very pleasant group – intelligent, unaffected, kind-hearted and hard-headed. At the Fishing Club the day was overcast with a gun-metal sky, the trees just beginning to turn. I think of this country not as young but as old as nature – ante-dating Athens and Rome – always these hidden lakes and waiting woods.

13 October 1944. Wolfville, Nova Scotia.[9]

The one street of Wolfville is lined with autumn trees – golden filters for sunlight, but there has not been much sun. It is overcast, cool and windless. The old-fashioned, white clapboard houses are so pretty that the village just escapes being a tourist picture postcard. Sandwiched between these charming, early Victorian, *Cranford* houses are the tall, fretted wooden villas of the eighties painted in liver and mustard and the comfortable, shingled, style-less, modern houses with big windows and roomy verandahs. Wolfville is built on a slope – from the woods the orchards spread down to the backs of houses on one side of the street. Behind the houses on the other side the slope ends abruptly in a steep bluff – below are marshes and mud flats stretching into the basin of Minas, an expanse of shifting tides and colours – a mirror for sunsets. Beyond this sea-inlet Cape Blomidon stands up nobly.

The old ladies whom Mother sees in Wolfville are forever spinning their web of daily living, of small worries and jokes, incidents and purchases, sympathies and antipathies, nerves and rests.

I have been re-reading my own early diaries written in my teens and at Oxford and I am so stifled by the fumes of my own personality that I have to overcome nausea to write at all. Yet I am glad to have the diaries. They bring before me a youth who appals me by his silliness and by the banality of his mind. Only the eager appetite for experience is attractive – the astringent notes on people are sometimes amusing, and there is a recurrent sense of the writer's own ridiculousness. The diary describes a life which I had only remembered in a blurred way. The endless succession of people coming and going at home, the dances, picnics and fiirtations. A 'social animal', one can see that. Personal relationships and aesthetic or literary impressions (rendered in an appalling pastiche style) dominate. There is nothing worthy to be called an idea from cover to cover, and not one single mention of politics or world events. There is a note of gush mixed with a cynicism about my own motives – altogether an impressionable animal.

20 October 1944. Ottawa.

The feeling in the Department of External Affairs is very pro-Russian and anti-Pole – they do not see this as being inconsistent with our emphasis on the rights of small nations and find it inconvenient to be reminded that it is so. Someone in the Department said to me today that he would be more fearful of a strong Poland than a strong Russia. I suppose it is a remark that he must have read somewhere. It seems extraordinarily silly. The truth is that the old left-wing prejudices still stick. Poland is 'reactionary' – Russia is 'progressive'.

1 November 1944. London.

I reflected coming over on the plane on how obsessed I have been all my life by my determination to forgo nothing. How gently but ruthlessly I have insisted on my pattern at the expense of other people's feelings and my own. Has it all been downright silly? Am I like the man in Henry James's story *The Beast in the Jungle* who found in the end that it was his singular fate to be the man to whom nothing happened?

London seems to me quite meaningless. The

illusion it provided has vanished. As Elizabeth says, 'It is no doubt an old and interesting city but for me it has come unstuck.'

1944 will stand in our memories as the year of fatigue and sorrow when 'the silver cord was loosed,' etc.

15 November 1944.

Dreamt that I was in the throes of an air raid and woke up to find that it was true. There had been a raid last night but these buzz-bombs and V2s have never made much impression on me, though God knows I was scared enough in the early raids.

I sat about all morning in my dressing-gown in a demoralised state talking about life with the Life Force (my name for the woman who cleans my flat because of her whirlwind energy). We agreed that soft, imaginative people go rotten and bitter much more certainly than those who start dull or hard.

3 December 1944.

The squirrel-faced lift-woman was talking away volubly last night about the English – 'The greatest race on earth,' she said. 'Never has been anythink like us – never will be. Look the way we borne the brunt of the war yet we never talk about ourselves – no swank – we just get on with the job.'

The Americans in London are a well-behaved tolerant army of occupation. They are so polite that one almost hears their thoughts and they are thinking, 'These poor, quaint people. They have guts but – backward, reactionary.' And the English with their kindly street directions thinking behind shut faces, 'These people have not got what it takes – no breeding – an inferior race but, damn them, they have the money and the power. We can only dominate them by character, our national asset from which we can always cut and come again.'

The two races and the two armies mingle in street and pub without ever touching except for the collaborating little factory girls who chew gum, wear their hair *à la* Lana Turner and queue up for movies hand-in-hand with their protectors. The American men are so different with the women. They fondle them in the street, always a hand splaying over breast or buttock. Loose-limbed they amble at the girl-friend's side whispering in her ear, pinching her behind, their two mouths rhythmically moving in unison – so different from the wooden Englishman walking side by side with his girl not seeming to see her except for covert glances and the occasional clumsy touch of his hand on hers.

20 December 1944.

Dined at the Masseys with Rab Butler.[10] I like him better each time I see him. He enjoys his own success so much. He is so malicious and under the don-like manner he is a born politician. He puts out so many tentacles into the conversation and never muffs or muddles what he is saying. He has a trick of praising in general terms before getting on to particular denigration. 'I admire X enormously – he is very nearly a great man, but what I think, don't you, has so far held him up has been quite simply lack of intelligence.'

All the same he and his fellow Tories understand nothing about Canada. It is discouraging to find this ignorance in the intelligent ones like Rab. A small instance – Rab was trying to show that he appreciated Canada's position in the Commonwealth and said to Mr. Massey, 'To show you what I mean I have several times in speaking of Canada to you referred to it as 'your country.' Quite separate from us.' This was said in good faith. Any Canadian's reaction would be, 'why the Hell wouldn't you – it *is* our country'. Isn't it or is it?

He was talking of the need for Canada becoming the second line of defence, the refuge of the British race, perhaps the future centre of the Empire. 'If,' he said, 'this was presented to the Canadian people on racial grounds they would understand it. Race after all, as Disraeli said, is fundamental.' But there are – I reminded him – two races in Canada. 'Oh, your French-Canadians,' he said, 'that would be all right if we had a much closer relationship with France.' The Foreign Office cannot get it out of their heads that the French-Canadians are politically devoted to France. Pure ignorance – I only hope to God that they know more about other foreign countries than they do about Canada.

I asked Rab if the country was restive at the delays in implementing social reforms. 'Everything in politics can be solved by not making up your mind in a hurry and not getting rattled – procrastination – or I should say – patience.'

26 December 1944.

Christmas at Loelia, Duchess of Westminster's. The house is so like a stage set that it engenders a stagey brilliance in people. It looked more unreal than ever in Christmas-card weather, with silver hoarfrost in the park – an interior of crystals and silks seen from the fogbound avenue. The party were Loelia (who had fits of impatience when she turned on us all and rated the nearest victim, but she is a wonderful creature; coming in from a walk in the cold showed her sudden dark flashing beauty) then the Sitwells and their son, Reresby, Angie Biddle Duke, very smooth – I thought too easy to the edge of insolence, Peter Quennell, emitting a phosphorescent charm.

We went over to the Christmas Ball at Sutton.11 The whey-faced Duke speaks and moves like a zombie. The ball was an odd mixture – fresh little country-girl neighbours, boy midshipmen, red-faced middle-aged hangers-on of the Duke, and our own group. Then there were American Colonels slapping Duchesses on their bottoms and feeding free lifts, free champagne, free cigars, free silk stockings to the aristocracy, seeing how much dirt they can make the English eat. One said to Loelia, 'Since I have come here I find that the Royal Navy stinks, the R.A.F. stinks and I always knew the British Army stank.' Loelia said she very *nearly* threw the bottle of Noilly Prat he brought her out of the door after him, but she had second thoughts. But when he said to young Reresby, 'Why do you Etonians go around with your hands in your pockets all the time,' he answered like a true Sitwell; 'If we had three hands we would keep them all in our pockets if we were inclined to.'

An exotic element was added to the ball by the arrival of the Spanish Embassy party, the Duke of Alba's daughter, the Duchess of Montero, cleverly dressed by some dressmaker to look like a Velasquez Infanta.

The house, Renaissance Italianate, is beautiful outside – lovely in its shape against the frost-silvered gardens. Inside it is 1912 Tudor – inescapable panelling everywhere, vast hotel-like rooms, buffets of heat from the grates in the floors, the library full of photographs of women in flower-pot hats and motoring veils.

31 December 1944.

After this war the most we can aim at is a breathing-space which, if we are lucky, might last a generation. It is a delusion to talk of permanent peace and there is no 'solution' of a 'political problem'. The latter is the language of mathematics not of politics.

The only new element in the permanent human situation is the technical one. As weapons become so much more destructive there is the possibility that the human race may outlaw the more deadly ones and carry on its struggle by common agreement with the less destructive. This would seem unduly optimistic but for one fact, that in this war gas has not so far been used, even by a Hitler.

1945

3 January 1945. Paris.[1]

New Year's Day was magnificent – sun and frost. From the roof of Saul's flat which faces on the Esplanade des Invalides you have a panorama of Paris through the sunny mist; the familiar silhouettes sharpened as the day went on and directly below us ran the Seine, the colour of chartreuse between the white bleached stone quais. The sun burnished the melodramatic gold statues on the Pont Alexandre III. Paris was preserved, untouched physically by the war.

At last I got an opportunity to get out alone into the streets and to look for Paris. It was like a dream in which you see the woman you love but cannot speak to her and cannot touch her. The untouched beauty of the city lying about me in burnished splendour under the winter sun made the emptiness more sinister. Paris is dead – there is no movement, no life, no crowds of talking, gesticulating people, no hum of assurance, no noisy erratic traffic of people and vehicles. Nothing but a spacious emptiness of the streets and the shabby, silent passers-by with drawn faces and hunched shoulders, grim, cold, hungry people. You look at their faces, and pity and nostalgia for the past seem out of place. The irony of the heroic arches and spectacular perspectives – the backdrop for their humiliation and their bitter unresigned endurance. This was how Paris seemed to me, and it would have been idle to think twice of my past youth there and memories of old loves when faced with this iron logic of defeat.

Everywhere in Paris you are haunted by the Germans. In the flat where I am staying two German diplomats had been living throughout the occupation. They had left in a hurry, their hair ointments and medicines were still in the cupboard, their calendar on the wall, and they had their own telephone switchboard in the salon with a direct line to Wilhelmstrasse. The maid who brought me my morning coffee had brought them every morning for four years their morning coffee. She was a Luxembourg peasant woman with a German accent. I asked her what she thought about the Germans and she said, like one who has sought the advice of a good lawyer and been told what she says might be taken in evidence against her, 'There were some who were bad and then naturally there were others who were less bad.' Saul says that you often hear people in the shops saying, 'Well, after all, the Germans provided coal, they kept the transport running, and when they were here one could buy things.'

There is resentment against the Americans and some practical cause for irritation. The American military authorities have demanded all the accommodation which the Germans had had. They are in all the best hotels with the only central heating working in Paris in this icy winter. They have money and, above all, and this is to the Parisians the unforgivable thing – they have food. The United States army rations are incredibly, almost scandalously abundant. They have the only cars in Paris, while Paris freezes and nearly starves. The Allies and a small fringe of rich French have everything they want and live from one party to the next.

In the shops it is not the contrast between French and American but between rich French and poor French which comes into play. No foreigner can afford the prices in these luxury shops, whose goods are, in fact, investments against inflation, but the rich French will buy anything by any means to get rid of currency in which they have no confidence. The astonishing thing is the beauty and variety of the luxury articles displayed. Coming to the shops fresh from wartime London I feel like a simple Russian soldier who has his first view of the western world and its amenities. It is so long since we have seen any object that tempts that we have almost forgotten the lures of vanity. This puritanism melts away at the sight of the Paris shop-windows. Here are jewels and clothes which would make you love your mistress more – simply because you had given them to her. We in England have missed a chapter in the history of taste. Everything is new to our eyes – the fantastic, sumptuous hats, pyramids and turbans of satin and velvet, of fur and of feathers, the new settings for jewels, the new colours of materials, the dramatic brilliance of the presentation in the shop windows.

In the empty boulevards the only traffic is United States army vehicles and a few ancient horse-drawn cabs, or bicycle-propelled hooded affairs which have been invented to try to fill the need for taxis – otherwise the Parisians have no transportation except the Métro.

The Raes' flat belongs to a rich Canadian woman. It is a typical modern luxury flat – great expanse of window, beige carpets, white china horses on the mantelpiece, imitation leopard skin on the bed and every modern device of comfort, only none of them working owing to the complete absence of fuel. The bathroom was an elaborate mockery with its showers and appliances – no one in the house had had a bath for two months. There was a large salon full of Empire furniture covered in striped satin, but it was too cold to contemplate as a sitting-room. As for my bedroom there could be no thought of sleeping in it. I slept on the sofa in front of the wood fire with a hot-water bottle, a sweater and all the windows closed. The family spent the day sitting on the floor to be as close as possible to the one minute wood stove in the sitting-room. We ate well on United States army rations.

12 January 1945. London.

Lionel Massey's farewell party for me. If you take twenty or thirty fairly adult and intelligent people and pump them full of alcohol from 6.30 until two in the morning you hear some pretty astonishing things. I do not think the English and Americans quite understand this kind of party. I sometimes think that Canadians, who are at heart a sensitive, pugnacious, voluble and amorous race, are only released by whisky.

3 February 1945. Ottawa.[2]

I suppose I could have gone on year after year representing my country abroad without knowing much about what was going on at home. I am in for an intensive bout of re-education. In the Department I feel like a new boy at school. They all seem to know so much more than I do. I asked myself what I can have been doing in these years when they were informing themselves so fully. Living through the war must be the answer.

18 February 1945.

Pavlov, an officer of the Soviet Embassy, came to a dinner for people from our Department and some foreign diplomats. He was out to *épater le bourgeois* and succeeded. Very cocky and on the offensive – looks like Harpo Marx but with fanatical eyes and a false mouth, nimble-witted and entertaining – the only one from the Embassy who talks freely, but then he is N.K.V.D., and so can say what he likes. He began by attacking, saying that Canada was owned by the Americans and why didn't we have a bigger population? Why didn't the Head of the European Division speak Russian? Why hadn't we provided houses for diplomats posted here as they did in the Soviet Union? Why did we allow the incubus of the church to stifle us? In fact, he thoroughly enjoyed himself at our expense. Norman Robertson[3] was good with him – ironic, sceptical – but he brushed aside argument. It was disconcerting to see how well our people took it. If an Englishman had dared half as much criticism there would have been a free fight, but the bourgeois fall for this proletarian line with inverted snobbery.

24 February 1945. Ottawa.

Staying with dear Aunt Elsie. I had breakfast alone in the dining-room among Elsie's glass tigers and cats and under the eyes of that portrait of the Admiral, her grandfather. The flat is full of tapestries, silver, nice 'bits' of furniture and in the hall a series of water-colours of the old Rowley family manor house in England. You have only to put your nose in the flat to be conscious of 'background'.

Elsie and I shout at each other at the tops of our voices (she is getting deafer and deafer). We carry on inconsequential conversations from room to room. We meet half-dressed in the hall – she in a silk slip, I in my shirt-tail. We inveigh against the Government, discuss love and the upbringing of children, rehash old scandals. She is incapable of getting into low gear, never wants to go to bed, never sleeps when she gets there, but lies all night listening to the wireless and worrying about her sons at the war.

3 March 1945.

Dinner last night for the Soviet Ambassador, Zarubin. Sat next to the Soviet Ambassadress and asked her how she liked Ottawa after Moscow. She replied with animation, 'Moscow wonderful, concerts wonderful, ballet wonderful, opera wonderful, Moscow big city – Ottawa nothing (*nichevo*) – cinema, cinema, cinema.'

21 April 1945.

On the train *en route* to San Francisco.[4] Luncheon with Mackenzie King and was charmed by the fat little conjurer with his flickering, shifty eyes and appliqué smile. He has eyes that can look like grey stones or can shine with amusement or film with sentiment. He chats away incessantly – he seems very pleased with himself, delightfully so, pleased with his own cleverness and with his own survival. He talked of the 'fun' of parliamentary tactics which cannot, he added regretfully, be so freely indulged in time of war. He talked of the conscription crisis and said that when it was viewed from the historical point of view its most significant feature would seem to be that the French-Canadian Ministers remained in the Government. That is what saved Canada's unity. I irritated him by remarking that our troops must be thoroughly tired by now. He replied, 'They have had two months' rest,' (*when?* I should like to know) and said, 'I knew during the recruitment crisis that they were due for that rest but this I could not reveal.'

He described Roosevelt's funeral at Hyde Park naturally and effectively, the silence in the garden and the rightness of the ceremony. He spoke affectionately but not over-sentimentally of Roosevelt himself, adding, 'When I last saw him I felt the end might come at any moment. When any subject came up about which he had a complex of worry he collapsed completely. When they called me from the White House to tell me of his death I did not even go to the telephone. I knew what had happened without being told.'

Talking of Mussolini he said, 'A remarkably finely-shaped head – the head of a Caesar – deep-set eyes full of intelligence. He did a lot of good – cleaned up a lot of corruption, but he had too much power for too long. They worship false gods in Europe – that is the trouble – Europe is too full of pictures of Napoleon and statues of the Caesars.'

26 April 1945. San Francisco.

The San Francisco Conference. San Francisco is as lively as a circus – the setting and the audience are much more amusing than the Conference performance. No one can resist the attraction of the town and the cheerfulness of its inhabitants. Nowhere could have been found in the world which is more of a contrast to the battered cities and tired people of Europe. The shock which I felt on arriving in the normality of Ottawa after England is nothing compared with what one would have felt coming from blacked-out London, Paris or Moscow to this holiday city. The Bay is a beautiful background, the sun shines perpetually, the streets are thronged, there are American sailors everywhere with their girls and this somehow adds to the musical comedy atmosphere. You expect them at any moment to break into song and dance, and the illusion is heightened because every shop and café wafts light music from thousands of radios. Colours too are of circus brightness, the flamboyant advertisements, the flags of all the Conference nations, the brilliant yellow taxis. This seems a technicolor world glossy with cheerful self-assurance. The people are full of curiosity about the Conference delegates. They crowd around them like the friendly, innocent Indians who crowded around the Spanish adventurers when they came to America and gaped at their armour and took their strings of coloured beads for real. The delegates are less picturesque than they should be to justify so much curiosity. There are the inevitable Arabs and some Indians in turbans who are worth the price of admission, and the Saudi Arabian prince who gleams like Valentino, but in general the delegates are just so many men in business suits with circular Conference pins in their buttonholes making them look as if they were here for the Elks' Convention. The exceptions are the Russians – they have stolen the show. People are impressed, excited, mystified and nervous about the Russians. Groups of wooden-looking peasant Soviet officers sit isolated (by their own choice) at restaurant tables and are stared at as if they were wild animals. They are painfully self-conscious, quiet, dignified – determined not to take a step which might make people laugh at the beautiful Soviet Union. The crowds throng outside the hotel to see Molotov, that square-head is much more of a sight than Eden. He is power. When he came into the initial plenary session he was followed by half-a-dozen husky gorillas from N.K.V.D. The town is full of stories about the Russians – that they have a warship laden with caviare in the harbour, etc., etc.

Meanwhile the local Hearst press conducts an unceasing campaign of anti-Russian mischief-making – doing their damnedest to start a new world war before this one is finished.

The Conference arrangements have so far been conducted with characteristic American inefficiency. The Opera House in the Veterans' Memorial Building where the sessions are to be held is like something out of a Marx Brothers' film. A mob of delegates, advisers and secretaries mill about in the halls asking questions and getting no answers. Where are they to register their credentials? Why have no offices been allotted to them? Where are the typewriters they were promised? To answer them are half-a-dozen State Department officials white with strain and exhaustion who have themselves not yet got office space, typewriters or the remotest idea of how the organisation is to work. Meanwhile, American sailors are shifting office desks through too-narrow doors. The San Francisco Boy Scouts are shouldering and ferreting their way among the crowd (what they are doing no one knows). Junior League young socialite matrons of San Francisco dressed up in various fancy uniforms lean beguilingly from innumerable booths marked 'Information', but as they charmingly confess they are just 'rehearsing' at present and can no more be expected to answer your questions than figures in a shop-window. All the babble of questions goes on to the accompaniment of hammering conducted in all keys by an army of workmen who are putting up partitions, painting walls, eating out of dinner-pails, whistling, sitting smoking with their legs outstretched in the overcrowded corridors. The only thing that is missing in this scene of pandemonium is Harpo Marx tearing through the mob in pursuit of a pair of disappearing female legs.

28 April 1945.

Second meeting of the plenary session again in the Opera House with powerful klieg lights shining down from the balcony into the eyes of the delegates, dazzling and irritating them. The session is declared open by Stettinius[5] who comes on to the dais chewing (whether gum or the remains of his lunch is a subject of speculation). His manner is one of misplaced assurance – unintentionally offensive. (Although the newspapers have described him as handsome, he looks like something out of the bird house at the zoo – I do not know just what – some bird that is trying to look like an eagle.) He makes the worst impression on the delegates. He reads his speech in a laypreacher's voice husky with corny emotion. The Chilean Foreign Minister reads a tribute to Roosevelt which being translated consists of an elaborate metaphor (which gets completely out of control as he goes along) comparing Roosevelt to a tree whose foliage spreads over the world which is struck by what appears to be the lightning of death but is actually the lightning stroke of victory so that its blossoms, while they may seem to wither, are brighter than ever.

Then comes along Wellington Koo of China, a natty, cool, little man in a 'faultless' business suit who reads a short speech about China's sufferings, written in careful English. After him Molotov mounts the tribune in an atmosphere of intense curiosity and some nervousness. He looks like an

employee in any *hôtel de ville* – one of those individuals who sit behind a wire grille entering figures
in a ledger, and when you ask them anything always
say 'no'. You forgive their rudeness because you
know they are underpaid and that someone bullies
them, and they must, in accordance with Nature's
unsavoury laws, 'take it out on' someone else. He
makes a very long speech in Russian which is translated first into English, then into French, and turns
out to be a pretty routine affair. The delegates are
by now bored and dispirited. Then Eden gets up
and at once the atmosphere changes – you can feel
the ripple of life run through the audience as he
speaks. It is not that he says anything really very
remarkable, but he sounds as if he meant it   as if
he believed in the importance of the Conference
and the urgency of the work to be done. He is quite
beyond his usual form, moved outside himself, perhaps, by exasperation at the flatness and unreality of
the proceedings.

I have developed a sort of rash on my chest and
rather all over. I am not disturbed by this, as I have
always been a great itcher, but the dolt of a hotel
doctor has diagnosed it as measles, which must be a
medical impossibility as I have had ordinary measles
once and German measles twice. However, the doctor is insistent that it is measles. He said he hoped I
knew that it was contagious and might spread rapidly
in the delegation. I propose to disregard this.

30 April 1945.

Miss Smithson, my secretary, says that agencies – the hotel authorities? or F.B.I.? – have put up a small photograph of me in the women's washroom with printed underneath, 'Avoid contact with the above person who is suffering from a contagious disease.' This will cramp my style in personal and diplomatic contacts.

22 May 1945.

The back-drop of San Francisco is gloriously irrelevant to the work of the Conference. The people of the town regard the whole proceedings with mixed benevolence and suspicion. Here is an opportunity to make the rest of the world as free, rich and righteous as the United States but it is hindered by the machinations of evil men. Of the uncertainties, worries and fears of the delegates they have no idea. They can swallow any amount of this sort of thing – 'The Conference is the greatest human gathering since the Last Supper.' In the end their appetite for ballyhoo is rather frightening.

But no one could resist the town itself or the luxuriantly beautiful countryside around it, or the spontaneity and chattiness of the inhabitants, or the beauty of the girls – who seem to unaccustomed eyes a race of Goddesses. The town is indeed remarkable for this tall radiant race of amazons; for thousands of sailors who all seem to be on leave with their pockets full and a roving eye for the girls – and for oceans of alcohol in which the happy population float. I suppose there are poor, sick and worried people here as everywhere else, but the impression is of people without a trouble in the world.

In the hotel dining-room a crooner with a voice like cream sings by request a number dedicated to Mr. and Mrs. Frank Lord because they are just married and on their honeymoon – cameras click – the happy couple bask – no self-consciousness – no sneers – it's 'a very lovely thought'. At the end of a drunken evening at the Bohemian Club's annual frolic the compère suggests that we should stand and sing two verses of Onward Christian Soldiers 'honouring our boys in the Pacific' – the audience responds without a blush.

The day is spent in a series of committee meetings which are teaching me several things – the necessity for patience. It is wonderful to see quick-minded men sitting quite still hour after hour listening to people saying at almost infinite length things which could be said in a sentence or two. One becomes, I suppose, inured to boredom. And in combination with this patience the old hands have great quickness. They have been playing this game so long that they know instinctively by now when and how to play the rules of committee procedure or to catch the point of some quite discreet amendment to a motion. They are always on the alert for such things even when they seem to be half-asleep. All this is rather fascinating to a tyro. These are the tricks of the trade. Most men of my age and length of service know them well already.

I mentioned my alleged measles (now vanished) to a newspaperman as a joke. Tonight there is a headline in one of the evening papers, 'Measles at Conference Hotel. Will it spread to the Russian Delegation?' It is true that the Russians are installed on the floor above us in this hotel, but I have no contact with them of any kind.

23 May 1945.

The Conference atmosphere is thick with alarm and despondency about Russia. Wherever two or three are gathered together in the hotel bedrooms and sitting-rooms, where more unbuttoned conversation is permissible there you can bet that the subject is the U.S.S.R. – speculation about their intention, argument as to the best way of dealing with them – whether to be tough and, if so, when – gloomy realisation that by unscrupulous conference tactics they may be courting and perhaps winning the favour of the 'working masses'. This fear of Russia casts its long shadow over the Conference. Meanwhile some of the Latin American and Middle Eastern States, by their verbose silliness and irresponsible sniping, almost induce one to believe that there is a good deal to be said for a Great Power dictatorship. But the Great Power representatives have no eloquent, authoritative or persuasive spokesman in the more important committees.

They repeat, parrot fashion, 'Trust the Security Council. Do nothing to injure unanimity.' There are no outstanding speakers – Evatt of Australia has ability – Berendsen of New Zealand has eloquence of a homespun sort – Rollin, the Belgian, has a clever, satirical mind (I take names at random) – but there is no one of whom you say – a great man – and few indeed of whom you say – a fine speaker.

The British Delegation seems pretty thin and undistinguished now that Eden and the other senior Cabinet ministers have gone. Cranborne[6] is skilful and authoritative in committee – Halifax does not attend – Cadogan seems a tired, mediocre *fonctionnaire*. Webster is always at his elbow with an impressive memory (he can quote the documents of the Congress of Vienna, of the Paris Conference, of the Dumbarton Oaks meeting). His heroes are Castlereagh and Wellington. He takes a donnish pleasure in argumentation and in snubbing people. An excellent adviser – but he should not be allowed his head in policy matters – I do not know if he is – one sometimes sees his hand. The delegation is weak on the economic and social side. There is a grave lack of authority – of men of solid experience, wisdom and moderation, who inform a committee – not so much by what they say as by what they are. Then there is the lack of any representation of the English internationalists or those who have devoted themselves to oppressed peoples and to social causes – that whole humanitarian and social side of

English activity goes unrepresented. There were representatives of it, but they have gone home – the brunt of the British representation is borne by a little group thinking in terms of political and military power and with not much feeling for public opinion. As they get more tired they may pull a serious gaffe. They produce no ideas which can attract other nations and are not much fitted to deal with Commonwealth countries.

American policy, or perhaps I should say more narrowly, American tactics in this Conference are similar to British – like the British they hew closely to the party line of support for the Great Power veto while allowing the impression to be disseminated among the smaller countries that they do so reluctantly, that their hearts are in the right place but that they dare not say so for fear of the Russians bolting the organisation. One incidental result of this line which the British and Americans may not contemplate is to increase the prestige of Russia. The United States delegation as a whole is no more impressive than the British. There does not seem to be much attempt to understand the viewpoint of the smaller nations or to produce reasoned arguments to meet their objections. On the other hand, the Americans are extremely susceptible to pressure from the Latin Americans who are not doing at all badly out of this Conference. The only American advisers I know are the State Department Team – shifty-eyed little Alger Hiss who has a professionally informal and friendly manner – which fails to conceal a resentful and suspicious nature said to be very anti-British – Ted Achilles – slow, solid, strong physically as an ox, a careful, good-tempered negotiator and a very good fellow – I should not think much influence on policy.

The U.S.S.R. have achieved a most unfavourable reputation in the Committees. This does not result from dislike for the methods or personalities of individual Russians – so far as the Conference is concerned there are no individual Russians – they all say exactly the same thing (and needless to say this goes for the Ukrainian and Bielo-Russkis). All make the same brief colourless statements – every comma approved by Moscow – from which every trace of the personality of the speaker has been rigorously excluded. Their reputation is one of solid stonewalling and refusal to compromise. On the other hand, they are continually blackmailing other governments by posing as the protectors of the masses against reactionary influence. This they have done so effectively that it is quite possible for them to produce a record at the Conference which would show them battling for the oppressed all over the world. The insincerity of these tactics is patent to those who see them at close quarters, but will not be so to the public for whom they are designed. They have great political flair – envisage every question not on its merits but entirely from the political point of view. This causes acute distress to (a) the legalistically-minded Latin Americans, (b) all social crusaders and liberal internationalists who see 'power politics' invading every aspect of the new organisation, the social, humanitarian and even purely administrative.

The intellectual defence of the Dumbarton Oaks[7] proposals has been left to Wellington Koo, which is rather hard on him, as he had nothing to do with drafting them. I sat opposite him and he fascinated me – he looks like a little lizard, darting lizard eyes and nose down close to his papers. When he speaks he displays a remarkable collection of *tics nerveux* – he blinks rapidly and convulsively, sniffs spasmodi-cally, clasps and unclasps his immaculately mani-cured little hands, pulls at the lapels of his coat and continually removes and then readjusts his two pairs of spectacles. This pantomime does not in the least mean that he is nervous of the work in hand – he is a very experienced professional diplomat, quick-minded, ingenious and conciliatory. But, of course, he has not – any more than any of the other Great Powers' delegates – the moral authority, eloquence and vigour which would be needed to carry the Conference – it would take a Roosevelt or Churchill to do that – or perhaps Smuts. The Chinese are an endearing delegation, polite and humorous – but then are they really a Great Power?

The French are among the disappointments of this Conference. The Big Power representatives, however undistinguished individually, *do* represent

314

Power and so carry weight. The French are in the position of having to depend on their tradition, their professionalism and that assurance of tough and violent precision of language which have always been at their command in international gatherings. But it is just this assurance that they lack. The French delegation here reinforce the painful impression that I formed in Paris – they seem to be *détraqués*. You do not feel that they have France, *la grande nation*, behind them. They are full of *petits soins* and handshakes to other delegates. They are full of schemes and combinations and suspicions. But there is no steadiness or clarity in their policy. They have no one who is a connecting link with the past and who still retains faith and vitality. The national continuity has been broken. They seem just a collection of clever, amiable, young Frenchmen – and old Paul Boncour is too old and too tired – so is André Siegfried. In fact, you can see the effects of fatigue in the drained faces of almost all the European delegates. Europe (I do not count Russia) is not making much of a showing at this Conference.

In our own delegation Norman Robertson and Hume Wrong are the two most influential senior officials. There could hardly be a greater contrast than that between them. Hume (under whom I worked when he was Counsellor at our Legation in Washington), pale and fine featured, stroking the back of his head with a rapid gesture which suggests mounting impatience. He inspires alarm on first encounter – an alarm which could be justified as he is totally intolerant of muddle, inanity or sheer brute stupidity. He has style in everything from the way he wears his coat to the prose of his memoranda. He is a realist who understands political forces better, unfortunately, than he does politicians themselves.

Norman understands them very well and has influence with the Prime Minister, but what does not Norman understand? His mind is as capacious as his great sloping frame. He has displacement, as they say of ocean liners, displacement physical and intellectual and he is wonderful company with his ironic asides, his shafts of wisdom and his sighs of resignation.

5 June 1945.

We are still tormented by the feeling in our deal-ings with the Russians there *may* be an element of genuine misunderstanding on their side and that some of their suspicions of some of our motives may not be so very wide of the mark. They on their side seem untroubled by any such scruples. They keep us permanently on the defensive and we wallow about clumsily like some marine monster being plagued by a faster enemy (a whale with several harpoons already in its side). Yet they do not want or mean war.

The struggle for power plays itself out in the Conference committees. Every question before the committees becomes a test of strength between the Russians and their satellites and the rest of the world. The other Great Powers vote glumly with the Russians and send junior members of their delegations to convey to us their discomfiture and apologies. This situation reproduces itself over matters which in themselves do not seem to have much political content. But to the Russians everything is political whether it is something to do with the secretariat of the new organisation or the changing of a comma in the Declaration of the General Principles.

Committee 1 of the Commission, on which I sit as adviser, deals with the preamble to the Charter of the United Nations (composed of pious aspirations) and the chapters concerned with the Purposes and Principles of the Organisation. It is presided over by a Ukrainian chairman, Manuilsky, said to be the brains of the Communist Party in the Ukraine. My first impression of him was of a humorous and polite old gentleman – an *ancien régime* landowner perhaps. He speaks good French. But I was wrong in everything except the humour – he is quite ruthlessly rude, exceedingly intelligent and moves so fast in committee tactics that he leaves a room full of experienced parliamentarians breathless. It cannot be said that he breaks the rules of procedure – rather he interprets them with great cleverness to suit his ends. And his principal end is to hurry these chapters through the committee without further debate.

6 June 1945.

We had nearly seven hours on end in our Committee on Purposes and Principles. The Chairman, Manuilsky, gave us a touch of the knout when the Latin Americans were just spreading their wings for flights of oratory. He rapped on the table with his chairman's gavel and said, 'Gentlemen, we must speed up the work of the Committee. I propose that no one shall leave this hall until the preamble and the first chapter of the Charter are voted.' The delegates gazed ruefully at their blotters – this meant cutting all dinner dates. Yet no one dared to falter in the 'sacred task'. Paul Gore-Booth, the British delegate, sprang to his feet and said in tones of emotion, 'Mr. Chairman I cannot promise that I shall be physically able to remain so long in this hall without leaving it.' Manuilsky looked at him sternly, 'I say to the British representative that there are in this hall men older than you are, and if they can stay here you must also.' So we settled down to hour after hour of debate.

We were after all discussing the principles of the New World Order. The room was full of professional orators who were ravening to speak and speak again. Latin American Foreign Ministers hoped to slide in an oblique reference to some of their local vendettas disguised in terms of the Rights of Nations. The Egyptian representative was hoping to see his way clear to take a crack at the Anglo-Egyptian Treaty under some phrase about the necessity for 'flexibility in the interpretation of international obligations'. The Syrian delegate saw an opportunity to embarrass the French. The representatives of the Colonial Powers were junior delegates (their chiefs were dining) who were frightened that any reference to 'justice' or 'human rights' might conceal a veiled attack on the colonial system. All afternoon and all evening until twelve o'clock at night we argued about the principles that must guide the conduct of men and nations. By eleven o'clock there were many haggard faces around the table. The room had got very hot and smelly – dozens of stout politicians sweating profusely in a confined space – outside the street-cars (and San Francisco is a great place for street-cars) rattled noisily and still the speeches went on. The Egyptian delegate was indefatigable in interpolations. He seemed to bounce to his feet on india-rubber buttocks, 'A point of order, Mr. Chairman' and he would fix his monocle and survey his helpless victims. The Peruvian was another inexhaustible plague; he was a professional lecturer who kept remarking, 'The Peruvian delegation regard this aspect of the question as very grave indeed, in fact fundamental.' Then he would remove his reading spectacles, put on his talking spectacles, brush the forelock back from his forehead and get into his stride. But it was the Norwegian who moved me to homicide by making lengthy interventions in an obstinate, bleating voice. However, thanks to the knout, thanks to the ruthless, surgical operations of the Chairman, we finished our task in time. The committee was littered with punctured egos, and snubbed statesmen glowered at each other across the tables. The eminent political figures and distinguished jurists of half the world had been rated by the Chairman like schoolboys; but we had finished on time.

12 June 1945.

Lunch in the country with rich, friendly easy-going Californians – a cool, roomy house – none of the stiff, interior-decorated look of so many expensive houses in the East. Californians do not seem to treat their houses very seriously. They are places to sleep and refuges from the heat of the sun. These people seem to swim through life, carried along effortlessly by their good nature and good health. One can hardly believe that they have ever been scared or snubbed or 'put in their place' or that anyone has ever exposed them to irony. There were three children bathing in the pool – perfect little physical specimens with nice, rich, easy-going, good-looking, sensible parents – what a way to grow up!

15 June 1945.

Last week I saw an advertisement in one of the San Francisco newspapers which described the attractions of 'a historic old ranch home now transformed into a luxury hotel situated in a beautiful valley in easy reach of San Francisco'. What a delightful escape, I thought, from the pressures of the Conference! Why not spend the week-end there? I succeeded in talking my colleagues, Norman and Hume and Jean Désy, the Canadian Adviser on Latin American Affairs, into this project, and our party was joined by a friend of Jean Désy, a French Ambassador, a senior and distinguished diplomat attached to the French Delegation. Last Saturday we all set forth by car in a holiday spirit to savour the delights of old-style ranch life in California as advertised to include 'gourmet meals, horseback riding and music in an exclusive atmosphere.' It seemed an eminently suitable setting for this little group of overworked and fastidious *conferenciers*. As we approached in the late afternoon up the long avenue, we saw the ranch house set amidst a bower of trees, but when we debouched at the entrance instead of the subdued welcome of a luxury hotel we were brusquely but cheerily propelled by a stout and thug-like individual towards a swaying tollgate which opened to admit us one by one on payment in advance for the period of our stay. Once in the entrance hall we found ourselves in the midst of an animated crowd, but what was unexpected was that all the men were sailors and young sailors at that, while the women were equally young and some strikingly luscious. This throng, exchanging jokes, playful slaps on bottoms and swigs out of beer cans, filtered off from time to time in pairs to mount the noble staircase leading to the rooms above. Our diplomatic quintet stood together waiting for guidance among the jostling throng and were soon the objects of remarks. 'Who the hell are those old guys?' Finally, seeing that no one was coming to our rescue we set off up the stairs, luggage in hand to inspect our rooms. Mounting floor by floor we found all the bedrooms in a state of active and noisy occupation, until we reached the top floor where we encountered a large female of the squaw variety. As she appeared to be in charge of operations we enquired for our rooms to find that only three rooms were available for the five of us.

It was decided among us that the French Ambassador should have a room to himself, while Jean Désy and Hume shared one and Norman and I the other. In our room we found an exhausted maid slapping at some dirty-looking pillows as she replaced them in position. 'This is the fifth time I have made up this bed today,' she observed. 'Are you two men sharing this room?' With a look beyond surprise she withdrew. Norman seemingly not in the least disconcerted sank with a sigh into the only available chair and addressed himself to the evening paper. The other members of our party were less philosophical. Hume and Jean appearing in the doorway rounded sharply on me. 'Why had I lured them into this brothel? Was this my idea of a joke?' I suggested that we should all be better for food and drink and we descended to the dining-room, a vast, panelled interior already packed with couples dancing to a blaring radio. After a lengthy wait we were squeezed into a corner table where we were attended by a motherly-looking waitress. 'Who are all these girls?' I asked her. 'And why all these sailors?' 'Well, I guess you might call it a kind of meeting place for the boys off the ships and the girls who work near here in an aircraft factory.' Meanwhile the French Ambassador was beginning to show signs of controlled irritation as he studied the menu that had been handed to him. Adjusting his spectacles he read out, 'Tomato soup, hamburger delights, cheeseburgers, Hawaiian-style ham with pineapple.' 'For me,' he announced, 'I shall have a plain omelette.' At this Jean Désy, in an attempt to lighten the gloom which was settling over our little party, clapped his hands together and in an almost boisterous tone called out to the waitress, 'The wine list at once – we shall have champagne.' 'Wine list,' she said, 'I do not know about any list but we have some lovely pink wine – it is sparkling, too.' 'Bring it,' said Jean, 'and lots of it.' It was not bad – both sweet and tinny but it helped. For a few moments our spirits improved and we began to laugh at our predicament. Then came the omelette. The Ambassador just touched it with the prong of his fork and leaned back in his chair with an air of incredulity. 'This an omelette!' He raised his shoulders with a shrug to end all shrugs.

At this Jean Désy, perhaps stimulated by the wine or pricked by embarrassment at having exposed his French colleague to such an experience, seized the plate with the omelette upon it and said, 'I shall complain to the chef myself about this outrage.' With this he hurled himself into the mob of dancers and made for a swinging door leading to the kitchen. Some uneasy moments passed at our table, then the swinging door swung open. Jean still holding the plate with the omelette upon it was backing away before an enormous Negro who was bellowing above the music, 'Get out of my kitchen. Who the hell do you think you are? Bugger off! Bugger off! Bugger off!' Jean returned to our table. 'I shall report him,' he said – but it was difficult to know to whom. Soon afterwards we repaired to our rooms. As I left the dining-room I heard a girl say to her sailor companion, 'Those are a bunch of old fairies sleeping together – the maid told me.' The sailor spat, not actually at us, but on the floor quite audibly.

The night was an uneasy one for me. I was kept restlessly awake by the beery hoots of laughter and the moans and murmurs of passion from the next room. Norman settled into his bed and slept peaceably with his deaf ear uppermost.

When I looked out of the window in the early morning the sun was shining, and a troop of sailors and their girls mounted on miscellaneous horses were riding by towards the adjoining fields, thus proving that horseback riding was as advertised one of the facilities of the ranch. Two small figures, Jean Désy and the French Ambassador, the latter sealed into a tight-looking overcoat, were proceeding side by side down the avenue. I later learned that they were on their way to Mass at a neighbouring church.

By mutual agreement for which no words were needed our party left the ranch before luncheon and returned to San Francisco.

On the way back in the car the French Ambassador raised the possibility that one of the assiduous gossip writers of the San Francisco press might learn where we had spent the week-end and he asked what effect this would be likely to have on the prestige of our respective delegations and indeed on our own reputations. My own colleagues reassured him by saying that in the event of publicity the episode could be attributed to my misleading them owing to my innate folly and vicious proclivities. This seemed to satisfy him.

18 June 1945.

The Conference is on its last lap. The delegates – many of them – are quite punch-drunk with fatigue. Meetings start every day at 9 a.m. and go on until midnight. In addition, we are having a heat wave. The committee rooms are uncomfortably hot and the commission meetings in the Opera House are an inferno. The heat generated by the enormous klieg lights adds to this and the glare drives your eyes back into your head.

We are in a feverish scramble to get through the work – an unhealthy atmosphere in which we are liable to push things through for the sake of getting them finished. The Russians are taking advantage of this state of affairs to reopen all sorts of questions in the hope that out of mere weakness we shall give in to them. Their tone and manner seem daily to become more openly truculent and antagonistic.

Once the labours of the committees are finished, the Articles they have drafted and the reports they have approved are put before the Co-ordinating Committee who plunge into an orgy of revision. There is no pleasanter sport for a group of highly intelligent and critical men than to have delivered into their hands a collection of botched-up, badly-drafted documents and be asked to pull them to pieces and to point out the faults of substance and form. This could go on forever.

However hot, tired and bad-tempered the other delegates may become, Halifax remains cool and Olympian and makes benevolent, cloudy speeches which soothe but do not satisfy. Senator Connally of the U.S. delegation roars at his opponent waving his arms and sweating. It is somehow reassuring to come out from the committee meetings into the streets and see the people in whose name we are arguing so fiercely and who do not give a damn how the Charter reads. Sailors hand in hand with their girls – (this is a great town for walking hand in hand) on their way to a movie or a dance hall.

If the people were let into the committee meetings they would have broken up this Conference long ago.

Alice was sitting across the table from me today at the committee meeting, in glowing looks from her week-end in the country and wearing an exceptionally low-cut flowered dress. I was not the only one to be distracted from the dissertation of our pedantic El Salvadorean rapporteur.

Every day going to and from the Conference we pass a Picasso picture in an art shop window – two elongated and distorted forms are in silent communion. They gaze at each other in trance-like stillness. I find that by looking for a few minutes at this picture I can get into a sort of dope dream.

19 June 1945.

The Soviet delegates have got very little goodwill out of this Conference. They use aggressive tactics about every question large or small. They remind people of Nazi diplomatic methods and create, sometimes needlessly, suspicions and resentment. They enjoy equally making fools of their opponents and their supporters. Slyness, bullying and bad manners are the other features of their Conference behaviour.

Their system has some unfortunate results from their point of view. They have no elbow-room in committee tactics – they cannot vary their method to allow for a change in mood and tempo of the Conference. They are paralysed by the unexpected. They always have to stall and cable home for instructions. It is unfortunate from our point of view as well as theirs that they should have made such a bad showing, for I think they are proposing to make a serious effort to use the organisation and are not out to wreck it.

28 June 1945.

Back in Ottawa the Conference is over. It is going to be a little disconcerting at first living alone again after our group existence in San Francisco. The hotel sitting-room which Norman Robertson and Hume Wrong shared was a meeting place for members of our delegation and there was a perpetual flow of drinks on tap. There we foregathered to talk Conference gossip. The pace of the Conference got more and more hectic towards the end. Meetings would end at four or five a.m., when we would fall into bed and drag ourselves up three or four hours later. It also became increasingly difficult to relate the Conference to other events going on in the world and form an estimate of the real importance in the scheme of things of what we were doing at San Francisco. While we were there the war against Germany was won, the occupation of Germany took place, the Russians installed themselves in Prague and in Vienna and made their first bid for a port on the Adriatic and bases in the Straits. We were preoccupied with the Battle of the Veto and with the tussles over the powers of the General Assembly and the provisions for amending the Charter. How much were these mere paper battles? How much was the

San Francisco Conference a smokescreen behind which the Great Powers took up their positions? These doubts were floating about in the backs of our minds but we had not much time for doubts – the daily time-table was too gruelling.

At any rate, if the Conference was a gigantic bluff, it bluffed the participants – at least some of them.

The final public sessions were decidedly too good to be true. The Opera House was packed with pleased, excited, well-fed people. There was a feeling of a gala performance. On the floodlit stage ranged in front of the flags of the United Nations were standing hand-picked specimens of each branch of the United States Armed Forces – very pretty girls from the Women's Forces made up for the floodlighting and wore very becoming uniforms – soldiers and sailors preserving even on this occasion an air of loose-limbed sloppiness.

One after another the speakers mounted the rostrum and addressed us – most of them in their native languages. The text of the speeches in English had been circulated to the audience, but this was hardly necessary as we knew what they would say, and they all said it – in Chinese, Arabic, French and Russian we were told that mankind was embarking on another effort to organise the world so that peace should reign. We were told that the success of the Conference showed that this ideal could be attained if unity was preserved – that we owed it to the living and to the dead to devote all our efforts to this end. Almost all the speeches worked in a reference to the inspiring example of Franklin D. Roosevelt and a flowery tribute to Stettinius (rather wasted as he resigned next day).

It all went off very well – there was really nothing to complain of – no outrageous bit of vulgarity or juke-box sentimentality. Even that great ape, Stettinius, was rather subdued and contented himself with grinning and signalling to his acquaintances in the audience during the playing of the United States National Anthem. The speakers were dignified and sincere – Halifax, Wellington Koo, Smuts, Paul-Boncour – all spoke out of long experience and were impressive. True, they said nothing, but this seemed an occasion when nothing was better than too much. President Truman made a sensible, undistinguished speech – just too long. (He looks like a sparrowy, little, old, small-town, American housewife who could shut the door very firmly in the face of the travelling salesmen and tramps.) He got the biggest hand from the audience and after him Halifax. They fell completely for Halifax's gilt-edged 'niceness'. What with tributes to the Great Deceased and bouquets to each other and commendatory remarks on the good work accomplished, the whole thing reminded one of speech day at school. In front of me the Argentine Ambassador and his pretty daughter applauded with polite enthusiasm. There were only two cracks in the surface – one was when Masaryk, the Czech Foreign Minister, said at the close of his speech, 'Let us for God's sake hear less talk of the next world war.' And the other (for me at least) was when Stettinius asked us to stand 'in silent memory of the dead in this war whose sacrifice had made this Conference possible'. I suppose it had to be said – it sounded as if we were thanking Lady Bountiful for lending her garden 'without which this bazaar would not have been possible'. As a matter of fact I did think of some of the dead – of Victor Gordon-Ives, who wanted to go on living and to enjoy country-house culture, collect beautiful things and make jokes with his friends – of John Rowley and Gavin Rainnie and the other Canadians whose prompt reaction would have been 'Balls to you, brother!' Still, I suppose it had to be said, but not by Stettinius in the San Francisco Opera House on a gala evening to the polite applause of the Argentine Ambassador.

5 July 1945. Halifax, Nova Scotia.

Back in my own country among my own people – how different from the easy-going superficial Californians. The surface layer here as everywhere is Americanisation – the climate that extends over the whole of this continent – the whole Anglo-Saxon world – babbitry but here it is a peculiar brand of babbitry without optimism, and it is not deep. Underneath is a queer compound of philosophical pessimism, of rooted old prejudice, of practical kindliness to the neighbour and the unfortunate, of unkindness towards the prosperous, something which has been ironed out in the prosperous fat lands of Upper Canada but which still grows on this rocky soil.

For me, Halifax is full of what Elizabeth calls 'mined areas'. As I am walking in its streets I am suddenly assailed by memories coming out of a past which is so far away as to be almost meaningless – a street smell, the sharp angle of a tall roof, the cracked, dark red paint on the shingle of a wall – they send me signals that I cannot read. I walk the sunny streets under the trees – everything registers, reminds, torments with hidden hints, sly remembrances, elusive little airs of memories. I am easily bewildered and tired here – it is too much to fit together, and while I observe the changes, the disappearance of shops and houses there surges a tide laden with old scraps – empty fruit husks, an uneasy wave that goes to and fro, the sensation of change, of time of change – comes so close that it is stifling.

7 July 1945.

Went to lunch at the Halifax Club. An old man sitting in his armchair said, 'When I get the fish smell coming up from the wharves and the oil smell blown across the harbour from Dartmouth and the smell of the nearby brothels, I ask myself whether I live in a very savoury neighbourhood.' The brothels

are usually ancient houses in Hollis and Water
Streets solidly built in the late eighteenth century,
once the homes of merchants, now encrusted with
filth, infested with bed-bugs and snotty-nosed brats.
Little girls of twelve and thirteen are already in the
business, with painted faces and gyrating bottoms –
they walk the streets in twos and threes giving a gig-
gle for a leer. This part of Halifax is the old port-
town shortly to be swept away. It is not far from
Hogarth's Gin Alley. In the midst of these smells of
fish, wharf and brothel lives my maiden cousin,
Susie, in the last of the old houses to keep its character. On its outer wall is a mildewed brass plate
with 'A' engraved in flowery longhand upon it. The
glass panel in the door is protected by a fortification
of twisted wire-work to prevent drunken lascars
from breaking in. This is a last outpost of gentility.
It has an obdurate defender. Susie's face is the
colour of a yellowing letter left in a desk. Her manner is gentle, her obstinacy does not appear on the
surface. She would be a happy martyr for her obsessions – she loves resistance – she is the woman every
underground movement is looking for. Thumbscrews
would avail her enemies nothing – and she sees her
enemies everywhere – the Catholic Church, the
American Nation, Modern Commercialism – she tilts
at all of them. As for the squalor around her, it shall
be kept at bay. It is provided in her will that this old
house is to be destroyed at her death. Meanwhile she
writes in her childish hand long rigmaroles of family

gossip to cousins in England or in Bermuda. She sits under the Copley portrait of the loyalist great-great-great-great-grandfather Byles. (Although practically penniless she refused to sell it to the Boston Art Gallery for $20,000 lest it should fall into the hands of the Americans.) She looks out between the yellow lace curtains at the life of Gin Alley and knows herself as strong as the drunken bullies or the hardened tarts.

8 July 1945. Wolfville, Nova Scotia.

This time it is different being in Wolfville. Perhaps I have been too keyed up and cannot relax, or else I am too well, and this place is only ideal for invalids and the old. The weather has been close and airless with low, suffocating, grey skies. There is to be an eclipse of the sun tomorrow and people say this queer weather has something to do with it.

I miss Elizabeth more and more. When I am working I banish her from my conscious mind by thinking of something that has to be thought of first because it must be tackled at once, so I manage to keep her image at arm's length but now that I am idle thoughts of her besiege me.

The main street of Wolfville which before seemed so idyllic has lost its charm – in fact it is stifling to me. So many old women spying at the passer-by from behind their muslin curtains – the tight, taut atmosphere of a small town waiting for an event, a scandal, a false step, anything around which to circle and scream like hungry seagulls. It makes me feel absurdly sulky, restless and adolescent, yet the people are very kind. It is just that the place gives me a mild attack of the disease of my youth – claustrophobia.

I wonder if the returned soldiers suffer from this disease. I saw two of them today sitting somewhat disconsolately in their hot uniforms on a park bench. What do they make of the home town after months of waiting and fear and exhilaration, after the wild welcoming crowds in the Brussels streets, after the years of their youth in Sussex towns and villages?

9 July 1945.

This is the season for the smells of cut hay and the sweetness of clover – the wild roses are out everywhere. I rush out of this house on a sudden walk streaking along Main Street past the neat white houses with their little lawns and pergolas and right up the hill among the orchards. From there you look down over the dike lands to Minas Basin.

Mother and I spend a good deal of our time with the Sherwoods who are as much a local product as the apples they grow in their own orchards. Gertie is earthy Nova Scotian – she can hardly open her mouth without some localism popping out. 'Some person told me' is the beginning of half her gossip, and 'Small town – small talk' she says of her own conversation. She notices that the clergyman is wearing a silk surplice instead of a linen one and does not believe that it is because of any wartime shortage of linen – no – it is because his wife thinks silk looks grander. She says of the bank manager's wife, 'She calls on everyone, she is the sort of woman who never gets offended.' (This is a devastating comment, as in her view people with proper pride are always in a state of 'being offended' with some of their neighbours.)

11 July 1945.

Main Street of Wolfville. The brownstone of the Post Office, the greens and reds of the municipal geranium beds. The street itself is still and dusty in the sun – awnings are down over the closed shops. It is Wednesday afternoon – early-closing day – an occasional car passes driven at a sleepy tempo or carts and horses moving at a walking pace. Twos and threes of small boys in overalls with bare feet scour the sidewalks in desultory search for sensation. Men in shirt-sleeves sit on the doorsteps – a woman in a white and mauve polka-dot dress passes with a basket of strawberries under her arm. The pulse of the small town beats slowly, rhythmically, steadily – a sense of summer contentment fills the streets.

15 July 1945.

The summer perfection of Wolfville is too much for me – there are too many smells – the rich smell of clover and the juicy, verdant, almost sexy smell of the new-cut grass in the fields behind the house, the wild roses and arbutus, the poppies and the peonies.

There are breezes all day long – nothing seems to stand still for a moment – the grass, trees and flowers shiver and skimmer in the wind and sun. I get hay fever from the smells. My eyes ache from the brilliance of summer colours – the breezes make me lascivious – the beauty makes me restless – there is nothing peaceful about this summer countryside. This indecent display of charms is a standing invitation to lust and venery.

4 September 1945.

Back to Ottawa on a train crowded with returning soldiers. Train after train travels across Canada from east to west laden with them, dropping them off by threes and fours at small towns and in their hundreds at the big cities. The train windows are crowded with their sunburned, excited faces. They lean out in their shirt-sleeves, whistling at the girls on the station platforms, making unflattering jokes about Mackenzie King. We passed through one little station where there were a few mugwumps standing about on the platform staring bemusedly at the train and a group of soldiers on the train began themselves to cheer, 'Hurray! Give the boys a welcome.' The stations are crowded with them striding about self-consciously – men of the world – having proved something about themselves that is plainly to be seen in their sun-paled divisional patches and the ribbons on their chests – the 1939-43 Star, the Africa Star, the France and Germany award, the Voluntary Service Ribbon.

The women look at them fondly, the men respectfully and perhaps enviously. Everyone says, 'It is a big moment for them.' These are our heroes – the 'Flowers of the Nation's Manhood', etc. This is the role – every man his own Hotspur – and they play it to advantage; good-humoured, cynical, knowing their way around – they make the other men look tame and 'stay-at-home'.

The streets are fuller every day of demobilised soldiers. They wear pinned to their civilian coats emblems of overseas service and rows of ribbons, but you could not fail to recognise them anyway – the straight up and down army back which they will never entirely lose – the sunburned necks and the new clothes. They go in for sporting jackets fresh off the hook – perhaps a souvenir of English fashions.

7 September 1945. Ottawa.

An office day – I get up with a slight hangover but feeling pretty healthy and not gloomy – not any-thing – just like a bloody clock wound up to run for another twelve hours and off I go to my office in the Department of External Affairs. I read the papers obediently skipping the story about the gangsters to concentrate on Keynes's statement on economic policy. I cast a wary eye at the social notes. I get down to work. All morning a stream of interesting and informative telegrams and despatches from missions abroad comes pouring across my desk. I am tempted to read them all and to try to understand what is really happening, but if I do that I have not time to draft answers to the most immediate telegrams and despatches crying out for instructions. I must skim through everything with my mind concentrated on immediate practical implications. If I try to be objective and to comprehend all the issues I am lost. I draft telegrams and speeches under pressure, short-term considerations uppermost – 'Will the Prime Minister sign this?' – 'Are we not too short of personnel to be represented at this or that international meeting?' This is the way policy is made on a hand-to-mouth basis out of an overworked official by a tired politician with only half his mind on the subject.

12 September 1945.

Sally Gordon-Ives is here on a visit. She has never recovered from Victor's death in the war. She said, 'I suppose he was lucky to be killed young when he was at the height of his enjoyment. Anything is better than being dead in life.'

I wish the dead could use our bodies, feel our sensations, see with our eyes. If Victor's spirit lingers in some limbo I should like to lend him this apparatus for living and when I have been dead a little while I should like someone to do the same for me.

22 September 1945.

How devastating it would be to find celibacy bearable – to get fairly comfortably into the habits of chastity and then to find it too much trouble to get out of it again.

I have just been reading a despatch about the difficulties of life in Moscow. I must say it sounds very much like Ottawa – 'For instance, the difficulty of finding a mistress and making arrangements for cherishing her.' But the pressure of work keeps me riveted to this spot under an uneasy spell. Just as I get to the point of saying to myself that I cannot stand this life a moment longer a crisis blows up – I am brought in – something has to be done in a hurry – a formula has to be found – a way of getting around things devised a situation met. I am on a stretch – my will and brain and judgement are called upon. I live on this stimulus.

23 September 1945. Ottawa.

I have come up against a blank wall. There is nothing to do but turn around and face things. I feel myself hardening. I will not be one of life's casualties, nor just a sympathetic character. Middle-age is the time when one is supposed to concentrate on the world's game, care about making a grand slam and watch other people's play. The game has always interested me but never enough to overcome my love of talking and of sensuous perception, but now I am bloody well going to have my fling at it. The trouble is that it is only for two or three days at a time that I can deceive myself that I do care about this success game. Then I long to throw my cards in and clear out.

EPILOGUE

The diarist did not 'throw in his cards and clear out'. On the contrary he played them for all he was worth. His diplomatic career is written in the sands of *Who's Who*. He was to become Canada's Representative to the United Nations which he had seen founded at San Francisco, to go as Ambassador to Washington where he had served his apprentice-ship, and finally as High Commissioner to the United Kingdom to find himself back again in the grand room at Canada House where standing under the chandelier Vincent Massey had announced to his staff the outbreak of World War II.

He had one undeserved piece of good fortune in a happy marriage. His wife, Sylvia, during more than twenty-five years has encouraged and supported him with her wit and wisdom in everything he has under-taken, including the publication of this book.

The diaries continue – compulsion dies hard.

ENDNOTES

1937-1938

1 Secretary at the British Embassy in Washington, now Tutor at Trinity College, Cambridge.

2 This house and its estate were presented for public use by former Ambassador Robert Woods Bliss; the conference which made the plans for the United Nations was held there in August 1944.

3 Levi Ziegler Leiter was a self-made man who amassed a fortune. His daughter married Lord Curzon and his granddaughter Sir Oswald Mosley.

4 The house now belonged to Gladys Vanderbilt who was married to Count Laszlo Szechenyi, Hungarian Minister in Washington.

5 The beautiful Magee sisters, Willa and Nora, decorated and enlivened the Legation as successive social secretaries to Lady Marler.

1939

1 I was acting as liaison officer between Canada House and the Foreign Office.

2 My mother was in England on one of her annual visits from Canada. While in London she took a flat in the same house in Tregunter Road in which I had a room.

3   The Canadian Government was supplied with a selection of telegrams exchanged between the Foreign Office and British diplomatic posts abroad.

4   The widow of Lord Oxford and Asquith, who had been Prime Minister 1908-16. She was a formidable personality in London political and social life.

5   The country house in Sussex of the Earl of Bessborough. He had been Governor-General of Canada from 1931-35. Moyra was his daughter.

6   Sir Samuel Hoare, who had been forced to resign as Foreign Secretary over the Hoare-Laval Pact in December 1935, had been brought back into the government the following June, and was now Home Secretary.

7   Travel-writer and aesthete, author of several books including *The Road to Oxiana*, killed at sea during the war.

8   The 5th Baron Redesdale, father of the six Mitford sisters, Nancy, Pamela, Diana (married Sir Oswald Mosley), Unity Valkyrie, Jessica, Deborah (Duchess of Devonshire).

9   He was, in fact, killed in the war.

10 Viscount Halifax had been British Foreign Secretary since Eden resigned in 1938. He became Ambassador to the United States in 1941 until 1946.

11 J. R. Colville had been Assistant Private Secretary to Neville Chamberlain since the out-

break of war, and was to hold the same post under Winston Churchill and Clement Attlee when they were Prime Ministers.

12 I was leaving my room in Tregunter Road and had taken a furnished flat in Arlington Street.

1940

1 Stanley Baldwin had been raised to the peerage when he ceased to be Prime Minister in 1937. He was popularly blamed for Britain's unpreparedness for war, and rather ostracised at this time.

2 He had just succeeded to the title on 11 February, when his father, John Buchan, first Lord Tweedsmuir, had died while Governor-General of Canada. He served with distinction in the Canadian army during the war. His younger brothers, William and Alastair, were also friends of mine.

3 Sir John Simon had been an M.P. since 1906 and was then Chancellor of the Exchequer.

4 The Earl of Athlone was about to take up his post as Governor-General of Canada.

5 He later came to England with the Canadian army and was wounded in Normandy in 1944, now a judge of the Supreme Court of Canada.

6 Formerly a Liberal M.P. and Parliamentary Secretary to Lloyd George, he was a keen supporter of the League of Nations.

7　The Dunkirk evacuation from 27 May to 3 June brought over 300,000 men, French as well as British, to England.

8　Bennett, who had been Canadian Prime Minister 1930-5, was now living in retirement. He was created Viscount Bennett in the Birthday Honours in June 1941.

9　The great house of the Dukes of Devonshire; it has in fact survived, and the present Duke lives there.

10　Younger son of the 4th Marquess of Salisbury, Fellow of New College, Oxford, and later Professor of English Literature at Oxford. The description is in his book, *The Young Melbourne*.

11　General A. G. L. McNaughton was officer commanding the First Canadian Division, and later the First Canadian Army. He resigned in 1944 to become Minister of Defence.

12　Part of my work at Canada House was concerned with the arrangements for transferring suspected enemy aliens from British internment camps to Canada.

13　I had moved again to a furnished flat off Pall Mall.

14　My cousin Mary Adlington.

15　Frank and Margery Ziegler; he is an old Oxford friend of mine.

1941

1 General Sir Archibald Wavell was then Commander-in-Chief of British forces in the Middle East and under the greatest pressure from Churchill to stretch his forces to the utmost. Field-Marshal Chetwode had been Commander-in-Chief, India, 1930-5, but was now retired.

2 Pierre Dupuy was Canadian Minister to the French Government at Vichy.

3 He was in fact killed in a plane crash while a training instructor with the R.C.A.F.

4 The representatives of the Allied Governments in exile in London.

5 Massey's appointment and Bennett's peerage were announced in the Birthday Honours. Bracken, who was to become Minister of Information on 20 July, was then Churchill's Parliamentary Private Secretary, and so may have been writing on Churchill's behalf. Bennett's actual title was Viscount Bennett of Mickleham and of Calgary and Hopewell.

6 An old friend from Oxford and Harvard days.

7 Germany had invaded Soviet Russia the day before.

8 The House of Commons had been bombed on the night of 10 May 1941.

9 Beatrice Lillie was in London after touring with E.N.S.A. entertaining the forces.

10 Leslie Hore-Belisha had been Minister for War from May 1937 until January 1940. He held no office in the Coalition Government.

11 Daughter of Lord Rosebery, wife of the former British Ambassador in Paris.

12 Second son of the 15th Earl of Pembroke. He served in the Navy during the war.

13 Then a member of staff at Canada House, subsequently Canadian Ambassador to the U.N. and the N.A.T.O. His elder brother Nicholas was in the Russian and Scandinavian section of British Military Intelligence, and was chief of M.I.3C 1943-5.

1942

1 Sir Stafford Cripps, left-wing Labour former Solicitor-General, had been British Ambassador to Russia since 1940. A few days after this entry was written he was recalled from Moscow to become Lord Privy Seal.

2 These two German battle-cruisers had been stuck in Brest from March 1941 until they escaped through the English Channel on 12 February, despite the R.A.F. and the Royal Navy.

3 He was now stationed with the Canadian army in Sussex.

4 A French ship, carrying 3,000 tons of explosives, collided with a Norwegian vessel in Halifax har-

bour on 6 December 1917 and devastated about one-tenth of the city.

5 Herbert Morrison, Labour Home Secretary in the Coalition Government, had been a pacifist in 1914-18; 12th Duke of Bedford, pacifist with sympathies for fascism; William Temple, Archbishop of Canterbury.

6 *Black Lamb and Grey Falcon,* which had just been published.

7 Novelist, playright and essayist, author of *The Fountain, The Flashing Stream,* etc., sometimes subject to similar disparagement in England, much respected in France.

1943

1 My diary lapsed during much of 1943.

2 Sir Oswald Mosley, founder of the British Union of Fascists, had been detained under regulation 18B in May 1940. He was released in November 1943.

3 In October 1943 the Lord Chief Justice quashed the sentence and severely rebuked a magistrate who had ordered an eleven-year-old boy to be birched.

4 C. M. Bowra, classical scholar, was Warden of Wadham College Oxford; Mortimer, a literary critic, was then working for the French service of the B.B.C.; he had long ago given up Roman Catholicism (see Bowra's remarks below).

1944

1 Halifax argued that for Great Britain to be an effective power in the postwar world, she would need a closely unified Commonwealth.

2 Mackenzie King repudiated Halifax's argument in a speech in the Canadian House of Commons. He rejected any notion of a shared Commonwealth foreign policy.

3 See above, page 56.

4 Lady Ottoline Morrell, patron of Bloomsbury writers and of D. H. Lawrence, died in 1938. A selection of her memoirs was eventually published in 1963.

5 My cousin, and now brother-in-law, Peter Smellie.

6 *The Heat of the Day.*

7 A niece of Winston Churchill, she later married Anthony Eden.

8 I was on a visit to Canada on leave and for 'purposes of consultation'.

9 I was staying with my mother at an hotel in this small town in the Annapolis Valley.

10 R. A. Butler was Minister (or President of the Board) of Education from 1941 until the end of the war. He had previously been at the Foreign Office, and was to hold many high ministerial posts (other than that of Prime Minister) later.

11 The home of the Duke of Sutherland.

1945

1 I was staying with Saul Rae, of the Department of External Affairs, then stationed in Paris, and his wife.

2 I had been posted back from London to the Department of External Affairs.

3 Norman Robertson was then Under-Secretary of State for External Affairs. He had been part of the original Department of External Affairs formed by Dr. O. D. Skelton.

4 We were on our way to the San Francisco Conference, which was to open in the Opera House there on 25 April and set up the machinery of the United Nations. I was an adviser to the Canadian delegation.

5 Edward R. Stettinius, was then American Secretary of State, and later United States Representative at the United Nations.

6 Viscount Cranborne (later 5th Marquess of Salisbury) was Secretary of State for Dominion Affairs; Sir Alexander Cadogan, Permanent Under-Secretary at the Foreign Office; Sir Charles Webster, a professor of history, was adviser to the delegation.

7 At the Dumbarton Oaks Conference in August 1944, the four Great Powers – Great Britain, China, the U.S.A. and the U.S.S.R. – agreed on a draft text for the creation of the United Nations.

INDEX